The Companion to
Hispanic Studies

The Companion to Hispanic Studies

Edited by Catherine Davies

Professor of Spanish, University of Manchester

A member of the Hodder Headline Group
LONDON
Co-published in the United States of America by
Oxford University Press Inc., New York

First published in Great Britain in 2002 by
Arnold, a member of the Hodder Headline Group,
338 Euston Road, London NW1 3BH

http://www.arnoldpublishers.com

Co-published in the United States of America by
Oxford University Press Inc.,
198 Madison Avenue, New York, NY 10016

British Library Cataloguing in Publication Data
A catalogue record for this book is available from the British Library

Library of Congress Cataloging-in-Publication Data
A catalog record for this book is available from the Library of Congress

ISBN 0 340 76297 7 (hb)
ISBN 0 340 76298 5 (pb)

1 2 3 4 5 6 7 8 9 10

Production Editor: Anke Ueberberg
Production Controller: Bryan Eccleshall
Cover Design: Terry Griffiths

Typeset in 10/12½pt Sabon by
Phoenix Photosetting, Chatham, Kent
Printed and bound in Great Britain by
MPG Books Ltd, Bodmin, Cornwall

What do you think about this book? Or any other Arnold title?
Please send your comments to feedback.arnold@hodder.co.uk

Contents

List of contributors

Jon Beasley-Murray is Lecturer in Latin American Cultural Studies at the University of Manchester and co-director of the MA in Latin American Cultural Studies. He has co-edited 'Culture and state in Latin America' (a special issue of *Journal of Latin American Cultural Studies*) and 'Subaltern affect' (a special issue of *Angelaki*). He has published several articles on Sendero Luminoso, Peronism and film theory among other topics.

Catherine Davies is Professor of Spanish at the Department of Spanish and Portuguese Studies, University of Manchester. She teaches and researches on nineteenth- and twentieth-century Spanish and Latin American literature and film, in particular the work of women writers such as Rosalía de Castro, Rosa Montero and Gertrudis Gómez de Avellaneda. She published a book on Cuban women writers in 1997 and another on Spanish women writers in 1998.

Derek Gagen is Professor of Spanish at the University of Wales, Swansea, and currently Dean of the Faculty of Arts and Social Studies. His research has centred on the poetry and drama of Spain in the twentieth century, concentrating on the works of Rafael Alberti and Buero Vallejo. He has published on a wide variety of authors, usually researching the historical and cultural contexts in which they work, aspects that he emphasises in his teaching.

David George is Senior Lecturer in Hispanic Studies at the University of Wales, Swansea, where he teaches Spanish and Catalan. He has published mainly on modern Spanish and Catalan drama, the commedia dell'arte in modern Hispanic literature and the Catalan playwright/director Sergi Belbel. He has co-edited a book on contemporary Catalan drama, *The Theatre in Madrid and Barcelona 1892–1936: rivals or collaborators?* (University of Wales Press, 2002). He has also edited translations of modern Catalan plays.

Louise M. Haywood is Lecturer in Medieval Spanish Studies at the University of Cambridge, and a Fellow of Trinity Hall. She teaches and publishes on medieval Hispanic literature, particularly the portrayal of women, medieval theatre and lyric in narrative. She is also co-author of a widely used manual on translation methodology. She is currently working on Don Juan Manuel and Juan Ruiz, lyrical modes in Medieval Epic and Romance, and a critical bibliography on Iberian drama.

Terence O'Reilly is Associate Professor in the Department of Hispanic Studies in University College Cork, Ireland. He has published widely on various Golden Age subjects, including San Ignacio de Loyola, Garcilaso, *Lazarillo de Tormes*, Montemayor, Luis de León, San Juan de la Cruz, Góngora, Calderón and the artist Diego de Velázquez.

John D. Perivolaris is Lecturer in the Department of Spanish and Portuguese, University of Manchester. His most recent major publications are *Puerto Rican Cultural Identity and the Work of Luis Rafael Sánchez* (University of North Carolina, 2001) and *The Cultures of the Hispanic Caribbean*, co-edited with Conrad James (Macmillan, 2001). He is currently preparing a book entitled *Photography and the Hispanic World*.

Geoffrey Ribbans was Kenan University Professor at Brown University, Providence, Rhode Island from 1978 and Emeritus since 1999. He has taught courses on eighteenth- and nineteenth-century literature for some 45 years in the UK and the USA, and has supervised much postgraduate work. He has published extensively on both centuries, especially on Benito Pérez Galdós, as well as *fin de siècle* poetry, modern Catalan literature, Miguel de Unamuno and Antonio Machado.

Rob Rix is Head of Modern Languages at Trinity and All Saints College, Leeds. His teaching and research interests include Spanish language skills and Spanish and Latin American cinema, literature, culture and society. Publications include an edited volume of essays on the Spanish detective novel, *Thrillers in the Transition*, and on Spanish and Latin American film studies (all in the *Leeds Iberian Papers* series). Current interests are in Spanish-Cuban cultural and cinematic co-operation and Argentine literature and film.

Peter Standish is Professor in the Department of Foreign Languages and Literatures, East Carolina University, Senior Research Fellow in the University of Glasgow, and President of the Philological Association of the Carolinas (1998–1999). He has published many books and articles on Latin American literature, in particular on José Luis Borges, Carlos Fuentes and Mario Vargas Llosa. In 1996 he published *The Hispanic Culture of Mexico, Central America and the Hispanic Caribbean*. His most recent book is *Understanding Julio Cortázar* (University of South Carolina Press, 2001).

Philip Swanson is Professor of Hispanic Studies at the University of Aberdeen, Scotland. He has written extensively on Latin American fiction and Spanish film, including books on Gabriel García Márquez, José Donoso, modern Latin American narrative, and politics and popular culture in the 'new novel'. He is currently writing a book on the detective and postmodernity in Latin America. He is also preparing a new companion to Latin American Studies for Arnold publishers.

Lynn Williams is Senior Lecturer in the Department of Spanish at the University of Exeter and currently Visiting Professor in Spanish linguistics at Brigham Young University, Utah. In addition to Spanish language, he teaches medieval Spanish literature, Spanish linguistics and aspects of Spanish history. His main area of research is in Spanish linguistics, especially Spanish sociolinguistics and orthographic theory and practice. He has also published on medieval Spanish literature, Cervantes, language and national identity, and seventeenth-century Spanish diplomatic history.

What is 'Hispanic Studies'?

Catherine Davies

HISPANIC?

There are two kinds of answers to this question. The first is simple, the second more complex. 'Hispanic', according to *The Shorter Oxford Dictionary*, means 'pertaining to Spain or its people'. The easy answer is this: Hispanic Studies is the study of the culture and society of Spain. But why 'Hispanic' rather than 'Spanish' studies? Because first not all the peoples of Spain consider themselves exclusively Spanish – the Spanish language is not the only official language spoken in Spain, and second, vast areas of the Americas that once 'pertained to Spain' (the Spanish Empire) may well share a language (though not exclusively) and a colonial history (until the nineteenth century) but they have quite distinctive identities and can hardly be accounted for under the rubric 'Spanish'. In this respect, Hispanic Studies is similar to 'English and American Studies' (which, just as problematically, often stretches its remit to Australia, Canada, Ireland and so on). As we shall see, there is no easy answer to the above question. The difficulties that arise have to do with complex processes of national autonomy in the aftermath of European colonialism, processes which are inseparable from the workings of language, culture and society.

A more accurate and interesting answer, though no less problematic, is this: Hispanic Studies is an institutionally recognised discipline (area of study and learning) taught in universities, the core subject of which is the languages and literatures of (Roman) Hispania, that is, the Iberian Peninsula (today's Spain and Portugal) and the former Spanish and Portuguese Empires. The focus on the Iberian Peninsula as a whole has a historical explanation. The modern nation states we refer to today as Spain and Portugal were not regarded as separate political entities until the eighteenth century; previously they were kingdoms, sometimes ruled by the same monarch (between 1580 and 1640), a part of the sprawling Habsburg Empire. In fact, before the eighteenth century sometimes 'Spain' referred to the whole of the Iberian Peninsula. The university discipline Hispanic Studies was established in Britain and the USA in the first years of the twentieth century, when Anglophone scholars were mainly interested in medieval and Golden Age (sixteenth- and seventeenth-century) peninsular studies. For them, the term 'Hispanic' was particularly apt.

But this raises a set of further problems: what about Portuguese? Portuguese is a global language, spoken not only in Portugal but in Brazil and the Lusophone (Portuguese-speaking) countries of Africa, including Mozambique and Angola (the former Portuguese Empire). To include the immense Lusophone areas of the globe under the rubric 'Hispanic Studies', as some kind of supplement to the Spanish core, is degrading (and provides further indication of the hierarchy of national standing implicit in British and US institutions). It is true that the Portuguese language and Lusophone cultures and societies are taught primarily in Hispanic Studies departments (in the UK, there are only two free-standing departments of Portuguese) but it is increasingly recognised that this practice stretches the 'Hispanic' discipline too far. The Lusophone world cannot be contained or subsumed under the rubrics 'Hispanic' or 'Iberian'; it has complex global, colonial and postcolonial identities of its own. 'Lusophone Studies' need their own disciplinary space, and this should be taken on board by academic institutions. This book, at least, limits itself to Spain and Latin America; 'Lusophone Studies' deserve a book in their own right.

How does Catalan fit in? For many, Catalonia, the Basque country and Galicia have distinctive national cultural identities, though politically they are not independent nation states. As noted above, Spanish (often referred to as Castilian in this context) is not the only language spoken in Spain. The other three languages officially recognised by the Spanish state are Basque, Galician and Catalan. Most Hispanic Studies departments include the study of Catalan (and the history, culture and society of Catalonia), though less so Galician (from which modern Portuguese developed) and Basque. Unlike the Germanic/Romance languages, Basque (spoken by about half a million people in Spain and France) is not an Indo-European language. But even if the Basque and Galician languages are not often taught, there is no doubt that the Basque and Galician cultures form a significant part of Hispanic Studies. For this reason, a chapter on these 'autonomous regions' has been included in this book.

Did you spot the deliberate error in the last sentence of the penultimate paragraph? There I referred to 'Latin' America. What is 'Latin America'? The term, invented in France in the nineteenth century to take account of the (minimal) French presence on the continent (Haiti, Guyana), was favoured by South American exiles living in Paris who were keen to give their newly independent territories a supra-national continental identity, and to differentiate it from that of Anglo-America. But 'Latin America' is a misnomer. There is Spanish America (*Hispanoamérica* in Spanish), comprising the following countries: Mexico, Cuba, Puerto Rico, the Dominican Republic, Guatemala, Honduras, El Salvador, Panama, Venezuela, Colombia, Bolivia, Peru, Ecuador, Paraguay, Uruguay, Argentina, and Chile. And then there is Brazil, where Spanish is not spoken but Portuguese. Brazil forms part of the Lusophone world. A more accurate term to refer to the southern part of the

American continent is *Iberoamérica*, that is, those areas of the New World that were colonised by the peoples of the Iberian Peninsula. As stated above, traditionally the discipline Hispanic Studies embraced the language, cultures and societies not only of *Hispanoamérica* (Spanish America) but also of *Iberoamérica*. This latter term is not synonymous with what is referred to in the English-speaking world as South America. South America is a geographical term and refers to the part of the American continent south of Central America. In other words, only the countries south of the Panama canal are strictly speaking in South America. Honduras, Guatemala, and Panama, for example, are in Central America, and Cuba and Puerto Rico, in the Hispanic Caribbean. That leaves Mexico. The United States of the Republic of Mexico is, like the United States of America and Canada, a part of North America. And, of course, after English, Spanish is the most widely spoken language in the USA. Then there is the term Mesoamerica, used to refer to the area stretching from northern Mexico to Nicaragua, a region of flourishing American-Indian cultures before the arrival of the Spanish.

There are further complications. In Spanish America, Spanish is not the only official or spoken language by any means. This is a sure indication of the survival of pre-Hispanic Amerindian cultures and social structures. In Paraguay Guaraní is recognised as a co-official language; Aymara and Quechua are widely spoken in the Andean zones, Nahuatl in Mexico and Mapuche in Chile. Hispanic Studies therefore may include the study of indigenous Amerindian languages and civilisations (inevitably the Aztecs and Mayas in Mexico and the Incas in Bolivia and Peru), though these are more often included in Latin American studies programmes. Of particular interest, for example, is the way these ancient cultures were mobilised in the nineteenth century to legitimise independence from Spain. Finally, we should not forget the impact of Rome and eight centuries of Islamic civilisation in the Iberian Peninsula, particularly in Spain. The development of Spanish (and of Galician, Portuguese and Catalan) from Latin, and the lasting influence of Arabic and Islamic culture (notably art and architecture), especially in Andalusia, also form a part of Hispanic Studies.

To sum up, 'Hispanic' refers to Spain (including Catalonia, Galicia and the Basque country), and sometimes Portugal and the Iberian Peninsula. It refers to Spanish America (North, Central and South America, and the Hispanic Caribbean) and sometimes Brazil (*Ibero-* or Latin America). It may refer to Roman and Islamic Spain, and pre-Columbian America. It may also refer to Spanish and Spanish American diasporas across the world, particularly in the USA (Cubans in Miami, Puerto Ricans in New York). It is a vast area of study and learning, extensive through time and space, and it is constantly shifting its areas of priority. The most noticeable developments in the past 30 years, at least in the UK and US, have entailed shifts of interest away from the medieval and Golden Age towards the modern and contemporary; and away from Spain (Castile) to the Americas (including the diasporas). Perhaps the most interesting developments of all, comprising all historical periods and geographical areas, have been a reappraisal of the study of language and literature in the context of other forms of cultural production, and the move towards interdisciplinary modes of analysis (see Chapter 10).

LANGUAGE

> Is there no method to tell her in Spanish
> June's twice June since she breathed it with me?
> (Robert Browning)

Hispanic Studies takes for granted that the key to knowledge of this immense area of human thought and activity is the mastery of the predominant languages through and by means of which such thought and activity take place. These languages are European: Spanish and Portuguese (the result of European expansion in the Americas). The most important language for Hispanic Studies is Spanish. The priority is to teach students Spanish, so that they attain near-native fluency in the spoken and written (literary) language. Language acquisition is the most obvious practical skill taught in this discipline. Why this insistence on language? As is the case for all language disciplines taught in universities (including English), it is assumed that language is inseparable from culture and society. You can never fully understand and use a language without a deep understanding of its culture and society. Conversely, you cannot hope to understand a culture without knowing the language through which it has developed. As we saw briefly, distinctive political identities are often predicated on language difference (such as Catalan in Spain); even more interesting perhaps is how distinctive local and national cultures are formed even when they share a language, even when former Spanish colonies (for example, Cuba) share the language of the once dominant power. These points regarding transcultural competence are obvious, but need repeating. And if you are interested in the history of the language, its structures or uses according to social, regional and other factors, you will study Hispanic linguistics. Universities are not language schools; they are much, much more.

To communicate effectively (orally and in writing) with native or other competent speakers of the target language (in this case Spanish), for specific purposes (for example, a job interview), using appropriate regional or social varieties (that is, being able to switch from a formal register to local colloquial slang) is extremely useful. For each situation there is a more or less appropriate language use. Take falling in love. This happens to many students during their year abroad. They find themselves in the situation described in the quotation above. How can the poet tell the girl that he loves her if he does not speak her language? If only he had known Spanish. But even if he did, would he have known the subtle difference between 'te quiero', 'te amo' and 'estoy enamorado de ti'? If he had known some poetry, Browning would have made a lasting impression quoting lines written by his Mexican contemporary, Manuel Acuña (1849–1873):

> ¡Pues bien!, Yo necesito decirte que te adoro,
> decirte que te quiero con todo el corazón;
> que es mucho lo que sufro, que es mucho lo que lloro
> que ya no puedo tanto, y al grito que te imploro
> te imploro y te hablo en nombre de mi última ilusión.

(I need to tell you I adore you, tell you that I love you with all my heart, that I suffer greatly and weep for ever, I need to tell you I can't go on. Aloud I implore you, I implore you, in the name of my last dream.)
('Nocturno', in P. Barreda and E. Béjar, eds, *Poética de la nación.* Boulder: SSSAS, 1999, p. 550)

Verbal communication, dialogue and conversation across languages is essential in today's world. It enables us to create relationships and build bridges, thus avoiding conflict and misunderstanding. No less important is to be able to communicate effectively in the written language (to read, comprehend and write). In fact, reading and understanding written Spanish is perhaps the most exciting skill of all. Reading in languages other than your own, across time and space, opens windows onto other peoples' lives, as they were in the past, and as they are now. When we read a novel, for example, especially if it is written in what for us is a foreign language, we can cross the seas, go back in time, look to the future; we might see different worlds and the world as we know it differently. This is the effect of language working on the powers of the imagination. At the most basic level, we can imagine (produce a mental image or conception of) what it might have been like to live in a medieval castle in Castile, to stumble across an unforeseen 'New World' with Columbus, to herd cattle on the Argentine pampas, to fight in the Spanish Civil War; we might understand more fully what it is like to be caught up in the Colombian drugs wars, serve in the Peruvian army, live in post-Pinochet Chile, experience the pop scene in Ibiza, from Colombian, Peruvian, Chilean, and Spanish points of view. Reading gives us the opportunity to immerse ourselves in these other, unfamiliar, times and spaces. Empathy from lived or imagined experience makes for communication. But literature offers even more than this.

The study of written texts still forms the backbone of Hispanic Studies. Many people refer to these texts as 'literature', by which they often mean a series of canonical 'set texts' which, it is thought, are worth reading, good for you and necessary to know about. In this way the *Poema de mio Cid* might correspond to *The Canterbury Tales*, Cervantes to Shakespeare, García Márquez to Salman Rushdie and so on. But the definition of what 'literature' consists of is not so straightforward and has resulted in an ongoing debate across the disciplinary spectrum, thus confirming John, Viscount Morley's much quoted view that literature is 'the most seductive, the most deceiving, the most dangerous of professions'.

LITERATURE, WRITING, WORDS

In Latin 'literatura' meant scholarship, and it is only in the twentieth century that the term has acquired its more specialist meaning; previously 'literature' referred to any type of written text. Sometimes 'literature' (from Latin *litera*, meaning 'letter of the alphabet') is referred to as 'writing' (from Anglo-Saxon *writan*, meaning to scratch, cut or score). These etymologies immediately suggest value judgements; writing is not perceived to be as scholarly (therefore, powerful) as literature. Shelves of books have been written discussing whether some texts are more special than others, and if so how. Some critics (people who engage in reasoned discussion of 'literary' works) point to the special use and effects of language, or 'literariness', in literary texts; others to the 'literary' intentions of the author (though the importance of the author is rapidly fading); others to the intentions of the reader – when we read what we are trained to expect to be 'literature' we read for further layers of meaning. The French thinker Jean Paul Sartre wrote, 'Reading is a pact of generosity between author and reader. Each one trusts the other and each one counts on the other, demands of the other as much as he demands of himself' (*Literature and Existentialism*. New York: Citadel Press, 1962, p. 56). Reading, like writing, is a process, and the reader is just as important as the text and the author (perhaps more). But what happens when an English reader reads, for example, a Peruvian text in Spanish, thus reading across languages? This is a question that has still to be fully explored.

Few critics have risked a brief definition of literature. Chris Baldick's in the *Concise Oxford Dictionary of Literary Terms* (Oxford: Oxford University Press, 1990) is:

> a body of written works related by subject matter, by language or place of origin, or by *prevailing cultural standards of merit*. In this last sense, 'literature' is taken to include oral, dramatic, and broadcast compositions that may not have been published in written form but which have been (or deserve to be) preserved [. . .] Until the mid-twentieth century, many kinds of non-fictional writing – in philosophy, history, biography, criticism, topography, science, and politics – were counted as literature [. . .], as that *body of works which – for whatever reason – deserves to be preserved* as part of the current reproduction of meanings within a given culture (*unlike yesterday's newspaper, which belongs to the disposable category of ephemera*). (124)

I have abbreviated Baldick's definition substantially, and italicised the more disputable statements. We might compare his view with the more contentious one of Canadian critic Kenneth Quinn in his book *How Literature Works* (Basingstoke: Macmillan, 1992).

> The difference between literary texts and other texts is like that between cars and trucks. Cars come in all sorts of shapes and sizes; many of the things they have in common (wheels, tyres, engine . . .) are found also in trucks. And yet, for us, cars and trucks are two quite different kinds of vehicle. A visitor from Mars might find the distinction hard to grasp. *But for us the distinction is obvious* because cars and trucks occupy different places in our lives: the different uses we put them to keeps them apart in our minds. It's the different place literary texts occupy in our minds that makes it easy for us to keep literary texts and non-literary texts apart. [. . .] *Recognising a text as literature means recognising that what we're being offered is a literary experience*, one that calls for a different kind of attention to the words used [. . .] a novel or a poem works the way it does because it has been put together to work that way. (9–11)

Again, some of these statements need to be qualified. Quinn echoes the Spanish dictionary definition of 'literatura': 'arte cuyo medio de expresión es la palabra oral o escrita y en el que el lenguaje no tiene la función de informar, sino de proporcionar placer estético' (art whose means of expression is the spoken or written word and in which the function of language is not to inform but to give aesthetic pleasure). (*Diccionario básico de la lengua*. Madrid: Anaya 1993). Both corroborate the much accepted view that literature is the art of words, and is written with (or examined as if it had) an aesthetic purpose. My own concept of literature is broader. For me literature is human thought, shaped, articulated and, if read in texts, communicated through and by language. In other words, it is the language you think in that shapes your thoughts. Language has a life of its own, and so do texts; you (author or reader) can only control them to an extent. This explains why each text is different for each reader, and why engaging with a written text in its language of origin is a radically different experience from engaging with it in translation. In short, language is not simply instrumental; language does not represent human thought but *is* human thought and each language (English, Spanish, Portuguese) configures a slightly distinctive version or vision of the world. Similarly, literature and language are inseparable from value judgements, ideologies, modes of feeling, general assumptions and the exercising of power. Through literature we can analyse how meaning is made, and we can value the subjective dimension of language and the expressivist dimension of culture. Another type of text studied is film, the written script and subtitles of which may be read. But the script is only a minor part of a film, and sometimes does not exist as such. A film is a series of moving images and sounds which are read and interpreted as visual and audio images. When you study film you will learn how to analyse filmic texts.

CRITICAL THEORY

Since the 1980s the study of 'literature' (in whatever language) has become increasingly embroiled in what is termed 'critical' or 'literary' theory. These theoretical discourses about and around literature attempt to formulate generalising systems of ideas, general principles, that may (in theory) be applied to all texts. Such theories in themselves have become models of knowledge, and the explosion of theories about literature has sometimes led critics to lose sight of the literary works themselves. This is an important issue in Hispanic Studies because almost all the established theories (for example, psychoanalysis, Marxist criticism, postmodernism, postcolonialism, feminism) have originated in Europe or the USA (predominantly in English, French, German, Italian, and Russian) and may not be entirely appropriate for reading Spanish or Hispanoamerican texts. Even so, the main point about theory, that no form of reading or criticism is theory-free, and that we need to be conscious of this, has been enormously beneficial to the discipline. Not only has it led to the radical reassessment of former ideas and approaches, but it has also opened up the field of enquiry to encompass new directions and subjects long neglected (for example, popular film culture in Franco's Spain). Gone are assumptions (now considered hopelessly naïve) such as: the innocent reader and his or her direct response to a text; the author as sole originator of the text; a single 'common sense' interpretation of the text, or seeing it as containing a message to be deciphered by the reader. All readers come with baggage, and should be aware of this; there is no such thing as an unmediated reading of a text. The author is only one of the elements that go into the creation of a work – language is another; there is no one correct reading, but many possible interpretations, although all need to be argued for and substantiated by the text. Nothing should be taken for granted, nothing assumed. In other words, the text is not just consumed but is actively produced by the reader. Literary texts are therefore sounding boards for a multiplicity of ideas on any subject under the sun.

The impact of these ideas may be judged with reference to two important books. In *British Hispanism and the Challenge of Literary Theory* (Warminster: Aris and Phillips, 1990), written in the mid-1980s, Barry Jordan made a spirited defence of critical theory. But, he wrote, 'despite some notable exceptions, British Hispanism in its institutional fabric and day to day working remains largely untouched by the theoretical revolution' (p. 4). Ten years later, *New Hispanisms: Literature, Culture, Theory* (Ottawa: Ottawa Hispanic Studies, 1994), edited by Mark Millington and Paul Julian Smith, took for granted that theory now formed a part of the Hispanic Studies curriculum. Theory needed no defence. The book simply draws attention to the diversity of new approaches existing within Hispanism, in particular a concern with class, gender, sexuality and nationality.

Nevertheless, the debate goes on – not least in English Studies. The outgoing President of the Modern Language Association of America, Edward Said, gave his valedictory speech on (English) literary studies in the USA in December 1999. Said is an enormously influential literary critic whose theories have demonstrated how the West had constructed the concept of the Orient. Yet on this millennial occasion he spoke of 'catastrophic disorganisation and disillusionment' in the US academy: 'we can't agree on anything [. . .] it is no longer clear what it is that English departments are supposed to be doing. We have lots of courses on Jacques Derrida, post-colonial studies, gay studies, ethnic studies, Afro American studies, but I find it very odd that very few courses address literature.' Linda Hutcheon (Toronto University), the incoming MLA President, struck a more optimistic note: 'I see real value in the richness and expansion of the field. We are heading towards a stage where nothing is dominant and everything is open to consideration' (reported in *The Times Higher Educational Supplement*, 17 December 1999). These critics refer to fields and sub-fields. Stages, and fields, bring to mind no more than open theatre, empty gestures, a great show, but for whose benefit? Who are the players? Who is the audience? The point is, how many of these sub-fields are plotted from 'Hispanic' perspectives? It is up to students of Hispanic Studies to make literary theory relevant to the discipline and to suggest broader theoretically informed modes of analysis. After all, if generalising principles are not relevant to the vast area of the globe outlined above, they can hardly be called theory.

CULTURE, LANGUAGE, POWER

In settling an island, the first building erected by a Spaniard will be a church; by a Frenchman, a fort; by a Dutchman, a warehouse; and by an Englishman, an alehouse.

(Eighteenth-century proverb)

Why are the Spanish associated with religion and the English with pubs? In what ways does Spanish drinking culture differ from the English? These questions might pertain to cultural studies. So far we have briefly discussed literature and film, but there are other forms of cultural production increasingly taught in Hispanic Studies. Cultural Studies does not have a clearly defined subject area or institutional base and for this reason it is not quite yet a discipline in its own right. Like critical theory it borrows from other areas of study such as philosophy, sociology, anthropology, linguistics and so on. But Cultural Studies does have an agenda, which is to expose the workings of power and power relationships in the cultural activities and products (including literature) of particular political and social contexts. In other words, it has a critical and political edge in that it reveals structures of dominance. Hispanic Studies shares many of the concerns of Cultural Studies (see Chapter 10). The Spanish-speaking world is not only criss-crossed with internal conflict resulting from diverse power struggles but it has been dominated *en bloc* for two centuries, at least in the political and economic spheres, by Anglo-American interests. The rapid increase of Spanish in the USA has great political significance therefore. In marked contrast to Edward Said's pessimism mentioned above were the upbeat comments of Mexican novelist Carlos Fuentes at the same MLA event.

Fuentes was pleased with the growth of Spanish in the USA: 'We have 450 million people who speak Spanish all over the world. Three out of every five Americans will speak Spanish by 2050.' He describes monolingualism (ability to speak only one language) as a curable disease; and he adds that the knowledge of other cultures will make the USA realise that 'powerful as it may be, its values are relative. There's an assumption that American values are universal, and it simply isn't true'. Obviously, speaking a particular language may be a political act.

Spanish has certainly caught the headlines in the USA. Spanish undergraduate enrolments accounted for 55 per cent of total language registrations in higher education in 2000. The increase is due to the growth of the US-Latin American community, with evidently subversive potential. People speak Spanglish or, according to Fuentes, Angloñol. At present Hispanics constitute 11 per cent of the US population. Spanish-speaking North America is the world's fifth largest Hispanic nation. In ten years, only Mexico will have a larger Hispanic population. Hispanic buying power has increased by 66 per cent in one decade, to almost $350 billion, more than the entire Gross National Product (GNP) of Mexico. What does this mean? Among other things, it means that Bill Gates will include the Spanish 'ñ' in all Microsoft products.

Yet to what extent is interest in Hispanic cultures in the USA a form of introspection, a recognition of the country's own indigenous population, ethnic minorities, and multiculturalism, rather than curiosity about outside cultures? The massive growth, in US universities, of native Spanish-speaking students has resulted, paradoxically, in dissension in the Hispanic Studies departments. The tension is between the traditional Hispanic Studies discipline that still concentrates on Peninsular literature, and the often more radical Latin American Studies programmes that focus on the Americas. Some commentators have referred to this apparent mutual hatred between lecturers as verging on 'apartheid'. It would seem then that in the USA Hispanic Studies is a fragmented, decentred, conflictive discipline undergoing rapid change.

What about the UK? The surge in Spanish is no less impressive. The number of applicants accepted for Spanish university courses in 2000 was 25 per cent higher than in 1994. 'A' level entries for Spanish have almost doubled since 1994. There was a 7% rise in the number of students taking Spanish 'A' level at school between 2000–2001 and 2001–2002 (compared with a 6% fall in those taking French 'A' level over the same period). The figures tell us that French and German are still the two languages usually taught in schools, with substantially more 'A' level entries than Spanish. However, students taking Spanish 'A' level tend to go on to study the subject at university – over half, compared with a fifth of those who take French at 'A' level. In other words the choice to study Spanish seriously, in the UK, is made at school, at the age of 15 or 16, or at university at the age of 18. In addition, some 8,000 students are accepted onto university *ab initio* (beginners) Spanish courses.

POPULAR CULTURE

What are the reasons for this 'boom' in awareness of things Hispanic in the UK? What explains the attraction of young people to the Spanish-speaking world? Is Spain still 'different'? Is Latin America suitably familiar yet still exotic? Is it to do with the influence of US youth culture? Hispanic awareness in the UK and Ireland is not the same thing as in the USA. The impact of the Hispanic community in the USA is comparable perhaps to that of the British-Asian or British-Caribbean communities in English Studies, and relates to the postcolonial developments foregrounded by Said. There is no noticeable increase in Spanish or Latin American immigration into Britain, though there is a more palpable EU-Spanish presence. Young people in Britain are attracted to the Spanish-speaking world often because of youth culture and pop music. The newspaper report I mentioned above, carried photographs of Jennifer López and Ricky Martin. It may well have featured Gloria Estefan, Madonna's 'La isla bonita', Elvis Crespo, Jennifer Delgado, Francisco Paz, Donato y Estefano, and Christina Aguilera, Ibiza music, and UK salsa club bands such as Salsasonica, Ricardo and Charlie Pla, Ramon Vallejo and His Orchestra, or the Leeds-based band Charanga del Norte. This is good. Popular culture is what cultural studies is all about. An area of research awaiting further exploration, for example, is the representation of the Hispanic world in British popular culture. I doubt if things are so different these days from 40 years ago. Who can forget beautiful Doña Victoria in the *High Chaparral*, and grinning Manolito, or life on the frontier in *Bonanza* ('Here in the West / We're living the best bonanza'), el zorro, the Lone Ranger and 'Tonto', Frank Sinatra and Sophia Loren in *The Pride and the Passion* pulling their cannon across the Spanish mountains, the Cuban Desi Arnez and *I Love Lucy*, Manuel in *Faulty Towers*, Dorothy Dandridge in the film *Carmen Jones*, and, of course, *West Side Story*? This underlines the point that those engaged in Hispanic Studies need always to reflect on what students might be taught, and according to whose agenda. If it is true that Hispanic Studies is an expanding discipline, what kind of boundaries should be set (if any), and according to which (European, US, Spanish, Mexican . . .) viewpoint?

To sum up, Hispanic Studies entails exploring the interface between the peoples, histories, politics, and languages of the mainly Spanish-speaking areas of the world. The emphasis is on cultural expression, in particular the words of written and spoken texts (novels, poetry, drama, cinema, history, performance, translation, television, youth culture, the press, comics, song lyrics, philosophy, biography and so on) and, increasingly, visual texts (photography, film, painting). Examples of undergraduate courses presently on offer at universities are: 'Politics and the writer in Spanish America', 'Afro-Cuban literature', 'Film in Spain', 'The linguistic history of Spain', 'Don Juan', 'Argentina from independence to Perón', 'From history to Hollywood: exploiting the Cid', 'Conquest and colonisation: Spanish America 1492–1700', 'The gaucho in Argentine literature', 'The films of Pedro Almodóvar', 'Love and lust in medieval Spain', 'The culture of the Hispanic Caribbean', 'The Spanish Inquisition', 'Women and writing in Spanish and Portuguese', 'Latin American cultural studies', 'Hispanic linguistics', 'The history of Spain', 'The making of modern Mexico', 'Romantic poetry in Spanish', 'Culture in post-Franco Spain' and 'Contemporary Catalan theatre'. Textual criticism may be practised in an ancient, modern or postmodern sense, fixing the text or undoing it. We may explore how cultural practices intersect, move texts across languages, and constantly reinvent them. This way we participate in the brokerage of knowledge and meaning across languages and cultures.

THIS BOOK

One of the purposes of this book is to provide you with the foundations of Hispanic/Spanish/Latin American Studies, that is, the commonly accepted ideas and knowledge that constitute the discipline so far. To come up with new ideas you have to identify the old ones; to make some sense of the particular, it helps to have an overview of the whole. The book is designed to give you a relatively quick and easy entry into Hispanic Studies as it stands today. All the contributors are university teachers with years of teaching to their credit, and active researchers in their field. They were each asked to describe their areas of interest in broad strokes and to indicate the main issues currently under discussion in an accessible and unpretentious way. Each has approached the challenge differently, presenting a mixture of facts, hypotheses, interpretations and story-telling. To assist you some maps, tables and photographs have been inserted (the photographs are not meant to merely illustrate Argentina and Chile, but to elicit commentary). We hope you will find the book useful: above all, we hope you will find it fun. We aim to make you curious to find out more.

1

Language

Lynn Williams

Spanish is one of the great languages of the world. It offers access to a rich culture that spans several centuries, two continents, more than 20 countries and all literary genres. Miguel de Cervantes, Lope de Vega, Federico García Lorca and Gabriel García Márquez are just a few of the authors whose names are familiar to us. In terms of the number of its speakers, Spanish ranks high among the world's languages. With some 400,000,000 speakers who use it as their mother tongue, it is the language of approximately 6 per cent of the inhabitants of the globe. This figure is smaller than the likely number of those who speak Mandarin Chinese (*c*.885,000,000) and, to some extent, of those who speak English (*c*.500,000,000). But if we remember that virtually all speakers of Mandarin reside in China and that Spanish and English are spoken as first languages in numerous countries across the world, our perception of the relative importance of the three languages alters: English and Spanish are global languages and allow much more freedom of movement. The importance of Spanish is further reflected in the fact that, along with a handful of other languages, it is an official language of the United Nations, UNESCO and, of course, the main official bodies of the European Union.

Spanish has its roots in Western Europe, but its centre of gravity lies today in the New World. Mexico has by far the largest number of Spanish speakers (*c*.90,000,000). It is followed by Argentina, Colombia and Spain, each of which has between 35,000,000 and 40,000,000 speakers of the language. Next come the United States (*c*.30,000,000), Venezuela (*c*.22,000,000) and Peru (*c*.20,000,000) and, some way behind, Chile (13,000,000+), Cuba (*c*.12,000,000) and Ecuador (*c*.12,000,000). With the exception of Guatemala (with a population of perhaps 12,000,000 but at most 7,500,000 speakers of Spanish), the remaining Spanish-speaking countries are considerably smaller. Despite rapid demographic growth in many of them, none has a population of more than 8,000,000 and some, like Costa Rica and Uruguay, have less than 4,000,000. Panama is smaller still with approximately 3,000,000 inhabitants.

The USA may well have the fifth largest number of speakers of Spanish. However, the Hispanic communities are concentrated mainly in California,

Arizona, New Mexico, Texas, Florida, Illinois and New York. Moreover, the kind of Spanish spoken in these areas is different. Whereas Cuban Spanish predominates in Florida, Mexican Spanish dominates the south-west, and Puerto Rican Spanish the city of New York. The US Census Bureau predicts that the Hispanic community will grow to 96,500,000 by 2050 and constitute a quarter of the total population of the country. It also predicts that by 2025, Hispanics will represent 43 per cent of the population of California. The linguistic implications of this are potentially enormous, although much depends on how successfully Spanish is transmitted to future generations. None of these figures includes Puerto Rico, with its population of *c*.3,800,000 in 1996.

AMERICAN SPANISH v. PENINSULAR SPANISH

Non-specialists sometimes assume that the language of the New World presents a fairly uniform set of features that permits a clear contrast to be drawn between American and Peninsular Spanish. They note, for example, that American Spanish has only one second person plural form of address, namely *ustedes* (you), which is used in combination with the third person plural of the verb (*ustedes van*, 'you go'). The specifically familiar plural form of address (*vosotros váis*, 'you go'), still current in standard Peninsular Spanish, is nowhere to be found in the New World. Another feature noted as common to American Spanish is *seseo*. This involves making no distinction between /s/ and /θ/ (the 'th' sound in English *th*in) and pronouncing words like *casar* (to marry) and *cazar* (to hunt) in exactly the same way, namely as [kasár]. *Seseo* and absence of *vosotros*, it would seem, symbolise American Spanish.

Such a simplistic division of the language into Old and New World Spanish is naturally open to a number of objections. (1) There are no other features common to all American Spanish. (2) The Spanish of Spain is not uniform. In a number of ways, so-called standard Spanish, which takes as its model the language of central and northern Spain, is nowadays a minority variety. There are plenty of educated speakers in southern Spain and the Canary Islands for whom *seseo* is as natural as it is for the inhabitants of the New World. Similarly, *vosotros* is no longer used in much of Western Andalusia. As in American Spanish, its function is now covered by *ustedes*, although in this part of Spain *ustedes* may be accompanied by either the second or the third person plural of the verb, depending largely on the level of education of the speaker: *Vds van* ('you go', educated Spanish) and *Vds váis* (less educated). In short, the two features common to all American Spanish are also characteristic of certain southern varieties of Peninsular Spanish. (3) The Spanish of the New World is itself richly diverse. For instance, marked differences exist between the language of the highlands and that of the low coastal areas. There is a tendency in the highlands for unstressed vowels to weaken and be lost (*viej'cit'* for *viejecito* or 'little old man'). In low coastal areas, on the other hand, it is consonants, especially /d/ and /s/, that sometimes weaken and even disappear. It is thus not unusual to hear in such areas *cantao* for *cantado* and *perro* for *perros*. To this we can add more particular divergences such as those that exist between, say, Mexico City and Buenos Aires. Not only are the intonation patterns of Spanish in these two cities strikingly dissimilar, but so too are the pronunciation, vocabulary, morphology and syntax. The most obvious difference to note is perhaps the way in which both cities handle the second person singular familiar form of address. Whereas Mexico City sides with Peninsular Spanish in using *tú*, accompanied by perfectly orthodox inflections or endings of the verb (*tú quieres, tú cuentas, tú sigues*, 'you love, tell, follow'), Buenos Aires prefers *vos* (you) accompanied by an archaic second person plural (*vos querés, vos contás, vos seguís*). Because the latter stresses the ending rather than the root of the verb, in some tenses and in the imperative (*contá* for *cuenta*), it shows no radical change of the root vowel where this might otherwise be expected. Many other parts of Argentina behave like Mexico City, preferring *tú* to *vos*.

A sample of Mexican Spanish

–*Siéntate*, Fulgor. Aquí hablaremos con más calma. (Sit down, Fulgor.)
  Estaban en el corral. Pedro Páramo se arrellanó en un pesebre y esperó:
–¿Por qué no *te sientas*? (Why don't you sit down?)
–Prefiero estar de pie, Pedro.
–Como *tú quieras*. Pero no se te olvide el "don". (As you wish.)
                                              (Juan Rulfo, *Pedro Páramo*)

A sample of Argentinian (Buenos Aires) Spanish

–¿Qué edad *tenés*? (How old are you?)
–Dieciocho años.
–¿Dónde has vivido?
–Por allí nomás.
–*Sos* argentino . . . *hablás* raro, distinto. (You are Argentine . . . you speak strangely.)
–Viví en Centroamérica.
–*Sos* de otro planeta vos. (You are from another planet.)
        (Beatriz Guido, *Rojo sobre rojo: el secuestro de un general*)

HISTORY OF THE SPANISH LANGUAGE

Having underlined the diversity of Spanish in both its American and Peninsular forms, I will now sketch the evolution of Spanish from its Latin origins to the present day and trace briefly its struggle for supremacy over a multitude of other languages sharing the same social and geographical space.

Latin and Romance

Spanish is a Romance language. This means that it is one of a number of related languages (Spanish, French, Italian, etc.) that derive from Latin. However, the kind of Latin out of which these languages emerged was not Classical Latin. They evolved instead from the spoken Latin of the empire, which was often significantly different from the language we find in the writings of Cicero or Virgil. The simple sentence *Peter buys a horse for his brother* composed in the kind of Latin Cicero himself might have used and contrasted with its modern Romance equivalents, will serve to illustrate the point:

Classical Latin	EQUUM EMIT PETRUS FRATRI SUO
	(Horse) (buys) (Peter) (for brother) (his)
French	Pierre achète un cheval pour son frère.
Italian	Pietro compra un cavallo per suo fratello.
Portuguese	Pedro compra um cavalo para o seu irmão.
Spanish	Pedro compra un caballo para su hermano.
	(Peter) (buys) (a) (horse) (for) (his) (brother)

A number of deductions may be made from this simple comparison:

1 Classical Latin uses systems of inflections (declensions and conjugations) to identify clearly the grammatical function of a word, as well as its relation to other words in the sentence. Whereas the ending of EQUUM identifies the direct object, that of PETRUS identifies the subject of the sentence. Similarly, the ending of EMIT indicates the person, number, tense and mood of the verb, while those of FRATRI SUO signal the indirect object or person for whom the horse has been purchased. Word order hardly matters. Although in this example the direct object precedes the verb and the subject follows it, almost any sequence of words is possible since the ending of each word removes all doubt over its role in the sentence. The Romance languages, on the other hand, exhibit a more rigid word order. In the example given, all of them naturally place the subject before the verb and the object after it. They also all rely on the use of a preposition to identify the indirect object. Word order (subject-verb-object or, occasionally, verb-object, with flexible positioning of the subject in the case of the southern Romance languages) and use of prepositions came at some point largely to replace the functions discharged in Classical Latin by endings. In fact, the only endings retained in Romance, as far as nouns and adjectives are concerned, are those that allow us to distinguish number (cas*a* v. cas*as*) and, in many instances, to predict gender (chic*o* v. chic*a*).

The situation is altogether different for verbs. Most Romance languages

(Spanish, Italian, Portuguese, etc.) have retained more or less a complete set of verb endings and this explains why they are able to function without the assistance of subject pronouns (I, you, he, she, etc.), except where emphasis is required (e.g. Spanish *canto, cantas, canta*, etc.). French stands apart in this respect. Radical sound change has led to the confusion of many verb endings in spoken French so that, as in English, the use of subject pronouns is absolutely essential if ambiguity is to be avoided (e.g. *je chante, tu chantes, il chante*). Interestingly, what has happened in French provides a clue to the disappearance of the declension system of Classical Latin. Sound change here also led to the confusion of a number of endings and helped to make the system unworkable. Hence the need to rely on word order and prepositions for the purpose of signalling grammatical function and relations between words within the sentence. A fairly reliable rule of thumb states that the presence of a feature in all the Romance languages strongly suggests that it formed a solid part of the spoken Latin of the empire. Accordingly, it seems safe to conclude that increased use of prepositions and a more rigid word order than is evident in Classical Latin are defining characteristics of spoken Latin.

2 Certain items of vocabulary characteristic of Classical Latin were not the preferred items of everyday speech in the Roman Empire. Although Classical Latin EQUA (English *mare*) survived in the Iberian Peninsula (Sp. *yegua*, Port. *égua*, Cat. *euga*), it is quite clear from our sample sentence that the masculine form EQUUS was at some point rejected in favour of CABALLUS, which is the source of the word *horse* in all the Romance languages. This word is, in fact, attested in Roman times, but it belonged, early on at least, to a colloquial register and meant *nag*. Gradually, it lost its negative connotation and acquired the neutral meaning of *horse*. It was then used in polite speech as well. In similar fashion, the verb EMERE (EMIT) was replaced in the spoken tongue. But whereas in the Iberian Peninsula and in Italy it was replaced by COMPARARE, which had as one of its secondary meanings 'to purchase', in Gaul it must have been replaced by something like *ACCAPTARE, a verb based on CAPTARE and probably meaning *to acquire*. Classical Latin FRATER, or some derived form of it (*FRATELLUS), on the other hand, fared rather better, surviving in Gaul and Italy, but not in the Iberian Peninsula. Here it was the adjective GERMANUS, used initially to describe individuals who share both parents but later becoming a noun meaning *full brother*, that ultimately triumphed (Sp. *hermano*, Port. *irmão*, Cat. *germà*). The feminine form GERMANA likewise came to replace Classical Latin SOROR (Sp. *hermana*; Port. *irmã*; Cat. *germana*). FRATER and SOROR survive in Spanish in religious contexts only: *fraile, Fray Luis, Sor María*.

3 Another difference thrown up by our sample sentence is the existence of an indefinite article (*un/um*) in all the Romance languages and its absence in Classical Latin. In fact, Classical Latin possessed neither an indefinite nor a definite article. In contrast, spoken Latin seems to have used the numeral UNUS, UNA, UNUM in a diluted sense as an indefinite article and one of

the demonstrative adjectives (usually ILLE, ILLA, ILLUD), also in a diluted sense, as a definite article (Sp. *el, la, los, las*).

4 The Romance derivatives of PETRUS (Fr. *Pierre*, It. *Pietro*, Port./Sp. *Pedro*) and CABALLUS (Fr. *cheval*, It. *cavallo*, Port. *cavalo*, Sp. *caballo*) suggest some obvious things about sound change in spoken Latin and Romance. First, it did not follow the same lines in all parts of the Roman Empire. Second, it often proceeded much more rapidly in northern Gaul, the cradle of standard French, than elsewhere.

Obviously, it is not easy to uncover direct evidence of spoken Latin. Although we can get some idea of it from inscriptions or scratchings like those preserved on the walls of Pompeii by the eruption of Vesuvius in AD 79, from contemporary grammarians who occasionally comment on language deemed to be incorrect, and from literary works of a colloquial nature like the comedies of Plautus, most of our evidence is indirect. It comes from comparing the different Romance languages and reconstructing, where they share the same feature, a likely common spoken Latin source. It also often comes from reconstructing different spoken Latin sources where the Romance languages differ. French *acheter* and its reconstructed source *ACCAPTARE, along with the Romance derivatives of PETRUS and CABALLUS that we have looked at above, strongly suggest that, in terms of vocabulary and pronunciation, the spoken Latin of Late Antiquity (*c*. AD 300–500) was hardly uniform. Although our sample sentence does not provide the necessary information, spoken Latin was no less diverse at the levels of morphology and syntax.

How may this variation exhibited by Latin in Late Antiquity be explained? Romanisation was certainly more intense in some areas (e.g. southern Gaul) than in others (e.g. the north-west of the Iberian Peninsula) and Latin was certainly imposed on speakers of very different pre-Roman languages in different parts of the western Roman world. Taken together, these two factors must have made some contribution to the differentiation of spoken Latin. Traditionally, it has also been considered significant that different areas were colonised at different times. The Iberian Peninsula was colonised at a very early date (early third/late second century BC) so that 'older' forms of Latin were taken there than were later taken to northern Gaul. Linked to this is a related issue: the remoteness of the Iberian Peninsula. It has been maintained that innovations emanating from the centre often did not reach the edges of the empire and that therefore the 'archaic' Latin spoken on the fringes was left relatively undisturbed. There is probably some truth in this view. Although innovations clearly occurred everywhere, the prestige of Roman Latin meant that innovations originating in the imperial capital were likely to spread more widely than those arising elsewhere. However, as the following examples confirm, they did not always become general.

When the Iberian Peninsula was colonised, spoken Latin tended to use MAGIS + adjective to express positive comparisons (MAGIS FORTIS =

'stronger'). Later, Roman Latin replaced MAGIS with PLUS (It. *più forte*). This innovation reached northern Gaul (Fr. *plus fort*), but seems to have run out of steam upon entering the Iberian Peninsula. Although its frequent occurrence in old Catalan (*pus fort*) is evidence that the construction did penetrate the eastern segment of Iberia, a glance at the modern languages of the peninsula confirms that nowhere did it succeed in displacing MAGIS (Sp. *más fuerte*, Port. *mais forte*, Cat. *més fort*). Its sporadic presence, in medieval times, in the Romance of La Rioja is probably due to the fact that the Roman administrative area known as Tarraconensis extended from the Mediterranean coast along the river Ebro in a north-westerly direction, seemingly taking in not only modern Catalonia, but also those areas that were later to become La Rioja and a north-eastern strip of Old Castile. The tendency for innovations to spread along rivers is amply attested, so that it is hardly surprising that there should be echoes of this construction further upstream.

A second case presents itself in the Hispano-Romance equivalents of the verb 'to speak'. Catalan *parlar* clearly has the same origin (PARABOLARE) as French *parler* and Italian *parlare*. In contrast, the rest of the Iberian Peninsula retained an older word (FABULARI) from which Spanish gets *hablar* and Portuguese *falar*. But if the verb PARABOLARE prospered only in the area that was to give birth to Catalan, the same cannot be said of the noun PARABOLA, which has survived in every Hispano-Romance language (Sp. *palabra*, Port. *palavra*, Cat. *paraula*). The situation is further complicated by the fact that, like French but unlike the other Romance languages of the Iberian Peninsula, Catalan possesses not only *paraula* but also *mot* (both meaning *word*). What is evident from all of this is that the linguistic situation in the western empire was extremely complex. Everywhere there would have been competing linguistic forms of one kind or another. Differentiation would thus have emerged naturally as some areas favoured one solution, while others favoured another or, perhaps, retained more than one solution, as illustrated by French and Catalan in the example given here.

The development of Romance writing systems

The most dramatic changes affecting the language occur sometime between the collapse of the western empire in the late fifth century AD and the appearance of the first texts in Romance. With no central power to hold Latin together, this is the time when the spoken idiom is able to develop more freely to produce the various Romance languages. The texts that survive from this turbulent era have all the appearance of being written in Latin. Because of this, it used to be thought that a peculiar type of bilingualism operated in these lands. The assumption was that whereas Romance was used for the purposes of everyday conversation, Latin survived as the language of culture and was used for writing and, perhaps, as the spoken language of the educated. In other words, the kind of bilingualism imagined was the kind that allocated separate functions to each language. Romance would have had a set of 'low' or vernacular functions, while Latin would have had a set of 'high' or learned functions. Many sociolinguists today apply the label *diglossia* to this kind of societal bilingualism.

Several years ago, this theory was challenged by Roger Wright. He argued that these communities were not bilingual in Latin and Romance, but monolingual in Romance. The texts that appear to be Latin are not really Latin at all, but Romance. The confusion arises simply because these communities continued to use Latin conventions for writing. As Romance moved further away from Latin, the disparity between the written and spoken forms of the language became increasingly pronounced. This eventually made the written and spoken forms of the language appear to some extent unrelated, but did not make the writing system any more unworkable than those of modern English and French which also often bear no relation to the spoken tongue. For instance, reading VERITATEM as Romance *verdad(e)* would have been no more difficult than assigning to English *knight* its current value in the spoken idiom. In other words, there is no reason to suppose that the words in these ancient texts were pronounced the way they were written.

Wright's theory is probably the biggest thing to hit Romance linguistics in recent years. In addition to rejecting the continuing existence of Latin as a separate language after the collapse of the western empire, he also addresses the emergence of separate writing systems for Medieval Latin and for Romance. As a result of the reforms instigated by the emperor Charlemagne in the ninth century, a new approach to reading and writing was developed. As Holy Roman Emperor, Charlemagne was keen to endow the church with a single language. His scholars did this by producing a writing system in which each letter of the alphabet was assigned a specific and separate phonetic value. The new system brought spelling and pronunciation close together and allowed those familiar with its conventions to read a text in much the same way even though their native languages might be different. The Medieval Latin of the church was based on such a system. In time, this approach to writing was exploited for the benefit of the Romance languages. But instead of starting with the letters of the alphabet and assigning to each of them a specific sound, scholars now started with the individual sounds of their language and assigned to each one a specific letter or combination of letters. Only subsequent to this development do we begin to find texts that are unmistakably Romance. And because scholars started, in each case, with the sounds of a very specific variety of Romance (presumably, the dominant variety in a given area) and allocated to them appropriate letters, the texts produced in France, Italy and Spain reflect for the first time the very different linguistic varieties underlying them.

The first substantial texts in Romance do not appear until the twelfth and thirteenth centuries. When they do appear, they tell us a lot about the way in which they would have been read aloud. In other words, they provide substantial information on the careful pronunciation of educated speakers. They also provide information on vocabulary, morphology and syntax.

Medieval Spanish

The sibilants of Medieval Spanish		
Symbol	Letter	Sound
/s/	pa*ss*ar	(like 's' in English sit)
/z/	ro*s*a	(like 's' in English rose)
/ts/	cabe*ç*a	(like 'ts' in English cats)
/dz/	ra*z*ón	(like 'ds' in English heads)
/ʃ/	di*x*o	(like 'sh' in English ship)
/ʒ/	fi*j*o, *g*ente	(like 'j' in French jambe)

These new texts in Romance reveal significant differences between medieval and modern Spanish. For example, the sound system of the medieval language possessed neither the *jota* (the initial sound in modern Spanish *jugar*, sounding like *ch* in 'loch') nor the *zeta* but did, on the other hand, have an aspirate *h*, seven distinct sibilant sounds (but because the *ch* sound in words like *chico* has remained unchanged, only the six sounds listed above will be discussed), and also kept *b* and *v* separate. In terms of vocabulary, modern Spanish is characterised by large numbers of borrowings from Italian, English and the indigenous languages of the New World, and by recent importations from French, Latin and Greek. For obvious reasons, the medieval tongue had none of these. However, it had borrowed heavily from Arabic and this set it apart from the other Romance languages of the day. It also sets it apart from modern Spanish, which has lost many of the arabisms current in earlier centuries. Besides the differences resulting from borrowing, there are those arising out of the process of word replacement that occurs naturally in all languages. For instance, whereas medieval *abiltar* (to insult) long ago dropped out of the language, *guardaespaldas* (bodyguard) entered it only recently. This constant process of renewal, essential for the language to function in an ever-changing world, means that, from time to time, we need to consult a specialist dictionary when reading older forms of Spanish. Finally, as an example of syntactic change, we can point to the verb *haber* (medieval *aver*). In modern Spanish, it functions almost exclusively as an auxiliary and is used to form compound past tenses: *he cantado*, *había cantado* (I have sung; I had sung), etc. In the medieval language, however, *aver* also operated as a fully-fledged verb, much like modern French *avoir*, and meant *to have* or *to possess*. In the early thirteenth-century epic poem entitled *El Poema de mio Cid*, we read in line five: 'Sospiró mio Cid, ca mucho avié grandes cuidados' (My Cid sighed for he had very great cares). There is no doubt that *aver* functions here just as *tener* does in modern Spanish.

> ### A sample of old Spanish
>
> Et vós, señor conde Lucanor, si queredes fazer lo que devierdes, quando viéredes que cumple para defendimiento de lo vuestro et de los vuestros, et de vuestra onra, nunca vos sintades por lazeria, nin por trabajo, nin por peligro. (And you, Count Lucanor, if you want to do what you ought, when you see what is necessary for the defence of your possessions, your people and your honour, never be deterred by adversity, trouble or danger.)
>
> (Don Juan Manuel, *El conde Lucanor*)

Spanish during the Renaissance

Castilian was first reduced to a set of grammatical rules by an Andalusian, Antonio de Nebrija, who published his *Gramática de la lengua castellana* in 1492. This was not only the first grammar of Castilian, but also the first grammar of a Romance language. Nebrija presented it to the Castilian Crown, saying that it would enable Isabella the Catholic's non-Castilian-speaking subjects to be taught the language of their sovereign. Even so, the grammar met with little success, partly because it was based on Nebrija's earlier Latin grammar and was not specifically designed for Romance and also because the Spanish monarchy was not at this time concerned to promote a standard variety of the language. The next few generations of grammarians seem, for the same reason, to have had no more success. However, one thing common to several of them is a preoccupation with spelling. In this respect, a number followed Nebrija in advocating a spelling system that closely reflected pronunciation, thereby underlining, in their view, the primacy of speech over writing.

One of the reasons for this preoccupation with spelling was that the sound system of Castilian had changed considerably since the medieval period without any general consensus over how it should be represented in writing. For example, in much of central and northern Spain, aspirate /h/ had become mute by the Golden Age, the once distinct and separate sounds represented by the letters *b* and *v* had merged, and the process of simplifying the system of six sibilants (see above) was well under way. The reorganisation of this system eventually left the language with just one sibilant (/s/), but also produced two entirely new sounds (the *jota* and the *zeta*). In contrast, the important city of Seville, Spain's principal link with the New World, reorganised the sibilant system differently. Here the dominant solution never came to include the *zeta*. The late appearance of this sound (not fully attested until the seventeenth and eighteenth centuries) and the continued use of *seseo* in the prestigious Spanish of urban Seville probably explain the universality of *seseo* in the Americas and its dominance in the Canary Islands.

> ### A sample of Golden Age Spanish
>
> En este tiempo, vino a don Diego vna carta de su padre, en cuyo pliego venía otra de vn tio mio llamado Alonso Ramplon, ombre allegado a toda virtud y muy conoçido en Segouia por lo que era allegado a la justiçia, pues, cuantas alli se auian hecho, de quarenta años a esta parte, an passado por sus manos. (At this time, Don Diego received a letter from his father, and I, in the same dispatch, a letter from an uncle named Alonso Ramplon. [My uncle was] a man who cleaved to all virtue and was well known in Segovia because of his connection with the justice system, for every act of justice carried out in the past forty years had passed through his hands.)
>
> (Francisco de Quevedo, *La vida del buscón llamado Don Pablos*)

The eighteenth century

By the early eighteenth century, Spanish had behind it the weight and authority of the outstanding writers of the Golden Age. Nevertheless, it possessed only one good monolingual dictionary (that of Sebastián de Covarrubias published in 1611) and spelling was still chaotic. In this sense, it compared unfavourably with Italian and French (which had half a dozen excellent monolingual dictionaries, including that of the French Academy published in 1694). Motivated principally by a desire to equip Spanish with a dictionary equal to those of French and Italian, the Marquis of Villena founded the Royal Academy of the Spanish Language in 1713. The new Academy took as its motto *Limpia, fija y da esplendor* (Purify, fix and ennoble) and immediately began work on an impressive dictionary to be published in six volumes between 1726 and 1739. This dictionary, entitled *Diccionario de Autoridades*, is so called because its entries generally contain quotations from the great writers of the Golden Age, who lend their authority to the usage recorded. The Academy produced a separate orthography in 1741 (revised in 1763 and 1815) and a grammar of Spanish in 1771. The orthography set a standard to be followed, but was not coherent in its philosophy. On the one hand, it sought to bring spelling and pronunciation closer together by eliminating graphies such as -ss- (*passar*) and ç (*fuerça*) that had long since ceased to have unique and separate functions; on the other hand, it retained, presumably for etymological reasons, letters like *h* (*hombre*) and *v* (*venir*) that no longer had any useful roles to perform, thereby pushing spelling and pronunciation apart. Nevertheless, the Academy's orthography (and grammar) eventually received the state's stamp of approval and became the models to be followed.

The nineteenth and twentieth centuries

The nineteenth century was an especially tempestuous time for Spain. Not only was the country plagued internally by political instability and military conflict, but it also lost all of its American colonies. The spread of Spanish over such a vast area, together with the break-up of the empire into some 20 countries, caused a number of linguists to fear that the language might disintegrate, just as Latin had eventually disintegrated into the Romance languages after the collapse of the Roman Empire. However, history has so far shown this fear to be unfounded. This is not to suggest that Spanish fails to display today, as in the past, important variation. There are certainly significant differences between the speech of, say, an Andalusian barrister and that of an Andalusian peasant; there are also differences between the Spanish of different geographical areas, as explained above. To these we can add the impenetrable jargons of numerous social groups such as the police, bureaucrats and politicians, criminals and drug addicts, and even users of the Internet, whose 'navegar la red' sounds just as odd to the uninitiated as does its English equivalent 'to surf the web'. Nevertheless, Spanish continues to constitute a single language. In fact, there is some evidence that it is converging rather than diverging. Educated speakers at least seem to have little difficulty understanding each other regardless of their country of origin. The rise of literacy, the existence of mass media in Spanish and a common set of conventions for writing have all helped to preserve the basic unity of the language. Collaboration between the different national academies of the Spanish language is today also an important factor. The current situation seems unlikely to change so long as individual Spanish-speaking countries continue to recognise the value of possessing a world language and resist the temptation to exploit local varieties of Spanish for the purpose of signalling separate national identities.

A sample of colloquial modern Peninsular Spanish

–¿Dónde andabais, que os he tenido que buscar con candil?
–En Ibiza, tío– dijo Magdalena muerta de risa.
–¡Cómo vivís!– se lamentó Jato.
–Calla, colega, que tuvimos que salir por pies.
('Where've you both been that I've had to hunt all over for you? [literally: 'I look for you with a lamp']
  'In Ibiza, man,' said Magdalena, killing herself with laughing.
  'It's alright for some!' [literally: 'How you live!'] lamented Jato.
  'Don't you believe it [literally: 'Be silent'], mate. We had to hightail it out of there.')

(José Luis Martín Vigil, *La droga es joven*)

SPANISH IN COMPETITION WITH OTHER LANGUAGES

Linguistic varieties sharing the same social and geographical space compete for speakers, functions and territory. Normally, the variety that proves most useful (because of its greater cultural prestige, because its speakers are more numerous or the political entity to which they belong is economically or militarily dominant) either partially or completely displaces its rivals. The history of Spanish exhibits numerous examples of competition of this kind. For example, competition started when Latin entered the Iberian Peninsula and swept aside the tongues of every pre-Roman people except the Basques.

Arabic

The Muslim invasion represented a considerable threat to Romance (see Chapter 2). The Christian north was monolingual in Romance, except for those areas where Basque was also spoken; the south presented a more complex picture. During the early period of Muslim occupation, Arabic was both the language of culture and the vernacular (or spoken language) of Arabs; different spoken varieties of Berber survived for a time, but were eventually displaced. Romance operated as the vernacular and language of culture of Christians, as well as the vernacular of some Muslims, especially those who had married local women; and Hebrew survived as the religious, and later literary, language of the Jews. As time passed, the prestige of Arabic proved conclusive. By the mid- to late tenth century, it had become the language of culture of all the cultivated inhabitants of the south, Christian and Muslim alike, and was bequeathing to Romance a host of new lexical items (see box). At this time, the future of Arabic in the peninsula seemed assured, while that of Romance seemed much less bright. However, political changes of enormous magnitude occurring almost simultaneously north and south of the Muslim–Christian political divide changed all this. Powerful Christian kingdoms began to emerge in the north just as the caliphate of Cordoba collapsed and the Muslim south became more and more fragmented. This shift in the balance of power from south to north made possible the Christian Reconquest of the peninsula and the ultimate removal of Arabic from Iberian soil.

Some borrowings from Arabic			
noria:	waterwheel	zoco:	Arab market or suk
albañil:	bricklayer or mason	alcalde:	mayor
almirante:	admiral	alfombra:	carpet

Latin and Romance in the reign of Alfonso X (1252–1282)

The 'invention' of Medieval Latin posed a new and, perhaps, unexpected threat to Romance. Medieval Latin came to be used as a literary and administrative language, as well as the language of religion and high culture generally. Sometime during the first half of the thirteenth century, Ferdinand III of León-Castile began to reverse this trend by ordering that the royal chancery should operate in Romance rather than Latin. Ferdinand's son, Alfonso X, also resurrected the school of translators that had flourished in Toledo during the twelfth century, but instead of following the earlier pattern of translating works originally in Arabic and Greek into Latin, he ordered that they should be translated into Castilian. Among these works we find treatises on chess, astrology and precious stones, as well as many other topics. In addition to translations, Alfonso arranged for original works to be composed in Castilian, including histories of Spain and of the world and impressive compilations of Castilian law. Although Alfonso did not set out consciously to create a standard language by establishing precise rules to be followed, one can nevertheless detect, over the course of his reign, a clear movement towards increased standardisation of what came to be known as *castellano drecho*. There can be no doubt that as a consequence of Alfonso's efforts, the language of Toledo became a kind of national standard that was to be acknowledged for centuries to come. Castilian had become, by the end of Alfonso's reign, the dominant language of culture in the kingdom of León-Castile, as well as the language in which the king administered all his domestic affairs.

Basque, Galician and Catalan

As the might of Castile grew, political expansion was accompanied by linguistic expansion. By the early thirteenth century, all Basque-speaking areas except for the kingdom of Navarre had accepted the Castilian monarch as their lord and the Basque language was displaced from the towns and pushed into the countryside. Similar processes may be observed in Galicia and in Valencia. In Galicia, the kings of Castile favoured Castilian administrators from the fourteenth century. Valencia belonged to the crown of Aragon but displacement of the local language (Valencian Catalan) followed the civil war of the 1520s, which produced a profound schism in Valencian society. The nobles, who had appealed to the Spanish monarchy for assistance, embraced the Castilian language and culture following the successful conclusion of the war and prompt establishment of a viceroyalty in their city. By the mid-seventeenth century meetings of the city council were no longer held in Valencian but Castilian.

The position of Catalan within Catalonia remained protected largely because of the attachment of Catalonia to the crown of Aragon and its good fortune in escaping the same kind of social schism as divided Valencian society. Whilst it is true that Castilian was adopted by a few writers dazzled by the brightness of its literature and its international status, most Catalans remained faithful to their language. However, the War of the Spanish Succession (1700–1714) marked a watershed as far as linguistic policy in Spain is concerned. In this war in which Habsburg (Austrian) and Bourbon (French) dynasties disputed the throne of Spain, the territories of the former crown of Aragon threw their weight behind the Habsburg pretender. He was defeated and Philip, Duke of Anjou, became the first Bourbon monarch of Spain. Philip punished the territories that had resisted him by dismantling their institutions and stripping them of their political autonomy. With this act, Madrid embarked on a deliberate policy, supported with legislation, to impose Castilian in the Catalan-speaking regions and, subsequently, in every region possessing its own language.

Movements in defence of Catalan, Galician and Basque emerged in the nineteenth century but did not achieve a significant breakthrough until 1931 when the Second Spanish Republic approved a constitution that gave formal recognition to regional languages. Catalonia was granted a statute of autonomy in 1932 and Catalan co-official status with Castilian within Catalonia (see Chapter 6). Galicia and the Basque Country were granted statutes of autonomy in 1936. After Franco seized power in 1939, however, the regional languages of Spain were proscribed from official, public domains and largely confined to the home until the 1970s.

Today, the local languages of Catalonia, the Basque Country, Galicia, the Balearic Islands, Valencia and Navarre all share official status with Castilian in those areas where they are spoken. In most cases, there is at least one television channel in the local language and there are often also newspapers and magazines. The local language is taught in schools and is the medium of instruction for some school subjects in a number of autonomous communities. In the Basque Country, children may even choose to be educated entirely through the medium of Basque; in Catalonia, there is currently a programme of linguistic immersion in Catalan for all those enrolled in the first phase of primary education within the state sector. Approximately a quarter of all Spaniards today speak a language other than Castilian. These languages are competing with Castilian for speakers and domains. In fact, fears are regularly expressed in some circles that Catalan may at some point displace Castilian in Catalonia.

The New World: Spanish and the indigenous languages

When Columbus discovered the New World, it was inhabited by hundreds of indigenous peoples who between them spoke hundreds of languages. Two of these languages were imperial languages: Nahuatl was the language of the Aztec Empire based in Mexico, while Quechua was the language of the Inca Empire based in Peru. Over time, Spanish borrowed many words from these languages, especially words denoting fauna and flora peculiar to the New World. From Nahuatl, it borrowed liberally, taking words like *aguacate* (avocado), *tomate*, *chocolate* and *cacahuete* (peanut); from Quechua, it took, for example, *alpaca* (alpaca or mammal similar to the llama), *cóndor* and *mate* (local infusion or tea). Some of these words were exported from Spain to the rest of western Europe. As we might expect, Amerindian words constitute a significant portion of the current lexical stock of Spanish. However, they are far more numerous in New World Spanish than in Peninsular Spanish.

During the early years of colonisation, there was much controversy over what rights, if any, the indigenous peoples of the New World had. Despite the best efforts of men like Bartolomé de las Casas on their behalf, the indigenous people secured only limited support in Spain. Nevertheless, Philip II ruled in 1580 that no one should be ordained to the priesthood who did not know the language of his parishioners. Missionaries and churchmen in the New World were henceforth obliged to learn the language(s) of the local inhabitants under their ecclesiastical jurisdiction. This situation continued until 1770 when Charles III ordered exclusive use of Spanish in the Americas.

The distribution of indigenous languages in the New World is today very uneven. Whereas Cuba and Uruguay seem to have no indigenous languages, countries like Mexico and Peru have a hundred or more. In some cases, these languages are clearly facing extinction. Mixteco is a language spoken in Oaxaca, Mexico. Apparently, it had in 1990 only 138 speakers and all were over 50 years of age. In contrast, other indigenous languages have several million speakers. For instance, some 90 per cent of the population of Paraguay speak Guaraní, with around 52 per cent of those who live in rural areas being monolingual in the language. This means, of course, that the spread of Spanish also varies enormously from country to country. While approximately 86 per cent of the population of Mexico knows Spanish, the figure for Guatemala hovers around 60 per cent and may be even lower for Paraguay. In addition to numbers of speakers, we need also to consider the status of the indigenous languages. Only in a few countries do they enjoy official recognition. This is so in Paraguay, which recognises Guaraní alongside Spanish, and also in Bolivia, which has three official languages (Spanish, Aymara and Quechua), and in Peru, which has two (Spanish and Quechua). It is safe to conclude that the threat posed to Spanish by these languages is substantial only in countries like Paraguay, where the local language enjoys official status and is spoken by a majority of the population. There would seem to be little to fear in countries like Mexico which do not recognise any indigenous language and are, from the point of view of these languages, linguistically fragmented.

Spanish in the USA

The rapid growth of the Hispanic community has been a cause of concern to many Anglo-Americans in recent decades. Part of their concern is that Spanish may soon pose a serious challenge to English in some states. Accordingly, in 1983, some Republicans founded the movement known as 'English Only'. It claims to be inspired by a desire to encourage immigrants to learn English and has successfully promoted English Only bills in some 25 states of the union. Its critics argue that its aim is to 'pick off' the states one by one until the entire union accepts English as its only 'official' language. They also argue that the movement is unconstitutional since one of the purposes of the US constitution is to protect minorities. Whatever its motivation or constitutional status, the success of English Only may certainly be considered a blow to Spanish in the USA. Another serious blow to Spanish was delivered in 1998 when the state of California voted to abolish bilingual education for Hispanic children.

The kind of Spanish spoken in the USA is often typical of situations of language contact. Speakers regularly insert English words into Spanish sentences ('Leo un magazine'). They also code switch. In some cases of code-switching, the two languages are ordered sequentially within the sentence, with an English clause followed by a Spanish clause or vice versa ('I'll start a sentence in English y termino en español'); in other cases, speakers exhibit intrasentential switching ('Si tú eres puertorriqueño, your father's a Puerto Rican, you should at least de vez en cuando, you know, hablar español'). This switching requires great skill and is often found in the speech of competent bilinguals.

The mixing of Spanish and English has given rise to a hybrid variety known as Tex-Mex in Texas and as Spanglish elsewhere. In addition to the kinds of features listed above, this variety hispanicises basic lexical items (*moguear* 'to mug'; *cuitear* 'to quit'; *chusar* 'to choose'; *el suiche* 'the switch'; *el mofle* 'the muffler/silencer') and translates English phrases literally into Spanish (*llamar pa' tras* 'to call back'). Defenders of Spanglish want it recognised as a distinct language on the grounds that it is an integral part of the identity of a community that speaks something that is neither English nor Spanish. As a linguistic variety, it is certainly sufficiently widespread for us to conclude that it poses a significant threat to Spanish in the USA.

Some recent Anglicisms	
ultrasonido:	ultrasound scan. Spain uses *ecografía*.
frisar:	to freeze (*comida frisada* 'frozen food'). *Frisar* also exists in Spain and the New World as a gallicism with a very different set of meanings.
chequear:	to check (*chequear el 'email'*). In Spain, *chequeo* exists as a noun meaning 'medical check-up'.
Chance/chanza:	chance (*deme un chance* 'give me a chance'). Spain expresses it as *deme una oportunidad*.

The impact of US English on Spanish is, of course, not limited to Spanish spoken in the USA. Much of the Spanish of Spanish America shows considerable borrowings from US English, especially in the domains of sport and technology. In many cases, Spanish derives new forms from the English base word, creating items that do not exist in the source language. A good example is *webear* ('to surf the web'), which may be heard in Panama as an alternative to the more standard *navegar la red*. Just as American Spanish is richer in Amerindian loanwords than is Peninsular Spanish, so too is it richer in Anglicisms. The insert above provides some further examples of recent borrowings in New World Spanish. However, it should be noted that they are not necessarily found everywhere in the New World and that some of them co-exist with more traditional ways of expressing the same concept.

CONCLUSION

Better than any other Romance tongue, Spanish has replicated the history of Latin. Once an insignificant linguistic variety spoken only in central northern Spain, it became the language of one of the world's greatest empires. Despite the break-up of that empire, its global importance has remained undiminished. Its past is exotic and fascinating; its future, bright and yet full of challenges. It will surely continue to open many doors to its speakers and provide students of linguistics with a host of exciting areas of research.

> ### Glossary of linguistic terms used in this chapter
>
> **Conjugation:** Verb class: *cantar, comer, vivir* represent the three conjugations or verb classes of Spanish. All Spanish verbs belong to one or other of these classes and are conjugated or given endings appropriate to the class to which they belong.
>
> **Declension:** Noun class: Classical Latin had five declensions or noun classes. All Latin nouns belong to one of these classes and are declined or given endings appropriate to the function they have within the sentence and the class to which they belong. Adjectives and pronouns are also declined.
>
> **Direct object:** Noun or noun equivalent denoting the goal or result of the action of a verb: 'The car hit *the boy*'.
>
> **Indirect object:** Noun or noun equivalent that benefits or suffers as a result of the action of a verb: 'Mary gave a present *to her mother*'.
>
> **Grammar:** The grammar of a language consists of those systems of rules that define its structures.
>
> **Intonation:** Modulation or change of voice pitch to produce a statement, question or exclamation, etc.
>
> **Morphology:** The part of grammar that studies word formation.
>
> **Phonetics:** Phonetics studies the production, transmission and perception of speech sounds.
>
> **Sibilant:** Sound resembling hissing or whistling like the 's' of English sit or 'sh' of English shop.
>
> **Subject:** The person or thing about which the verb makes a statement: '*The man* runs'.
>
> **Syntax:** The part of grammar that deals with the arrangement of words into clauses and sentences.

FURTHER READING

Green, J. N. 1988. Spanish. In Harris, M. and Vincent, N. (eds) *The Romance languages*. London and Sydney: Croom Helm, pp. 79–130.

Klee, C. and Ramos García, L. (eds) 1991. *Sociolinguistics of the Spanish-speaking world: Iberia, Latin America, USA*. Tempe: Bilingual Press.

Moreno Fernández, F. and Otero, J. 1998. Demografía de la lengua española. In *El español en el mundo. Anuario del Instituto de Cervantes 1998*. Madrid: Arco Libros and Instituto Cervantes, pp. 59–86.

Penny, R. 1991. *A history of the Spanish language*. Cambridge: Cambridge University Press.

Penny, R. 2000. *Variation and change in Spanish*. Cambridge: Cambridge University Press.

Poplack, S. 1982. 'Sometimes I'll start a sentence in English *y termino en español*': towards a typology of code switching. In Amastae, J. and Elías-Olivares, L. (eds) *Spanish in the United States: sociolinguistic aspects*. Cambridge: Cambridge University Press.

Siguan, M. 1992. *España plurilingüe*. Madrid: Alianza Universidad.

Silva-Corvalán, C. (ed.) 1995. *Spanish in four continents: studies in language contact and bilingualism*. Washington, DC: Georgetown University Press.

Williams, L. 1994–1995. Orthographic theory and practice and the diplomatic Spanish of the seventeenth century. *Journal of Hispanic Research* 3, pp. 13–29.

Williams, L. 1997. The act of reading: how straightforward is it? *Bulletin of Hispanic Studies (Liverpool)* 74, pp. 265–74.

Wright, R. 1982. *Late Latin and early Romance in Spain and Carolingian France*. Liverpool: Francis Cairns.

Wright, R. 2000. The future of Spanish: convergence or divergence? *La Marca Hispánica* 11, pp. 1–19.

ELECTRONIC SOURCES

Grimes, B. F. (ed.) 1996. *Ethnologue*. Summer Institute of Linguistics: http://www.sil.org/ethnologue

United States Census Bureau: http://www.census.gov

2

Medieval Spanish Studies

Louise M. Haywood

Ayer era rey de España,
hoy no lo soy de una villa,
ayer villas y castillos,
hoy ninguno posseýa,
ayer tenía criados,
hoy ninguno me servía,
hoy no tengo una almena
que pueda dezir que es mía
¡Desdichada fue la hora,
desdichado fue aquel día
en que nascí y heredé
la tan grande señoría!
Pues lo lavía de perder
todo junto y en un día.

(Yesterday I was King of Spain, today I don't even rule a town. Yesterday I possessed towns and castles. Today I have none. Yesterday I had servants. Today no one serves me. Today I don't even have a battlement I can call my own. Cursed was the hour, cursed was the day I was born to inherit such a great lordship, since I had to lose it, all at once in a single day!)

(Wright 1987: 46)

The contributions of Islam are very much in evidence in modern Spain, not only in its famous buildings, most notably the Alhambra at Granada and the Mosque at Cordoba, and in the cuisine, for example, Spain's famous meatballs, *albóndigas*, but also in the names of everyday foods and institutions, for example, *aceitunas, ayuntamiento, alcalde* (olives, town hall, mayor) (see Chapter 1). All of this reveals the importance of Spain's medieval past. Evidence about medieval Spain survives not only through these material and political reminders but also in written texts, such as poetry, historical chronicles, and medieval charters and legal documents. The Hispanic Middle Ages was a rich and complex society, whose organisation and structures fluctuated a great deal over the seven centuries, in which the peninsula was occupied by the three major religions of the modern world: Judaism, Christianity and Islam. At times the peoples of these religions lived in conflict and at others they enjoyed relative peace. However, each group also passed through extensive periods of internal civil unrest and warfare, and their allegiances often changed. The ethnic mix of the medieval past was viewed with suspicion by many nineteenth-century thinkers who saw the Christian struggle for dominance as an expression of indigenous Hispanic character, on the one hand, under threat of dilution through racial mixing and, on the other, as capable of impressing its own identity on invaders. Legends based around the lives of historical figures were used to justify the view of the true Spaniard as a warrior in need of strong leadership and this image of the Spanish national character was much promoted in the twentieth century by Franco's Nationalists. Many medieval legends and literary themes continue to be of considerable significance in the development of modern national identity, and incidentally also of consequence in European, Anglophone and Spanish-speaking American society. A sound grasp of Spain's past is essential in developing an understanding of its modern culture.

The largely nineteenth-century view of Spanish national character was challenged in the mid-twentieth century by the argument that Spain was actually a product of the interaction, or *convivencia*, of the three great religions. After Franco's death, critical discussion of these ideas moved away from the notion of national character and towards a more realistic assessment of the accomplishments of medieval Iberian civilisation. Remarkably, in contrast with our knowledge of other medieval European cultures, previously unknown materials, often of considerable importance, continue to come to light. Many documents have received little or no attention and a large number are not yet published in modern editions. This means that our understanding of the period is developing gradually as more information is discovered revealing a society whose organisation and mentalities differ greatly from our own. Many topics illustrate this difference but here the focus will be on a selection of written texts, on multiculturalism or *convivencia*, the struggle for dominance between Christian and Muslim Spain, and on the structure of society, and love and marriage.

WRITTEN TEXTS

Medieval Iberian culture straddled the divide between Western European Christian and Islamic civilisation and this enriched it and made it unique. Consequently, whilst medieval Iberian literature provides examples of familiar genres from other European languages, it also often deals with the conflicts between and amongst the Iberian peoples, as in the epic and ballad traditions. However, on occasions the survival and even existence of its literature is due to the interactions of these groups, as is the case with the *kharjas*. Epic poems are long poems (often several thousand lines) that sing the deeds of an exemplary hero who undergoes a test or challenge. Ballads, or *romances* in Spanish, are anonymous narrative songs often sung by many people in different versions, and with romantic, historical or supernatural settings. *Kharjas* may have first appeared in the ninth century and may be the first examples of lyric poetry in a language derived from Latin. They are brief snippets of song, often in the female voice and about love: 'What will I do, mother? / My lover is at the door!', 'So much loving, so much loving, beloved, so much loving! / My shining eyes became ill and they hurt so much.' They were composed in a mixture of Spanish and spoken Arabic but only survive because they were written down in Arabic or Hebrew script as concluding counterpoints to longer poems in Classical Arabic or Hebrew. The Arabic or Hebrew poems are known as *muwaššaḥat* and were often on subjects other than love, such as the praise of a patron. The *muwaššaḥa* form went on to enjoy great popularity throughout the Islamic world, where the *kharja* was couched in the locally spoken variety of Arabic.

Literature in all the major medieval genres survives: narrative and lyric poetry, epic and romance, exemplary literature, saints' lives and miracle collections, prose fiction and historiography, and early drama. The survival patterns for these genres do not always follow those for other European literatures but this in itself is a fascinating and intriguing object of study. For instance, women writers seem not to have been active as early in the peninsula as elsewhere nor are there documents supporting the performance of medieval theatre from such early dates as in, say, France. Much of the literature of the Hispanic Middle Ages is of the highest artistic quality, including several literary monuments that rival the finest and most exciting writing produced to date.

Epic and ballad

The *Poema* or *Cantar de mio Cid* (Song of the Cid, *c*.1207) is the earliest surviving epic poem in Castilian Spanish although there is some evidence suggesting that earlier epic poems did exist but have not survived. The *Poema*'s hero is Rodrigo Díaz de Vivar (*c*.1043–1099), known as the Cid, an Arabic title for Lord. The poem opens as the hero rides into exile, sadly looking back towards his deserted home but bravely accepting his fate:

> De los sos oios   tan fuertemientre llorando,
> tornava la cabeça   e estávalos catando;
> vio puertas abiertas   e uços sin cañados,
> alcándaras vazías,   sin pielles e sin mantos
> e sin falcones   e sin adtores mudados.

(From his eyes silently weeping copious tears, he turned his head and looked back at them: he saw doors left open and unlocked, bare hooks, without cloaks of cloth or leather, without falcons or moulted hawks.)

(Poema de mio Cid 1973: 75)

On account of this opening and the *Poema*'s survival in only one manuscript with a missing first page there is considerable debate about whether this emotionally affecting beginning is deliberate or just an accident of manuscript transmission.

The *Poema* is a finely structured account of the Cid's attempt to regain his honour. In its first half, after being exiled by his feudal lord, King Alfonso VI (1065–1109), the Cid re-establishes his public honour through the conquest of new territories from the Muslims and by giving gifts of booty to Alfonso, whilst in the second half he is forced to contend with the restoration of his family honour through the due process of medieval law after his sons-in-law brutally assault and desert his daughters. These two challenges test to the full the traditional strengths of an epic hero, his military skill and bravery, *fortitudo*, and his wisdom and political know-how, *sapientia*, and reveal the Cid as a truly exemplary individual.

The legend of Rodrigo Díaz de Vivar has inspired many adaptations, including a classic Hollywood film. *El Cid* (1961), starring Charlton Heston and Sophia Loren as the Cid and his wife Ximena, was restored by Martin Scorsese in the late 1990s. In grand Hollywood style, the film has sumptuous settings (with many scenes filmed in Spain) but takes considerable liberties with its sources and develops the love interest. The *Poema* also takes artistic licence with the Cid's life by conflating his two exiles into one episode and erasing mention of the Cid's service as a mercenary in the service of the Muslims.

Despite its bipartite structure, the *Poema* comprises three sections or *cantares*. The significance of this is linked to questions concerning whether the epic was sung popularly and passed on by memory or composed as a written poem by a learned author. A linked debate rages about Hispanic ballads on epic subjects, which have overlapping subject matter and a shared verse form. Ballads survive in two main ways: (1) in fifteenth- and sixteenth-century copies; and (2) in the modern folk tradition throughout the Spanish-speaking world. The crux of the debate is that many historical chronicles include snippets of verse about heroic topics written out as if they were continuous prose. The great Spanish scholar Ramón Menéndez Pidal argued that these were the vestiges of lost epic poems from a memorised tradition of sung (rather than written) epic, some of which antedated the life of the Cid. More recently Roger Wright has challenged this view by showing that many ballads pre-date their first appearance in script or print. Consequently he proposes that ballads rather than epics could be the source of the snippets of verse in prose chronicles thereby undermining the case for the existence of an early oral epic tradition.

The living traditions of Hispanic balladry and of the oral epic in Yugoslavia provide a reservoir of comparative material for testing these hypotheses.

Another noteworthy feature of the epic and ballad tradition is the extent to which female characters play important roles. Indeed most of the singers of the modern ballad tradition are women and many of their songs deal with issues about women's lives. In Spanish epic material, women characters play stronger and more diverse roles than in other Western and Northern European epics. For example, a female character is often linked to one of epic narrative's antagonists, the traitor. This is seen in the legend of the *Siete Infantes de Lara* (Seven noble sons of the house of Lara) in which Ruy Velázquez is manipulated by his bride into betraying his nephews into the hands of the Muslims, or in the ballads of La Cava which tell how Count Julián betrayed Spain to the Muslims as revenge for the rape of his daughter.

Narrative poetry and prose

Juan Ruiz's *Libro de buen amor* (Book of Good Love), written in the second quarter of the fourteenth century, is quite unlike almost any other book you will read. It contains a great diversity of material within an autobiographical frame-story about the frustrated sexual adventures of the narrator, who is largely, but not wholly, identified with the author, and who claims to be the Archpriest of Hita (near Guadalajara). The pseudo-autobiography frames other sorts of material such as short exemplary tales demonstrating how one should (or should not!) behave, many in the form of animal fables; didactic passages, some designed to instruct but others lampooned; lyric poetry, including serious secular and religious as well as parodic, comic and even obscene genres; and a number of *fabliaux*, bawdy metrical tales. In short, the *Libro* contains a variety of genre (narrative, lyric, didactic) and of tone and as such is a challenge and a pleasure to read. There is much debate about whether we should consider its message serious, to put aside sinful sexual love for divine love whether the frame is a vehicle for the Archpriest's literary dexterity or whether the *Libro* holds a message in celebration and acceptance of sexual love.

La Celestina

Fernando de Rojas's *Tragicomedia de Calisto y Melibea*, known as *Celestina* (comedy version, 1499; tragicomedy, 1502), is equally ambiguous. It tells how the seduction of a young virgin, Melibea, through the offices of a go-between and witch, Celestina, leads to the death of the lovers, many of their servants, and the bawd herself. In a concluding soliloquy Melibea's father, Pleberio, laments the loss of his daughter and the transitory nature of this world. As Fernando de Rojas was a *converso*, a Jewish convert to Christianity, the didactic content has been questioned. Should Pleberio's speech be regarded as reflecting the misery and meaninglessness of the world for a forced convert or does it contain a serious Christian message concerning the value of worldly goods and deeds? What does seem certain is that Rojas depicts a world in which sexual love corrupts all levels of society and leads to destruction.

Regarded by many as the first European novel, *Celestina* is entirely in dialogue and so resembles a modern play script on the page but it was probably intended for a partially dramatised reading by a single person. Another of its notable features is the space it gives to the portrayal of two fast-growing urban groups: salaried servants and marginalised lowlife, the latter operating on the fringes of legality as prostitutes, healers and henchmen. These characters are the forebears of the *pícaros*, or rogues, of the Golden Age picaresque novel (see Chapter 3).

FROM THE MOORS TO COLUMBUS

The verses at the beginning of this chapter come from a medieval ballad which recounts the lament of Rodrigo, the last king of the Visigoths, for the fall of Spain to the Moors. Although there are some documents and architectural remains from the rule of the Visigothic kings, medieval Hispanic studies usually begins with the events of 711 and ends around 1492: two dates which mark epoch-making events. In AD 711 the Moors, North African Berber Muslims with Arab leaders, invaded the Iberian peninsula, bringing with them an advanced civilisation. The history of al-Andalus, or Muslim Spain, falls into a series of periods: the establishment of the Umayyad dynasty, the Caliphate of Cordoba, the first period of the Taifa kings, the Almoravid Empire, the second Taifa period, the advent of the Almohads and the fall of Granada.

The events of 1492 laid the foundations from which Spain and Portugal came to dominate the world map and to be at the head of European Christendom: (1) Ferdinand and Isabella, the Catholic Monarchs (1474–1516) (whose daughter, Catherine, was Henry VIII's first wife), pushed the Christian/Muslim frontier out of Western Europe for the first time in seven centuries; (2) increased religious intolerance led to the expulsion of Jews; and, (3) the Genoese explorer Christopher Columbus returned to Spain from his voyages with news of a remarkable discovery. In many ways, 1492 marked the beginning of the modern age, for which the mentalities of the medieval world ceased representing everyday reality and instead were represented in comic or idealised notions about chivalry, as in *Don Quijote* or the legend of King Arthur.

Yet the seven centuries of history and five centuries of Spanish literature prior to 1492 reveal an extraordinary complexity and diversity which engages and perplexes us by being at once familiar and alien. For example, take the question of love. The medieval view of romantic love laid the foundations for our own. In literature, love was often represented as an ideal, and yet romantic love was not considered the primary reason for marriage and was viewed as sinful by theologians and as a sickness by physicians. Paradoxically women, thought to be a morally weaker and physically imperfect type of man, were viewed as the epitome of sin and yet were also the object of passionate, in some cases idolatrous, adoration. Eve and the Virgin Mary represent the two poles of this dichotomy.

MULTICULTURALISM AND CHANGING MEDIA

Historically the peninsula has been a site of successive waves of invasion and colonisation so that its culture encompasses pagan, Christian, Judaic and Islamic influences. From *c.* AD 1000 on, it was a melting pot of Jewish, Muslim and European Christian cultures and a main conduit bringing the learning of Ancient Antiquity into medieval Europe. The issues of cultures in contact and conflict that arise from this mix are of immediate interest and relevance to the twenty-first century. Further, as our own age teeters on the brink of the domination of a new information medium with the implications that this has for our relationship to the world, so too did the Hispanic Middle Ages move from a culture whose literary production was oral, then to one based largely on the written word in manuscripts, and then finally into the age of the printed word. Accordingly the shifts in the organisation, presentation and thematics of the written language can tell us much about cultural production at times of such fundamental change.

One characteristic of such cultural change in the Middle Ages is a polarity between innovating tendencies and conservative ones: two examples will serve to illustrate this point. First, in the second quarter of the fourteenth century, Don Juan Manuel (a courtier of royal blood) made a conservative defence of medieval feudal society in which he described the fixed nature of its three groups or estates: churchmen, the nobility and peasants, particularly focusing on the first two. Yet at the time he made these observations a new group of powerful town and city dwellers was rapidly increasing and gaining in influence. Despite this social conservatism, in his famous collection of tales, *Libro del Conde Lucanor* (The Book of Count Lucanor and Patronio, his adviser, finished 1335), he expresses a new concern with accurate transmission. His interest in accuracy may be linked to the fact that as more people learnt to read there was an increased demand for books, which had to be copied by hand and into which errors consequently slipped. Secondly, in the fifteenth century there emerged a new genre, the sentimental romance, which combined elements from pre-existing forms such as letters, the university debate tradition and chivalric romance, placing these within a narrative of frustrated or tragic sexual love. The result was the creation of a genre that deals self-consciously with its own nature as fiction and its relationship to lived experience and as such is a precursor of Miguel de Cervantes's *Don Quijote* and the modern novel.

A medieval international bestseller was Diego de San Pedro's sentimental romance, *Cárcel de Amor* (Prison of Love, 1492). Printed at least 15 times in

Spain, it was translated into Catalan, Italian, French, English and German over the next 150 years. The tragic tale, in which a young man (Leriano) dies of love, is narrated by the 'Auctor' who directly reports the speeches and actions of the other characters. The romance contains a number of superb rhetorical speeches and set pieces, such as many letters, Leriano's mother's lament for her dying son, and the description of the Author's first encounter with Leriano in the title's imaginary prison of love, each of whose features allegorically represents an aspect of love-sickness. His jailer, for example, is Desire.

ISLAMIC SPAIN TO CHRISTIAN SPAIN

The history of the peninsula from its invasion in 711 until the expulsion of Jews and the capture of Granada from the Muslims in 1492 is often described as if it were a struggle towards unity and renewed Christian dominance of the peninsula. For this reason it, and particularly 1212–1492, is often referred to as the Reconquest; however, this is not really an accurate view. There was only limited unity, with Christian control of certain regions, before the Muslims arrived, and afterwards dominance of the peninsula was not always the focus of individual monarchs or peoples.

The Umayyad dynasty

After their arrival, the Muslims soon overran the peninsula, penetrating into France. Islam was then in the ascendancy as the Umayyad dynasty (756–1031) was established. Although the reasons for the rapid success of the invasion are unclear and may be attributable to the disintegration of the Christian forces due to dynastic rivalries, another explanation continues to occupy popular imagination. Arabic historiography and Christian legend tell of Count Julián and his revenge for the rape of his daughter, La Cava. The legend of La Cava was recently enacted on the London stage as a musical, directed by Steven Dexter. In the legend Count Julián has sent his daughter, La Cava, to the court of the Visigothic King Rodrigo only for her to be seduced by the king. In revenge, Julián betrays Spain to the Muslim forces. The legend is radically reworked by Juan Goytisolo, one of Spain's leading modern novelists, in his classic novel *Vindicación del conde don Julián* (1970).

Perhaps driven by the memory of the Visigothic Empire, Christian resistance to the Muslims was strongest in the north-west (now Asturias) and the Asturian leader Pelayo (718–737) achieved the first major rout of the Muslims in the battle of Covadonga (722). Over several generations, in the east and west, Christian rulers capitalised on the Muslim withdrawal from the frontier zone to south of the River Duero and put additional pressure on the area around Barcelona. Part of their success derived from the antipathy between the leading Arab aristocrats of al-Andalus, Muslim descendants of Christians, and other ethnic groups, which gave rise to inter-ethnic conflicts, or *fitnas*, similar to those experienced in the Balkans in the 1990s.

From the Caliphate of Cordoba to the taifa kings

At the beginning of the tenth century a member of the Umayyad dynasty, Abd al-Rahman III (912–961), declared himself Caliph of Cordoba (929), that is chief Muslim leader as successor of Mohammed. During the Caliphate period (912–1031) some of the religious tensions amongst the peoples of al-Andalus were resolved: non-aristocratic frontier Muslim families finally accepted Umayyad sovereignty whilst the rebellious sentiments of the Mozarabs (assimilated Christians living under the Moors) and *muwalladun* (second generation Muslim converts) were reduced. An ambitious first minister Ibn Abi Amir, known in the North as Almanzor, usurped much of the Caliph's power and tried to establish his son Sanjul as successor. This attempt met with failure but the resultant in-fighting effectively ended the Caliphate of Cordoba. Al-Andalus broke up into around 23 small kingships, called taifas, the larger of which proceeded to take over the smaller until the advent of the Almoravids (1086). Despite constant warfare between the taifas and the Christian kingdoms, Muslim civilisation flourished.

Christian kingdoms in the eleventh century

During most of the period of the Caliphate, although individual Christian kings did make incursions into and seize some Muslim land, they seem more concerned with strengthening their own territories and developing their individual patrimony through annexation rather than with a religiously motivated conquest or with attempts to unite the crowns permanently. This can be seen in the tendency of a monarch who successfully united the kingdoms not to pass them on to his eldest male heir but to re-divide them amongst his offspring. Where this happened, frequently the partition gave way to a dynastic crisis until one of the siblings defeated or deposed the others, and in the meanwhile, the Muslims exploited the civil unrest to make territorial gains.

Perhaps the best example of this concerns the struggle between Sancho II of Castile and Alfonso VI of León. Their father, Ferdinand I of León and Castile (who reigned between 1035 and 1065), expanded the western frontier considerably but he divided amongst his heirs his kingdoms and the major taifas from which he collected tributes: Sancho II held Castile and Zaragoza; Alfonso VI had León and Toledo; García, Galicia and Portugal; whilst his daughters received dominion over all monasteries in these three kingdoms. Sancho deposed and defeated his siblings (García in 1071 and Alfonso in 1072) until his assassination resulted in the uniting of the kingdoms under Alfonso in 1076.

The internecine rivalry that preceded Sancho's assassination was of sufficient impact to pass into Hispanic legend and literature. Alfonso was accused of his brother's assassination and was forced to take an oath of denial which was overseen by the Cid, then standard bearer and commander to Sancho's Castilian army. This act, and Leonese suspicion of the Castilian forces, resulted in the Cid's exile to serve a Muslim master in Zaragoza. These events and others associated with the Cid furnished a number of literary and historiographic accounts of his life, including the *Poema as* discussed above.

Alfonso's reign established a new period in the struggle for Iberia. By 1085 he occupied Toledo, taking much of the Tagus valley. This at once established the core of New Castile but also led to a fresh danger for the Christians: the taifa kings invited a sect of North African military ascetics, the Almoravids, to come to their aid. The Almoravids came and left in a wave of Christian and Muslim deaths. When Alfonso received support from the French, the Almoravids returned, this time against the weakened taifas, which they regarded as degenerate.

From the Almoravids to the Almohads

The Almoravids (1086–1157) established themselves in al-Andalus and North Africa but civil unrest produced a new generation of taifa kings thus exposing the Almoravids to attack from a new Muslim sect, the Almohads, during the last ten years of their dynasty. The Almoravids seemed on the verge of victory over the taifas when the crusading forces of Alfonso VII (1126–1157) of Aragon and Navarre took several major towns and fortresses in the south, including the major port of Almería (1147), thereby weakening them sufficiently for the Almohads (1157–1229) to take much of the South with the first incursions from 1146. There followed a critical period in the struggle for control in the peninsula marked by two great battles: a massive Muslim victory at Alarcos (1195) over Alfonso VIII of Castile (1158–1214), reopening the road to Toledo to the Muslim forces, and their rout at Las Navas de Tolosa (1212), a turning point in Christian favour which hastened the decline of the Almohads and opened the path to the most significant Christian advance until the reign of the Catholic Monarchs. Many of the advances and retreats of the intervening years form the subjects of ballads on the frontier conflict.

Almost every Spanish region boasts its own *Ruta de los Castillos*, or touring route around the many medieval castles that populate the landscape. The castles are physical evidence of the moving frontiers between Christian Spain and al-Andalus. The first castles were built by the Muslims to deflect incursions from the north. As the border moved south the Christians seized and modified these fortresses to suit their own needs. Later the Christian lords built their own castles in lands taken from the Muslims, to vaunt their wealth and power and as a defence against civil upheaval as much as against the Muslims.

EARLY CHRISTIAN SPAIN

In the centuries between Las Navas de Tolosa and Christian victory there are historical moments in which prominent political figures came to play important roles in literary history. In the thirteenth century, Alfonso X of Castile established his court as an internationally important cultural centre. In the fourteenth century, Don Juan Manuel, grandson of Ferdinand III of Castile, became involved in court intrigue and produced a significant body of written texts, much of which deals with political themes. In addition, at the end of the fourteenth and for much of the fifteenth century, the struggle for control of the Castilian and Aragonese thrones resulted. Many ballads and much political writing dealt with this struggle.

Alfonso X of Castile

Despite an uneven political career with periods of marked unrest Alfonso X of Castile, the Wise (1252–1284), made a great contribution, probably unparalleled amongst Christian peninsular rulers, to learning and intellectual activity. Alfonso championed the use of Castilian Spanish in all aspects of life as the common language of peoples of the peninsula's three religions. He initiated the compilation of two encyclopaedic histories, the *Estoria de España* and the *General estoria*, which made use of a wide range of source materials other than the standard Latin histories, including sources from across the Pyrenees, al-Andalus, and beyond. Of several legal works, perhaps the most influential was the *Siete partidas*, finally promulgated in 1348 and of lasting impact. The *Partidas* deal with all aspects of law and its application to all the peoples of Alfonso's kingdoms and they make an excellent starting point for an understanding of mentalities in this period. At Alfonso's court, Muslims, Christians and Jews translated a vast array of non-literary works, including astronomical tables, treatises on mathematics, philosophy, science, medicine and surgery as well as literary works and the Bible.

Curiously, among the output of his court is a collection of over four hundred Marian miracle poems written in Galician Portuguese rather than Castilian (see Chapter 1). His decision not to use Castilian may derive from the fact that there was not yet a tradition of Castilian court lyric whereas Galician Portuguese was well established thereby offering a sufficiently prestigious language in which to address the Virgin. Other than religious verse, there were three genres of Galician-Portuguese lyric. The *cantigas de amor*, poems of courtly love, and the *cantigas d'escarnho e de maldizer*, satirical poems usually attacking a named victim, both clearly derived from the Occitan tradition from south-western France, whereas the third group, *cantigas de amigo*, are semi-traditional female-voice love lyrics, possibly linked to the *kharjas* and to the fifteenth-century *villancicos*, which together may reflect an indigenous tradition of women's song. In modern Spanish a *villancico* is a Christmas carol but in the Middle Ages the term referred to a traditional song, often in the female voice and with a rural setting. A *villancico* begins with a short introductory refrain (*estribillo*), followed by one or more stanzas (*mudanzas*) whose last few lines (called the *vuelta*) reprise the e*stribillo*:

Que no me desnudéis,	'Don't undress me,	
amores de mi vida,	love of my life,	*estribillo*
que no me desnudéis	don't undress me,	
que yo me iré en camisa.	I'll wear my under shift'.	
–Entrastes, mi señora,	You entered, my Lady,	
en el huerto ajeno,	A stranger's garden,	
Cogistes tres pericas	You picked three little pears	
Del peral del medio:	From the tree in its midst,	*mudanza*
Dejaredes la prenda	You shall leave a token	
De amor verdadero.	Of true love.'	
–Que no me desnudéis,	'Don't undress me,	*vuelta*
que yo me iré en camisa	I'll wear my under shift.'	

FOURTEENTH-CENTURY SPAIN

The fourteenth century was much troubled with warfare, the advent of the plague (1348), and the resultant changes in social conditions. Don Juan Manuel's machinations in the courts of Castile, Portugal and Aragon sowed a great deal of strife without ever achieving his dynastic ambitions and instead gave rise to one or two notable court scandals. His interest in court politics is reflected in his significant body of literary works mentioned above. He succeeded in making a royal match for his daughter Constanza with Alfonso IV of Portugal's son Pedro; however, the prince had a long, passionate affair with Inés de Castro, a member of Alfonso's wife's entourage.

Inés de Castro, who bore Pedro four children out of wedlock, was a childhood friend of Constanza. Infuriated that Pedro refused to marry a suitable bride after Constanza's death, King Afonso had Inés murdered. When Pedro became king he exacted vengeance and erected two marble tombs at Alcobaça depicting her life story. Legend holds that he had Inés's corpse exhumed and crowned her as queen. This dramatic version of events was immortalised in a play, *Inés de Castro*, by Juan Ruiz de Alarcón and more recently in John Clifford's play and opera libretto, with music by James Macmillan, for Scottish opera (and later translated into Spanish).

THE CATHOLIC MONARCHS AND RELIGIOUS INTOLERANCE

After almost a century of civil strife Ferdinand and Isabella restored order: they formally constituted the *Consejo de la Santa Hermandad* in 1476 to impose law and order; reorganised the governmental structures in 1480; gained the right to appoint bishops in conquered territories; and reformed the church. However, their three most significant acts were: (1) the establishment of the Spanish Inquisition, the *Consejo de la Suprema y General Inquisición*, in 1483 to enquire into the activities of *conversos*; (2) the seizure of Granada in January 1492; and (3) the expulsion of Jews who refused to convert to Christianity, later the same year.

- How long
- upgrade

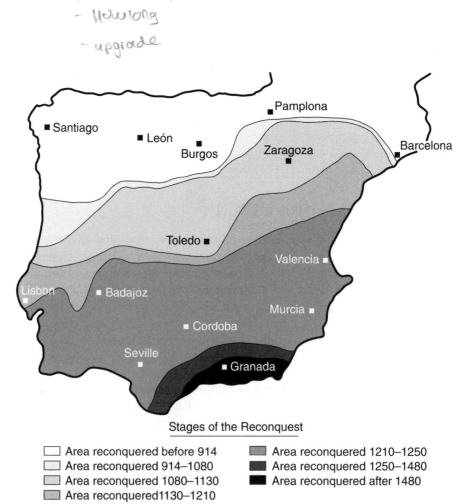

Stages of the Reconquest

- ☐ Area reconquered before 914
- ☐ Area reconquered 914–1080
- ☐ Area reconquered 1080–1130
- ☐ Area reconquered1130–1210
- ▨ Area reconquered 1210–1250
- ▨ Area reconquered 1250–1480
- ■ Area reconquered after 1480

Map 1: Stages of the Reconquest

Many Jews fled to Portugal where they were received on payment of a poll tax but they were harshly treated, reduced to slavery, had their children removed to Christian care and were finally expelled in 1496. Despite promises of tolerance from the Catholic Monarchs, in 1502 the first group of Muslims who chose not to convert to Christianity were exiled. Like *conversos*, Muslim converts were often treated with suspicion, even contempt, and barred from certain offices whilst in the Muslim territories: the fortunes of Jews and Christians depended very much on the attitudes of the group in power.

CHRISTIANS AND JEWS UNDER ISLAM IN AL-ANDALUS

Under Koranic law, Christians and Jews, as peoples whose sacred writings contained divine revelation, were permitted to practise their religion on payment of a poll tax (*jizyah*) rather than being subject to enslavement as other conquered peoples were. Nonetheless the Almoravid and the Almohad dynasties were highly intolerant of the diversity of religious practice, even amongst Muslims. In al-Andalus slaves formed a large group involved in military, domestic and administrative rather than agricultural service, as in the Christian north. Jewish families flourished under the Umayyad dynasty in the trade of luxury goods and in the fields of medicine and political administration, with many rising to hold high court positions. However from the mid-eleventh century there was a decline in their legal status from parity with Christians, including a pogrom of Granadan Jews in 1066 during civil unrest. Acculturated Christians, Mozarabs, married into Muslim families at the highest and lowest social levels and a considerable number of them converted. Their children, the *muwalladun*, rapidly became a major part of the population.

Jews probably first established themselves as a community in the peninsula as part of the Phoenician trading network, but their numbers swelled after the destruction of Jerusalem (70 BC). They participated fully in the intellectual life of al-Andalus as poets and scholars writing in Arabic, Hebrew and Latin and also occupied powerful positions in Christian courts, often as administrators or physicians. When Jewish communities in al-Andalus suffered at the hands of the Almohads from 1171 on, many chose to enter the Christian kingdoms rather than convert to Islam, frequently acting as conduits of philosophy and science from south to north.

FEUDALISM AND SOCIETY IN CHRISTIAN SPAIN

The dominant model of social organisation in the Christian Middle Ages was feudalism, based on the grant of land tenure in exchange for an oath of fealty and military service. A great lord would pledge fealty to the king as his vassal in return for heritable land rights but he in turn had his own vassals who held lands for service. A key element in Western European feudal society was weak regal authority but in the peninsula central authority remained strong on account of the king's role as permanent military leader. The feudal system reached its fullest apogee in the peninsula in Catalonia where, although the nobility were hierarchically ordered through bonds of vassalage, the ruler nonetheless retained considerable authority. In Castile and León a weakly feudal model arose in the later eleventh century. In these areas, large numbers of mobile, rather than land-bound, freemen in the newly settled territories meant that it was difficult and unnecessary for the monarchy to link the pledge of fealty to large land tenures as these freemen naturally felt some allegiance directly to the king who had led the capture of the lands they held.

During the rapid territorial expansions of the eleventh and twelfth centuries the Islamic and Jewish population increased. Simultaneously a new aristocracy arose on the basis of military or governmental service. The higher nobility, *ricos omnes*, held large estates whilst the lower nobility comprised knights, *infanzones*, who enjoyed smaller holdings or were remunerated in coin and booty. By the thirteenth and fourteenth centuries non-noble knights, *caballeros villanos*, had gained control of municipal administration and government but they were later replaced as an urban patriciate by merchants and professional men, such as lawyers, notaries and physicians. During the fourteenth and early fifteenth centuries, the theory of the three feudal estates gained considerable ideological acceptance although it presented, in fact, an inaccurate picture of contemporary society. Each of the estates – the nobility, clergy and peasants or *defensores*, *oratores* and *laboratores* – had a different area of social responsibility: warfare, religion and the production of food and other necessities. Acceptance of estate theory may have fed into pro-aristocratic feeling amongst the oligarchy and contributed to the rise in interest in the literature of chivalry.

Jews under Christianity

The first outbreak of the Black Death in 1348, the concomitant decline in population, and the need for a scapegoat increased religious intolerance in Castile and Aragon: the populous and prosperous Jewish communities were subjected to a horrific massacre in 1391. This marked the beginning of the decline in the fortunes of the peninsula's Judaic communities towards the abysmal nadir of 1492. The debt of medieval Hispanic culture to its Jewish contributors is significant. In particular, the Judaic community is partly responsible for two remarkable survivals: that of many *kharjas* and of a significant portion of the living tradition of Spanish ballads, which the Sephardim, Hispanic Jews, carried into exile with them.

THE CONTRIBUTION OF ISLAMIC CIVILISATION

The debt of peninsular, and European, civilisation to Muslim Spain is considerable. Many Islamic immigrants came from agriculturally-developed countries such as Syria and Egypt and introduced techniques for advanced agricultural and mineral exploitation as well as a wide variety of crops. The Muslims improved on irrigation methods and extended their use, running waterways from the Sierra Nevada into Cordoba. They kept open and maintained Roman roads, and improved upon postal services. As mentioned above, many aspects of agriculture, trade and civic organisation passed into the Christian kingdoms, often along with their names: *arroz*, rice; *arroba*, originally a liquid measure whose symbol @ is now familiar from e-mail addresses; *alcalde*, mayor; *alguacil*, bailiff or constable. The Muslims contributed greatly to architecture and art with magnificent building programmes such as the mosque at Cordoba and the royal palaces of the Alhambra in Granada, introducing non-figural decorative styles used in architecture and crafts and developing characteristic horseshoe-shaped arches, inspired perhaps by Roman aqueduct design or the mosque at Damascus, sometimes used to support second tiers of arches and uniquely-structured domed roofs. They were also responsible for the introduction of a number of instruments such as the lute, the guitar and the *rebec*, an early form of the fiddle.

The European debt to Hispano-Muslim literature is more controversial. Unusually for Muslim countries a court lyric tradition in colloquial (rather than Classical) Arabic developed quite rapidly. Scholars debate hotly whether this tradition and its metric forms were influenced by a pre-existing tradition of peninsular, perhaps Europe-wide, popular song or whether this innovation in al-Andalusian poetics passed into the European tradition, particularly into Occitan troubadour lyric. Most controversial of all is the possibility that the ideology and literature of courtly love, often considered a quintessentially medieval European development, found one of its points of origin in the culture of the Hispano-Islamic courts.

COURTLY LOVE AND MARRIAGE IN CHRISTIAN SPAIN

Although the validity of the term 'courtly love' has been questioned, given the differences between attitudes to sexual love portrayed in the literature of the medieval peninsular courts and modern European views, it remains useful. In Hispano-Medieval courtly love literature both the lover and the lady are noble in birth and conduct; the marital status of the lady is not often mentioned and the relationship between them does not preclude marriage nor the lady's passionate reciprocation. However, the affair is usually kept secret. The lover, regardless of his actual social status, views himself as inferior to the lady, experiences his suffering as ennobling and hopes for physical reciprocation. Due to prevailing moral and medical views, however, it is often a frustrated or tragic experience in which either some obstacle prevents consummation or, after consummation, the match is thwarted through death. The lovers may marry and, if the result of the union is not death, then much suffering is endured. In Hispano-Islamic literature several of these traits also appear: love heightens the lover's virtue; he assumes the role of a submissive servant and declares his beloved's superiority.

In reality, marriage formed the basis of the lives of most adult women living in Christian Iberia. Although the consent of both parties was expected, most marriages were arranged. Widows were considered legally competent individuals and could thus contract their own marriages after a year of mourning. The bridegroom provided *arras*, a dowry in the form of property or goods, which remained the wife's property if her husband predeceased her, and a proportion of which was heritable by their children. The bride-to-be contributed an *ajuar*, or trousseau of domestic equipment and necessities. Termination of the betrothal was rare and only permitted for legal reasons such as consanguinity or the bride's adultery. The wedding consisted of a blessing on the union and the bridegroom was held responsible for the nuptial celebrations, often lasting up to three days. Priests were enjoined only to bless marriages in public but nonetheless secret marriages did take place and were recognised.

In marriage women were often responsible in part or in whole for family businesses, shops, inns or trades and crafts, and in some cases even had military or civil responsibilities. Nonetheless men were considered the head of the family and wife-beating was permitted under canon law. A wife caught in adultery could be killed in revenge provided her lover were also severely punished but she could not accuse her husband of adultery. If, on the other hand, he kept a mistress, a *barragana*, he was guilty of informal bigamy, whose penalty was also often death. These penalties seem only to have applied to married townsmen and not noblemen or kings, who, along with bachelors and clerics, often kept *barraganas*. In many cases being a *barragana* provided a young woman and her family with a means of social mobility. Her offspring were regarded as natural children rather than as illegitimate and could be formally recognised by their father or, if he died intestate, by the community. Indeed, many priests kept *barraganas*, as suggested by Juan Ruiz's satire of the bitter response of the clergy of Talavera to an injunction to put aside mistresses, found in his *Libro de buen amor*.

FURTHER READING

Burckhardt, T. 1972. *Moorish culture in Spain*. London: George Allen and Unwin.

Deyermond, A. D. 1971. *A literary history of Spain: the Middle Ages*. London: Ernest Benn.

Dillard, H. 1984. *Daughters of the Reconquest: women in Castilian town society*. Cambridge: Cambridge University Press.

Fletcher, R. 1989. *The quest for El Cid*. New York: Knopf.

Frenk, M. 1990. *Lírica española de tipo popular: Edad Media y Renacimiento*. Madrid: Cátedra.

Glick, T. F. 1979. *Islamic and Christian Spain in the early Middle Ages*. Princeton: Princeton University Press.

Imamuddin, S. M. 1981. *Muslim Spain, 711–1492 AD: a sociological study*. Medieval Iberian Peninsula Texts and Studies 2. Leiden: Brill.

Mackay, A. 1989. Religion, culture, and ideology on the late Medieval Castilian–Granadan Frontier. In Bartlett, R. and Mackay, A. (eds) *Medieval frontier societies*. Oxford: Clarendon Press, pp. 217–43.

O'Callaghan, J. F. 1975. *A history of Medieval Spain*. Ithaca: Cornell University Press.

Poema de mio Cid. 1973. Michael, I. (ed.), 2nd edn. Madrid: Castalia.

The Poem of the Cid: a bilingual edition with parallel text. 1984. Michael, I. (ed.). Trans. by R. Hamilton and J. Perry. Harmondsworth: Penguin.

Ruiz, Juan. 1989. *Libro de buen amor*. Gybbon-Monypenny, G. B. (ed.) Madrid: Castalia.

Wright, R. 1987. *Spanish ballads*, 2nd edn. Warminster: Aris and Phillips.

Wright, R. 1995. *Early Ibero-Romance*. Newark: Juan de la Cuesta.

3

Golden Age Studies: Spain and Spanish America in the sixteenth and seventeenth centuries

Terence O'Reilly

What are the challenges facing Golden Age Studies? First, a large number of the texts we need in order to form a clear view of this period remain unstudied. Many survive in printed form, but have not been examined closely in modern times; many more are still in manuscript; most have yet to be reproduced in trustworthy critical editions. And secondly, interpretation of the texts we do know has been bedevilled by modern controversies about three events that shaped the Golden Age: (1) the unification of the Iberian kingdoms around Castile, (2) the conquest and colonisation of the New World, and (3) resistance within Spain to certain aspects of the European Renaissance and Reformation. At the time of the Spanish Civil War and in its aftermath, these events were viewed positively, on the whole, by Franco's Nationalists, who found in them models to imitate, but negatively by Republicans, for whom they signified an erosion of freedom. Strange as it may seem, both sides sought in the Golden Age the origins of the conflict in which they were involved. But since the death of Franco the situation has changed. The task of editing texts, known and unknown, has been energised by a new generation of scholars. In a stream of studies, both historical and literary, many of our received notions about the period have been rethought. These studies have also underlined a basic truth: the literature of the Golden Age is informed by a mentality very different from our own. To read it with understanding, therefore, we must be sensitive to its otherness, otherwise we shall find in it no more than a reflection of our own concerns.

UNITY AND DIVERSITY

The Golden Age witnessed the ascendancy of Castile, especially in the century before 1580 (see Chapter 2), when the medieval kingdoms of Iberia came together as a political unit, namely *la monarquía española* (the Spanish monarchy). The process began in 1469 with the marriage of Ferdinand of Aragon and Isabella of Castile, an alliance which resulted ten years later in the union of Castile and the Crown of Aragon (as Catalonia, Aragon and Valencia were collectively known). It continued with the annexation of the Moorish kingdom of Granada (1492), Navarre (1512) and eventually Portugal (1580–1640). The heart of the monarchy lay in Castile, which was initially more prosperous and populous than its neighbours, and when the royal court ceased to be itinerant the machinery of government became fixed in Madrid (apart from a brief period in Valladolid).

But ascendant though Castile was, it would be mistaken to see Spain at this time as a centralised state in the modern sense. In their economies and systems of government the various kingdoms continued to be distinct. To Castilians, moreover, it sometimes seemed that the unity of the monarchy was far from assured. Two poems by Fray Luis de León, a university teacher in Salamanca, convey this. Both were written about 1570 for a clerical friend, Don Pedro Portocarrero, who had been entrusted with government responsibilities. In the first (Ode 2) the poet looks north to Galicia, and sees there a harsh, uncultured population, to whom his friend is bringing order and learning. In the second (Ode 22) he looks south to Granada, where an unruly people, the *moriscos* (converted Moors), are fighting a war (the Second Rebellion of the Alpujarras) in which his friend is becoming caught up. In both poems Old Castile is portrayed as the locus, in a barbarous world, of civilisation and Christian faith. During the century that followed such perceptions were sharpened as Castile, her population declining and her economy in disarray, struggled to cope with the revolt of Catalonia (1640–1652) and the secession of Portugal from the union (1640).

LANGUAGE AND LITERATURE

One factor that gave unity to the *monarquía española* was the popularity of Castilian, which spread during the late fifteenth century to all parts of Spain, and became the medium in which political, religious and literary activities were normally conducted. This development was made possible by the printing press, which arrived in Iberia early in the 1470s. Concentrated in the towns of Castile, it created a demand for books in Spanish which writers throughout the peninsula sought to meet, even when Castilian was not their native tongue. A case in point is Juan Boscán (d.1542), a Catalan from Barcelona, whose translation of Baldesar Castiglione's *Cortegiano* (The

Courtier) became a model of Castilian prose. Portuguese writers contributed too, among them some major figures such as Gil Vicente (d.1536?), more than half of whose plays are wholly or partly in Castilian, and Jorge de Montemayor, who wrote the first Spanish pastoral romance, *Los siete libros de la Diana* (*c.*1559).

At this point, Castilian was not imposed on Spain politically, as it was to be later, in the eighteenth century and beyond. In Catalonia, for instance, Catalan continued to be the official language of government and the medium of instruction in schools, while in the north the *fueros* (law codes) of the Basque provinces remained in *euskera* (Basque). And at the popular level the songs and ballads of the oral tradition continued to flourish in the various languages of the peninsula.

Map 2: The Iberian Peninsula in the Golden Age

RACE AND CLASS

Spaniards in the Golden Age often wrote about the society in which they lived as if it were a homogenous community, united in its loyalties and beliefs. In reality, however, it was divided by social tensions rooted in class and race. The co-existence (or *convivencia*) of Christians, Jews and Moors (Muslims) came to an end in the early Golden Age when the Crown imposed religious unity on its subjects (see Chapter 2). In 1492 it decreed that the Jews should accept baptism or be expelled, and ten years later the same measure was applied to the Moors. The result was a sudden growth in size of two racial minorities, both Christian in name, whom it was hoped initially to assimilate, if possible by peaceful means. In the event, however, recourse was had in both cases to coercion, with appalling results of which contemporaries were aware, and which many of them deplored.

The first generation of convert Jews (*conversos*) was persecuted by the Inquisition, which was established in Castile (1478) and the Crown (or Kingdom) of Aragon (1487) in order to ensure that they had abandoned their traditional faith. The next generation was more integrated, and even produced from within its ranks a number of Christian reformers, including San Juan de Avila, whose introduction to the Christian life, *Audi Filia* (1556), was read widely. But in 1547 the cathedral chapter of Toledo ruled that no one of *converso* descent should hold a dignity or prebend, and within a few years the requirement of *limpieza de sangre* (purity of blood) had been adopted by many corporations, civic and religious.

The privileging of non-Jewish ancestry divided Spaniards deeply. It was opposed, on the whole, by the nobility, many of whom had Jewish forebears, and also by sections of the Church, notably the Society of Jesus, whose founder, San Ignacio de Loyola (d.1556), set his face against anti-Semitism. It was supported, on the other hand, by the rising class of *cristianos viejos* (Old – that is, pure-blooded – Christians), from among whom the Crown tended to draw the civil and ecclesiastical administrators it required. In time the Crown became critical of the insistence on *limpieza*, and the Inquisition tried to eradicate it, though with limited success. Gradually, and under duress, the *conversos* became assimilated, in some cases so completely that nowadays it is hard to trace them in the family records that have survived.

The bitterness that the *converso* problem caused may be glimpsed in *La vida del buscón* (The life of the rogue), a picaresque novel (from *pícaro*, or rogue) whose low-born anti-hero, Pablos, is satirised mercilessly for aspiring to rise in society and become a *caballero* (gentleman) despite his Jewish ancestry. Its author, Francisco de Quevedo (d.1645), was a nobleman of Old Christian stock.

The *moriscos*, on the other hand, resisted assimilation fiercely, and on two occasions (in 1499–1500 and 1568–1570) they fought to defend their customs in the Alpujarras mountains near Granada. Both uprisings were crushed, and after the second, the *moriscos* of Granada were dispersed throughout Castile. A generation later (1608–1614) most of the *moriscos* in Spain were expelled, ostensibly because of the security threat they were felt to pose at a time of conflict in the Mediterranean between Christians and Turks. Reaction to the expulsion was mixed. Some supported it enthusiastically, while others had reservations, including those in the government and Church who had favoured a policy of peaceful assimilation. Many, it seems, accepted that it was necessary, but were aware of the suffering it caused. This latter view is the one conveyed, shortly after the expulsion was completed, in the second part of *Don Quixote* (Chapter 53), where Miguel de Cervantes portrays a chance meeting between Sancho Panza and Ricote, a *morisco* neighbour and friend. Deeper reservations surfaced later. They are apparent in *Amar después de la muerte* (To love after death, *c*.1632–1633), a play by Pedro Calderón de la Barca about the Second Rebellion of the Alpujarras, which indicates that the *moriscos* had genuine grievances and were not treated fairly by their foes. It also implies that, handled wisely, they might have been assimilated after all.

HONOUR AND SHAME

The social tensions in Golden Age Spain, and the competing identities that underlay them, may be discerned in the notions of honour that occur in the literature of the time. Traditionally honour was associated with noble birth and behaviour, particularly constancy in love and valiant deeds, and this view of it was central to the chivalric romances, which narrated the adventures of knights and ladies in the legendary world of the Arthurian tales. The first, *Amadís de Gaula* (1508), quickly became a bestseller, and it was imitated in countless sequels for nearly a hundred years.

Another view, however, located honour not in blood that was aristocratic or 'blue', but in blood that was 'clean', the *limpieza de sangre* of the Old Christians. The friction that could arise between this notion and the traditional one (class v. race) was explored in various works, among them the peasant-honour plays of Lope de Vega (d.1635). In the first of these, *Peribáñez y el Comendador de Ocaña*, the conflict between a young nobleman and Peribáñez, the villager he has wronged, is presented as a clash between two social classes, whose differing concepts of honour (noble and Old Christian) are contrasted and opposed. The play is set in the medieval past, but the tensions it depicts were contemporary.

A further view of honour identified it with the outward signs, rather than the substance, of respectability. *Lazarillo de Tormes* (1554), a work of fiction whose author is unknown, portrays the comic consequences of such a notion in one of its characters, the *escudero* (squire), who goes to hilarious lengths in order to seem well-born and well off, whereas in reality his origins are shrouded in mystery and he does not have a penny. The potentially tragic consequences of the notion of honour, on the other hand, are explored in the wife-murder plays of Calderón. In the most disturbing, *El médico de su honra* (1635), the noble protagonist, Don Gutierre, hires a surgeon to bleed his wife to death, rashly surmising that she has been unfaithful and has put his honour at risk. Her innocence, which the audience sees, drives home the point of the play: when honour is separated from right judgement and love it becomes a savage force.

Cutting across all these views there was the further belief that honour is not, essentially, a matter of class, race or reputation, but of inner virtue. This notion, which had roots in both Classical and Christian Antiquity, was often articulated in the writings of religious authors and humanists, most memorably, perhaps, in those of Santa Teresa de Avila (d.1582), a contemplative nun and foundress, whose family origins were *converso*. In the anonymous *Lazarillo de Tormes* it plays a crucial role. The narrator and anti-hero, in many respects a forerunner of the *pícaro*, boasts that his life is a success, for from lowly origins he has risen to become a man of honour. But the honour he claims to possess has been attained at the cost of his integrity, as the ending makes plain: in order to keep his job in Toledo he has married the mistress of his employer, a well known cleric in the town. This glaring fact, of which he seems, disingenuously, unaware, imbues the narrative with an irony that undermines the image he projects, calling into question the values of the world in which he lives.

THE OLD WORLD AND THE NEW

The Atlantic voyage of Christopher Columbus in 1492, and the conquest and colonisation of the New World that followed, gave Spain vast territories overseas, and made Castilian, in the long run, a world language (see Chapter 1). They also inspired the *Chronicles* of the New World, a body of writing which includes eye-witness accounts by conquistadors, ethnographic studies by early missionaries, and general histories penned in Spain. At first sight it is not easy to trace the impact made by these events on the literary imagination of Spain, which remained in many ways focused on, and shaped by, the cultural traditions of the Mediterranean. But their influence may be detected at a deeper level, in two areas in particular: mystical works and prose fiction.

Mystical poetry and prose

When Columbus and the first chroniclers tried to convey their experience of wonder at the marvels they had beheld, they drew on biblical and classical images of paradise, including the Old Testament image of the islands at the end of the world that the Word of God was destined one day to reach (e.g. Jeremiah 31:10). These images recur later in the Golden Age in mystical writings about the inner journey to God, in which the divine presence within the soul is evoked in paradisal terms that reflect early descriptions of America. In the *Cántico espiritual* of San Juan de la Cruz (d.1591), for instance, the soul's exploration of the mystery of God is compared to a journey through 'strange islands' (*insulas extrañas*) whose unfamiliar features provoke wonder. And in the *Carta para Arias Montano* of Francisco de Aldana (d.1578), the interior world of the contemplative is described, in detail and ecstatically, as 'God's Indies' (*las Indias de Dios*).

Prose fiction

Golden Age writers cultivated fiction assiduously, producing in the process a series of experiments in narrative which modern critics have divided into 'genres': the chivalric romance, the picaresque novel, the pastoral romance, the exemplary tale, the Byzantine novel, and so on. Many of these experiments were brought together by Cervantes in the pages of *Don Quixote* (Part 1, 1605; Part 2, 1615). This work is, in many ways, a 'book about books', and it has been justly described as the first great novel of modern times. What provoked these experiments, and why did they occur in Spain rather than elsewhere? Recent scholarship has sought answers in the non-fictional narratives that the New World inspired, and has drawn attention to the fact that when writing their accounts the early chroniclers had to face a number of technical problems that were later confronted as well by writers of fiction. One of these problems is the crucial issue that Cervantes placed at the centre of his work, that is, how to bring together reality and make-believe, or 'the reconciliation of verisimilitude with the writer's obligation to surprise and delight his readers, to provoke wonder' (see Ife and Butt 1991: 204).

The New World left its mark also on Spain's conscience, thanks largely to the efforts of Fray Bartolomé de Las Casas (d.1576), who dedicated his life to defending the natural rights of *los indios*, as the native inhabitants of Spanish America were called (because Columbus thought he had found a new route to India). In pursuit of his goal Las Casas lobbied for legislation to protect them, and documented as fully as he could the greed and cruelty of the colonists. He also combated the arguments of those, like the humanist Juan Ginés de Sepúlveda, who held that the *indios* were not fully human and could therefore be treated as slaves. The results of his campaign were mixed. He did not put a halt to the abuses he deplored, for the laws passed at his instigation were not enforced. But he did make contemporaries aware of the suffering that colonisation had caused, publicising it in his best known work, *Brevísima relación de la destruición de las Indias* (A short account of the destruction of the Indies). He won support for his views in influential quarters of the government and the Church, including the Dominican order to which he belonged.

The influence of Las Casas may be sensed in *La Araucana*, an epic poem by Alonso de Ercilla (d.1594) which was widely read in its time. Set in the New

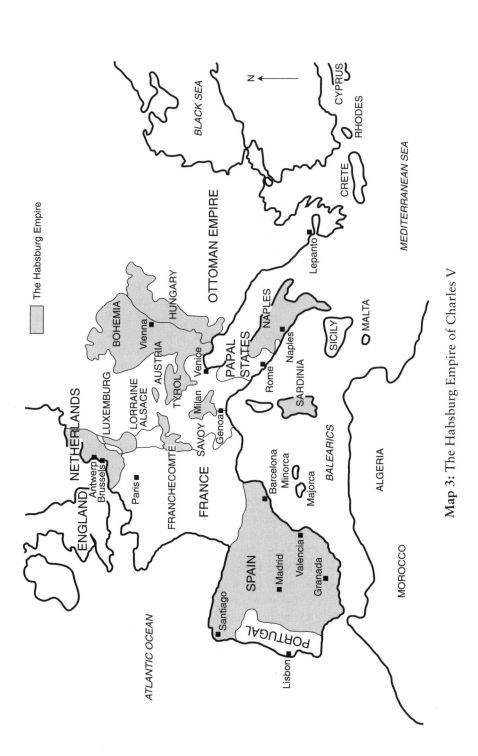

Map 3: The Habsburg Empire of Charles V

The Habsburg Empire

ATLANTIC OCEAN

ENGLAND
NETHERLANDS
Antwerp
Brussels
Paris
LUXEMBURG
FRANCHECOMTE
LORRAINE
ALSACE
FRANCE
SAVOY
TYROL
AUSTRIA
Vienna
BOHEMIA
HUNGARY

Santiago
PORTUGAL
Lisbon
SPAIN
Madrid
Valencia
Granada
Barcelona
Minorca
Majorca
BALEARICS

Genoa
Milan
Venice
PAPAL
STATES
Rome
SARDINIA
NAPLES
Naples
SICILY
MALTA

MOROCCO
ALGERIA
MEDITERRANEAN SEA

OTTOMAN EMPIRE
Lepanto
BLACK SEA
CRETE
RHODES
CYPRUS

N

World, it depicts the armed conflict that took place in Chile (then part of the Vice-royalty of Peru) between the Araucanian Indians and their Spanish foes, a conflict in which Ercilla himself had taken part. At no point does it call into question the legitimacy of the colonists' cause, but it does criticise harshly their cruelty and greed, and in general it portrays the Indians as a noble people, worthy of the Spaniards' respect.

SPAIN AND EUROPE

While the Spanish monarchy was expanding westwards into the New World, it was also opening up intellectually to the European Renaissance. The humanism of Italy and the Low Countries had begun to make an impression in Castile and Aragon during the fifteenth century before the Golden Age began, but in the sixteenth century its influence deepened. A key event occurred in 1517, the accession to the throne of Charles of Ghent, a Flemish prince who two years later was elected Holy Roman Emperor. This gave Castile an important role in the Habsburg Empire, which covered the Low Countries and large parts of modern Italy, Germany and Austria. It brought Spanish courtiers, students and scholars into closer contact with their European counterparts.

An early sign of the influence of humanism in Spain was the appearance of a substantial amount of writing in Latin shaped by the two ancient traditions that the humanists were anxious to restore: the literature of ancient Greece and Rome, and the Christian Bible with the commentaries of the Fathers of the Church. This neo-Latin writing, as it is known, consists not only of works of scholarship but also of original compositions, among them histories, biographies, poems and plays (see Chapter 1). Until recently it was neglected by scholars, but now it is receiving their attention, partly because of a growing awareness of the many connections that existed at the time between Latin and literature in Castilian. The importance in Spain of the Latin tradition was to some extent a result of its role in the universities, whose male students (women were not admitted) included two large social groups: members of the religious orders whose training required advanced studies, and laymen who wished to serve the Crown, in the peninsula or overseas, as *letrados* (jurists). To meet the demand for places, over 20 new universities were created in Castile before 1600, and since in all of them the instruction and course books were in Latin it became necessary to expand Latin teaching at second level as well. Grammar schools for boys were accordingly founded, including a significant number run by the Society of Jesus.

The degree of latinity acquired by educated men in Spain no doubt varied enormously, but the fact that for most of them Latin was their second language had its effect on literature in Spanish. Writers could take for granted, at least, a certain familiarity with classical and biblical allusions, and at best, a sensitive response to the Latin texts that often underlay their work.

POETRY IN SPANISH

In Renaissance Italy humanism had stimulated writing not only in Latin but in Italian as well, the exemplar of this being Petrarch (Francesco Petrarca, d.1374), a Latin scholar and stylist who sought in his Italian poetry to surpass the lyric poets of Antiquity. In Spain, similarly, the humanist movement gave rise to a literature in Castilian shaped by classical models, and the writer in whose work it first became apparent was a lyric poet, Garcilaso de la Vega (d.1536), who drew inspiration from Petrarch's work. Garcilaso based his poetry on the imitation of several models, blending together themes and motifs from the Latin, Italian and Spanish poetic traditions. Earlier poets had done this too, but with his friend Juan Boscán he devised new tools for the task, and introduced into Spanish verse fresh genres (the eclogue, elegy, verse epistle) and strophic forms (the sonnet, the Renaissance *canción*), as well as a poetic line (the hendecasyllable, or eleven-syllable line) which made possible the imitation in poetry of the cadences of a speaking voice. His own voice is distinctive: clear, intimate, confiding, and so is the rhetorical self portrayed in many of his poems, which owes much to the *Cortegiano* of Castiglione.

Many features of Garcilaso's verse appear in this fine sonnet (Sonnet 23), in which the poet urges the woman he loves to respond to him now, before time passes and her beauty disappears. The theme, which goes back to Classical Antiquity, inspired numerous medieval and Renaissance poets, and Garcilaso's models included works in Latin (Horace, Ausonius) and Catalan (Ausias March) as well as Italian (Pietro Bembo and Bernardo Tasso):

> En tanto que de rosa y azucena
> se muestra la color en vuestro gesto,
> y que vuestro mirar ardiente, honesto,
> enciende el corazón y lo refrena;
>
> Y en tanto que el cabello, que en la vena
> del oro se escogió, con vuelo presto,
> por el hermoso cuello blanco, enhiesto,
> el viento mueve, esparce y desordena;
>
> Coged de vuestra alegre primavera
> el dulce fruto, antes que el tiempo airado
> cubra de nieve la hermosa cumbre.
>
> Marchitará la rosa el viento helado,
> todo lo mudará la edad ligera,
> por no hacer mudanza en su costumbre.

(While the rose and the lily suffuse your complexion, and your glance, burning and pure, sets fire to the heart and checks it; and while the wind,

> with a sudden gust, moves, scatters and disorders your hair, mined in a vein of gold, across your lovely neck, white and erect; pluck the delicious fruit of your happy Springtime, before furious Time covers the lovely heights in snow. The icy wind will wither the rose, and fast-moving age will change all things, so as to be unchanging in its custom.)

Garcilaso composed his works so seamlessly that it takes a learned reader to detect the subtle allusions they contain to earlier poems in Spanish, Italian and Latin. One such reader was Fernando de Herrera, whose edition of Garcilaso's poems with a commentary (1580) presented him as an example whom younger writers should emulate. But in spite of Herrera's prestige as a poet and a critic, the concept of poetic diction in which he believed did not prevail. Like Garcilaso himself, Herrera drew inspiration from the courtly love songs of the medieval *cancioneros* but he did not include among his recommended models two other kinds of medieval Spanish verse: the popular lyric (*poesía de tipo tradicional*) and the traditional ballad (*romance viejo*) (see Chapter 2). Throughout the sixteenth century, however, these continued to flourish alongside the new style that Garcilaso had introduced. Like the *cancioneros*, they were collected, published and imitated in fresh adaptations and versions, and by the end of the century they had become an accepted part of the corpus of conventions on which poets could draw. The result was a poetic language that contained within itself not only the Latin and Italian traditions of the Renaissance, but older types of song and storytelling bequeathed by medieval Spain.

The formation of this language was accelerated by the popularity of two genres in which poetry had a central part: the pastoral romance and the *comedia*. In the *Diana* of Montemayor, for instance, where shepherds and shepherdesses move through an Arcadian landscape and ponder the nature of love, the prose narrative pauses repeatedly to include poems and songs composed in an astonishing variety of metres, both traditional and new. A similar range of conventions occurs in plays written for the public theatres that began to flourish in the towns of Castile during the 1580s. These plays were normally in verse, and the metres and strophes they employed were varied to match alterations in mood, situation and scene. Here the acknowledged master was Lope de Vega, a fine lyric poet in his own right, who established the polymetric system that the *comedia* used.

QUEVEDO AND GÓNGORA

The rich possibilities that the poetic idiom contained were exploited by Lope's contemporaries, Francisco de Quevedo and Luis de Góngora (d.1627). Both moved with ease between the two styles, traditional and new, often combining in individual poems features of each. At the same time, both were aware that the elements of which the idiom was composed were becoming hackneyed through overuse and needed to be renewed. The ways in which they tackled this problem, however, were quite distinct.

Quevedo's love sonnets draw on the full range of motifs that the Petrarchan tradition had made familiar. Often it is possible to trace them back, through myriad imitations, to the lyrics of Petrarch himself. But for an attentive reader the experience of recognition is accompanied by a sense of difference. Verbal forms, images and themes are juxtaposed dramatically, often in unexpected ways. The portrayal of the suffering lover, a commonplace of the courtly love convention, is taken to unprecedented extremes of existential anguish. This inventiveness enabled him to keep a certain distance from his models without ceasing to be faithful to Petrarchanism itself, and to give new life to the tradition by reanimating its language from within.

Góngora's solution may be seen in his unfinished sequence, the *Soledades* (Solitudes), whose sketchy protagonist, a nobleman in flight from the Court, is depicted within a strange landscape of haunting beauty. The poem is impossible to classify, for it draws inspiration from several genres without belonging wholly to any of them. Its language, too, transgresses long-standing conventions. In line with the tradition that Garcilaso had established, it comprises imitations of classical poets, notably Ovid, but it eschews a speaking voice that simulates the tones of conversation, offering instead an intriguing style that draws attention to its own complexity. The lexis (or vocabulary) is strongly influenced by Latin, and so is the syntax, which subverts the structure of the Spanish sentence, and the strangeness this causes is compounded by extended metaphors whose audacity is often startling. Góngora aimed to produce a text whose enigmas compel intense scrutiny, before yielding, once they are resolved, to a sense of *admiratio* (Latin) or wonder, in which ancestral truths that had become trivial over time are apprehended anew. His achievement was greeted by some of his contemporaries with adulation, and by others, such as Quevedo, with derision. But it set the poetic agenda for a generation, and was imitated by many subsequent poets, including a Mexican nun, Sor Juana Inés de la Cruz (d.1695).

THE BIBLE AND LITERATURE

Most Golden Age Spaniards who took an interest in the Christian scriptures were able to read parts of them in their own language, but not the whole Bible, which was not available in a Spanish translation. The only complete version in Castilian was by a Protestant exile, Casiodoro de Reina (d. 1594), and it was banned by the Inquisition, which feared the spread of heresy in the peninsula. Those who knew Latin, however, had access to the Vulgate, the Latin version of the Bible attributed to St Jerome (d.420), and to biblical scholarship by Catholic authors of the time, many of whom were Spanish. In the sixteenth century Spanish philologists took the lead in preparing editions of the original text of the scriptures and of its ancient translations into Latin and Greek. In the process they produced two polyglot bibles, each in its own way a masterpiece of printing, the first in Alcalá de Henares (1514–1517), the second in Antwerp (1569–1572). Later, in the seventeenth century, most of the important biblical commentaries that circulated in Catholic Europe were written by Spanish theologians.

The influence of these biblical commentaries has been traced in religious paintings by Spanish artists of the seventeenth century, including Diego Velázquez (d.1660), who became official painter at the royal court in Madrid, Francisco de Zurbarán (d.1664) and Bartolomé Esteban Murillo (d.1682), and although their literary impact has not been fully explored there can be little doubt that they also underlie the religious drama of the period, the *autos sacramentales*, which were performed in public on the feast of Corpus Christi, and the *comedias* based on stories of the Bible. A good example is *La venganza de Tamar* (Tamar's Revenge), a *comedia* by the Mercedarian friar Gabriel Téllez (d.1648), who wrote under the pseudonym of Tirso de Molina. Its subject is the account in the Second Book of Samuel of Tamar's rape by her half-brother Amon, and his subsequent death at the hands of her full brother Absalom. The play, which follows the biblical version closely, assumes that the audience is familiar with the story of King David's family, to which the main characters belong, and it shows in its subtle imagery that the author was well aware of contemporary exegesis of the Old Testament.

The renewal of biblical studies left its mark also on poetry and prose in Castilian, as may be seen in the writings of Fray Luis de León, a teacher of scripture who wrote extensively in Latin and Spanish. The humanist training he received led him to translate poems by classical authors, both Latin and Greek, as well as certain books of the Hebrew Scriptures (Job, some of the Psalms, the Song of Songs). In his poetry, mainly odes in the style of Horace, he delights in bringing together whenever he can images and themes that are common to the two traditions, classical and Christian. The same interests inform his great prose work, *Los nombres de Cristo* (The names of Christ), in which three friends gather in a garden near Salamanca to discuss the names by which Christ is designated in the Bible, and to consider in doing so the nature of the wisdom summed up in his person and teachings.

The case of his contemporary, San Juan de la Cruz, is rather different. He attended university, and may well have heard the lectures of Fray Luis, but he was not an academic or a humanist. Instead he led the cloistered life of a contemplative that his Carmelite rule required. But like Fray Luis he was steeped in the Bible, which he read in Latin, and it shaped the mystical poetry he composed. He was drawn, in particular, to the Song of Songs and to its theme of marriage, which like many Western mystics before him he applied to the relationship between God (the bridegroom) and the soul (the bride), and in his poetry he combined its images with others from the love poetry of his day, notably the popular lyric and the *cancioneros*. His prose works, which he wrote for his friends to help them interpret the poems, are also influenced by scripture, not least in their format, which is modelled on Latin commentaries on the Song of Songs.

RELIGIOUS RENEWAL AND REFORM

Spain in the early Golden Age was affected deeply not only by humanism but by the movements of religious renewal that swept through Europe before 1550. Their impact may be seen in the reform of the religious orders, which began in Castile and Aragon in the late fifteenth century, and in the popularity of religious literature in Spanish, including translations of classics such as the *Imitation of Christ*. After 1517 this peninsular renewal became caught up in the more general European call for Church reform in which humanists everywhere played a leading part. Particularly popular in Spain were the writings of the Dutch humanist Erasmus (d.1536) in which he mocked the monastic tradition for being too attached to ritual, and urged an interior piety instead.

This interest in religion inspired not only translations but a large number of original works in Spanish, including some which became well known throughout Europe. One was the *Ejercicios espirituales* (Spiritual exercises) of San Ignacio de Loyola, a text shaped by his own mystical experience, which was disseminated by the Society of Jesus. Another was the *Libro de la oración y meditación* (Book on prayer and meditation), a meditation manual by Fray Luis de Granada (d.1588), which became an international bestseller. The influence of such writings may be seen in the case of Teresa de Avila. When she became a Carmelite at the age of 20 she had received a rudimentary education which naturally did not include Latin. Accordingly she fed her intense interest in prayer on the religious literature available in Castilian. When she was asked by her confessors to write an account of her life she drew on the books she had read for many of her themes, images and rhetorical techniques. Later, on founding a reform of her order that spread throughout Spain, she wrote guides to the spiritual life for her followers, most of whom were 'unlettered' women like herself. It was then that she composed in Castilian her most considered description of mystical experience, *El castillo interior* (The interior castle).

The flood of writings on prayer, and the enthusiasm with which they were received, were monitored by the Inquisition with growing concern. It was anxious to avoid in Spain the religious divisions that were convulsing other countries, and when in 1559 it uncovered Protestant cells in Seville and Valladolid it took firm steps: many of the works in question were included in an index of prohibited books, and students were forbidden by the Crown to study in most universities abroad. The result was an air of crisis that deepened in the years that followed as Spain became involved in a fruitless religious war in Northern Europe, initially against Dutch rebels who espoused the Protestant cause, and later against England as well.

A CLOSED SOCIETY?

It used to be thought that the repressive events of 1559 were a decisive moment in the intellectual history of Spain, after which it became a closed society, hostile to dissent and cut off from European thought. Some modern historians, however, have challenged this view, and its underlying assumption that the Crown had a coherent ideology which it used the Inquisition to impose. The literature of the period suggests they are correct, for its vitality continued unabated for more than a hundred years, declining only as the seventeenth century came to an end.

In religious writing, it is true, some restrictions were introduced to protect beliefs and practices that the Protestants had attacked. But this did not prevent the survival in a new context of radical ideas that had been championed earlier in the movement of reform. In *Rinconete y Cortadillo*, for instance, a short story by Cervantes, two lads who get to know the criminal life of Seville are amazed and amused by devotional practices which have lost their inner meaning. Here the satire of mere ritual is as pointed as anything written by the reform-minded Erasmus. The context, however, has changed: the criminals are described ironically as a religious order, but there is no suggestion that the monastic tradition is responsible for the shortcomings of their piety. Mystical writings, similarly, continued to arouse misgivings, especially when they were by women, or by laymen who had no training in theology. For this reason the works of Teresa de Avila were subjected to the most searching examination. Yet in the event they were granted official approval, and when they appeared in print in 1588 they were greeted with acclaim.

In matters political and social, restrictions existed too. The Spanish monarchy, like its European neighbours, was hierarchical and authoritarian. But criticism was not impossible, as the public theatre showed. A *comedia* usually begins with a breakdown of normality, a crisis in which social conventions collapse: a king discovers evidence that his son is unfit to govern (*La vida es sueño*, 'Life is a dream'); a young man falls in love with his stepmother (*El castigo sin venganza*, 'Punishment without revenge'); a devout hermit loses his faith (*El condenado por desconfiado*, 'Condemned for mistrust'); an aristocrat rapes a country girl (*El alcalde de Zalamea*, 'The mayor of Zalamea'). The crisis, if successfully represented, seizes the audience's attention. Its consequences, and attempts to counter them, generate suspense. And the ending often brings a reaffirmation of social norms, a restoration of the moral order that had been disturbed. But not always. Sometimes the ending is ambiguous, puzzling or charged with irony, for the *comedia*, though conservative, was not predictably conformist, as modern studies have shown, and it could serve as 'an outlet for anxieties, a source of warnings and advice . . . a restraining influence' (see McKendrick 2000: 213).

In the realm of ideas many Spanish people remained in touch with European thought, and new developments continued to be received with interest. One of these was the recovery of classical scepticism, a philosophy that emphasised in an anti-dogmatic way the limitations of human knowledge. During the late sixteenth century, when it was being welcomed in France by Montaigne, it was also an influence in Spain, provoking Fray Luis de Granada to write his famous work, *Introducción del símbolo de la fe* (Introduction to the Creed, 1583). And in the seventeenth century, when Descartes took further the issues it raised, it became an important theme in the writings of Lope de Vega and Quevedo. Its impact is apparent too in *Don Quixote*, where the story of a madman who does not see things as they are prompts Cervantes to raise humorously some basic questions about how we know anything at all. Often the reader and even the narrator are as confused as Don Quixote himself about how to interpret the events around him, and Cervantes repeatedly presents situations from several points of view without indicating that one is right, another wrong. The reader is thus led to ponder in passing some serious questions, whose complexity he or she is not allowed to forget. The active cultivation of the intellect, moreover, is a hallmark of many works in Spanish of the seventeenth century, especially those by an Aragonese Jesuit, Baltasar Gracián (d.1658). His novel *El Criticón*, where the journey of two friends from a remote island to Rome may be read as an allegory of their journey through life, is in many respects the equivalent in prose of the combination of verbal and visual elements that one finds in emblem books of the day. Like an emblem it repeatedly arouses the reader's curiosity by presenting incongruities that can be resolved only by intense mental effort.

List of terms

Auto sacramental: An allegorical play concerned with the central tenets of Christian belief and performed in honour of the Eucharist on the feast of Corpus Christi.

Byzantine novel: A form of prose fiction, popular in the Renaissance, modelled on fictional narratives of the Ancient World, notably the *Aethiopica* of Heliodorus (third century BC).

Canción: The medieval *canción*: any kind of courtly poem set to music and intended to be sung. The Renaissance *canción*: a poem of variable length composed of a combination of 11- and 7-syllable lines.

Cancionero: A songbook or anthology of medieval *canciones*.

Chivalric romance: A work of prose fiction, set in the legendary world of medieval knights, which recounts the heroic deeds of noble characters in love and war.

Comedia: A three-act play in verse written during the Golden Age for performance in the public theatres of Spanish towns or in the court theatre in Madrid.

Eclogue: A poem with a pastoral setting and characters, written in the form of a dialogue or soliloquy.

Elegy: A poem that mourns the death of an individual or laments a tragic event.

Emblem: An allegorical picture, often an engraving or a woodcut, accompanied by a motto and an explanatory text.

Exemplary tale: A collection of subtle and thought-provoking short stories, the *Novelas ejemplares*, written by Miguel de Cervantes.

Ode: A lyric poem, often meditative in tone, concerned with a notable event, either public or private.

Pastoral romance: A work of fiction in prose and verse which recounts the amorous adventures of its characters in an idealised pastoral landscape, and which focuses on the nature of love.

Picaresque novel: A work of prose fiction, set in Golden Age Spain, which recounts the adventures of a *pícaro* (or rogue).

Poesía de tipo tradicional: The popular lyric of medieval Castile, usually concerned with the joys and sorrows of love seen from a woman's point of view.

Romance: A ballad. *Romance viejo*: a traditional ballad, medieval in origin and anonymous. *Romance nuevo*: a ballad composed by a Golden Age poet in conscious imitation of the *romance viejo*.

Sonnet: The Petrarchan sonnet popular in the Golden Age consists of fourteen lines, each eleven syllables in length, divisible into two quatrains (lines 1–4, 5–8) and two tercets (lines 9–11, 12–14).

Verse epistle: A poem in the form of a letter, usually concerned with a serious subject of a philosophical or moral kind.

FURTHER READING

Dixon, V. 1997. Spanish Renaissance theatre. In John Russell Brown (ed.) *The Oxford illustrated history of theatre*. Oxford: Oxford University Press, pp. 142–72.

Ife, B. W. and Butt, J. W. 1991. The literary heritage. In J. H. Elliott (ed.) *The Hispanic world*. London: Thames and Hudson, pp. 41–56.

Ife, B. W. 1994–1995. The literary impact of the New World: Columbus to Carrizales. *Journal of the Institute of Romance Studies* 3, pp. 65–85.

Kamen, Henry. 1991. *Spain 1469–1714. A society of conflict*. London: Longman.

McKendrick, Melveena. 2000. *Playing the king. Lope de Vega and the limits of conformity*. London: Tamesis.

Parker, Alexander A. 1985. *The philosophy of love in Spanish literature 1480–1680*, edited by Terence O'Reilly. Edinburgh: Edinburgh University Press.

Robbins, Jeremy. 1998. *The challenges of uncertainty. An introduction to seventeenth-century Spanish literature*. London: Duckworth.

Terry, Arthur. 1993. *Seventeenth-century Spanish poetry. The power of artifice*. Cambridge: Cambridge University Press.

4

Spain and Spanish America in the eighteenth and nineteenth centuries

Geoffrey Ribbans

Compared with the exuberance and imaginative fertility of Golden Age culture and the attractiveness of the contemporary period, the eighteenth century and perhaps even the nineteenth century may at first seem less exciting. Yet there are plenty of issues yet to be resolved and cultural endeavours of permanent interest. The eighteenth and nineteenth centuries played a vital part in the development of the modern world, both physically and intellectually, and the role of Spain and its empire was by no means as negligible as has often been assumed. Spain's intellectuals and their writing are fully representative of wider patterns of thought and accomplishment, as this chapter seeks to demonstrate.

THE EIGHTEENTH CENTURY

As it happens, the year 1700 is more than symbolic, for it counts as the year of a new political start, with the accession of the grandson of the magnificent French sun king Louis XIV to the Spanish throne as Philip V. But the French Bourbons did not succeed in replacing the Austrian Habsburgs as the Spanish royal dynasty without a struggle, and the war known in European history as the War of the Spanish Succession lasted until 1714. It was both a European conflict concerned with the balance of power, and a civil war within Spain. The distinct states of the Kingdom of Aragon (Catalonia, Valencia and Aragon itself) took the side, with Austria and Great Britain, of the Austrian claimant, the Archduke Charles, but when he became Holy Roman Emperor, the balance of power changed. Accordingly, Britain, living up to its name as perfidious Albion, abandoned the alliance, taking Gibraltar (and, for the time being,

Menorca) for itself. Barcelona resisted the French in a heroic siege, until 1714. The subsequent pacification was oppressive; the Bourbon political philosophy of centralised rule took away the autonomous institutions of the old kingdom of Aragon and imposed a new centralist order. Catalonia and Barcelona suffered particularly; the latter lost its university and had a military fortress, the Ciudadela, imposed on it. This action, comparable in some ways with the subduing of the Highlands after the Jacobite risings in Scotland, was to have long-term repercussions: Catalan nationalist claims invariably recall these events.

Neoclassicism

Culturally, the new Bourbon dynasty took a long time to make its distinctive mark and seventeenth-century characteristics continued to be a force for much of the first half of the eighteenth century. Neoclassicism, the cultural criterion introduced by the French dynasty, arouses little sympathy today. It is difficult to justify curtailing literary expression by stifling and arbitrary rules; in drama, the most seriously affected genre, modern consciousness knows no limit to the free range of the imagination, and the famous rules of time, place and action seem absurd today. Yet it is worth making an effort to understand why intelligent men, like the principal neoclassical theorist Ignacio de Luzán (1702–1754), believed in them. Partly it was a question of an undue deference to authority (going back, ultimately if inaccurately, to Aristotle) and partly it was a false interpretation of rationality that denied the human imagination the degree of flexibility we now take for granted. The belief in authority also gave rise to the establishment of those typical neoclassical institutions, the Royal Academies, to regulate language, history and the arts, and corresponding publications like the *Diccionario de autoridades* (see Chapter 1).

To catch a glimpse of neoclassical prejudices, it is instructive to read the notes the finest dramatist of the century, Leandro Fernández de Moratín (1737–1780), wrote for his translation of Hamlet; the ghost of Hamlet's father, Polonius, the play-within-a-play, and the gravediggers are all roundly condemned as entirely inappropriate to a serious drama. Not surprisingly, neoclassical tragedies never had much appeal. But by the end of the century comedies, notably those of Moratín, had achieved much more enduring success. Moratín was astute enough to find a model in the French dramatist Molière, and his finest play, *El sí de las niñas* (The maidens' consent, 1805) is comparable with Sheridan's *The Rivals*; the loquacious Doña Irene has something of Mrs Malaprop about her. Set in an inn and lasting less than twenty-four hours, it amusingly if rather obviously demonstrates the inadequacy of the education of girls, who are taught hypocrisy rather than sincerity, as well as condemning arranged marriages, especially between old men and young girls.

Poetry, too, suffered from artificial restraints. The pastoral convention, didactic verse and fables are not the most appealing forms to modern taste. Nonetheless a flourishing poetic school established itself at Salamanca in the second half of the century, and the lyrics of its best poet, Juan Meléndez Valdés (1754–1817), have considerable charm and skill; he has the merit of reviving the expressive romance or ballad metre. In a representative poem, 'La tarde' (The evening), the poet shows us the heightened sensibility of the age as he declares his enthusiasm for the peace of the countryside:

> Todo es paz, silencio todo,
> todo en estas soledades
> me conmueve, y hace dulce
> la memoria de mis males.
>
> (All is peace, all is silence,
> everything in these solitudes
> moves me and sweetens
> the memory of my sorrows).
> (Polt: 246–47)

The Enlightenment

The other major ideology of the century is more attuned to the modern world. It is the Enlightenment: *Ilustración* or *Las luces* in Spanish. The word itself declares its purpose: to bring light into the darkness of ignorance and superstition. Many of our notions of rationality and scientific method derive from the Enlightenment, with which we can relate directly. The first and most prolific of the Enlightenment figures in Spanish was Fray Benito Jerónimo Feijóo (1676–1764), a Benedictine friar who from his cell in Oviedo commanded a wide array of correspondence throughout Europe. His main concern is to extirpate common fallacies and superstitions and to spread information about scientific and medical advances. The exuberance of his essays remains infectious today, as he recounts for example the experiments of the Royal Society to measure the weight of air and the utter incredulity of his fellow friars at such a ridiculous enterprise. He is not always as scientific as he makes out, especially when attempting to reconcile rational objectivity and inborn prejudices (about Islam, for instance). But he is enlightened enough to embark on quite a modern defence of women and condemnation of their subjection, indicating that since each gender is by its nature prejudiced, if it were a question of women judging men, the result would be reversed. Women in the eighteenth century made significant if modest advances, and one, Josefa Amar y Borbón, penned a spirited defence of sexual equality, her '*Discurso en defensa del talento de las mujeres y su aptitud para el gobierno*' (Discourse in defence of the talent of women and their aptitude for government, 1786).

Feijóo's voluminous works were so much in tune with the progressive ideology of the monarchy by the middle of the century that any criticism of his work was banned by royal decree by Ferdinand VI. On the other hand, Ferdinand's brother, Charles III, who succeeded him (and reigned from 1759 to 1788), counts as one of the most notable enlightened despots of the age. It is not surprising that following the end of the Franco regime, the restored constitutional monarchy of Juan Carlos I should have chosen to place a statue of Carlos III in Madrid's Puerta de Sol.

Charles III

Nevertheless, Charles III was no democrat. He believed in and exercised absolute royal authority, expelling the Jesuits as belonging to too independent-minded an institution and curbing the Inquisition, which nevertheless persecuted one of the most radical of the *ilustrados* (enlightened thinkers), the Peruvian Pablo de Olavide (1725–1803). The expelled Jesuits, meanwhile, made notable contributions to learning from their new residence in Italy.

As a reformer, Charles III surrounded himself with a series of serious and dedicated ministers devoted to public service and 'benevolence'; these were called *hombres de bien* (men of good will). Instruction in modern methods in agriculture and manufacture were carried out through local institutions typical of the period, the *Sociedades de Amigos del País* (Societies of friends of the country). In the space of some 20 years many useful reforms were initiated in the mechanical arts, such as ceramics and tapestry, and in public services, transport, urban development, law, and university education. A major effort at agricultural recolonisation was undertaken under Olavide in the Sierra Morena. Culturally, Charles's court vied with those of other countries in its considerable artistic achievements, in painting, music and architecture.

Far-reaching reforms in the Spanish Empire included the opening out of trade with America and widespread administrative reorganisation, such as the establishment of the Vice-royalty of the River Plate, today's Argentina and Uruguay. The rapid increase in commerce and facilities in the New World produced a new middle class who by the end of the century, under the stimulus of Francisco de Miranda, the 'Precursor', would seek independence from the Mother Country.

Jovellanos and Cadalso

The finest representative of the Enlightenment in Spain was Melchor Gaspar de Jovellanos (1744–1811), a man of high-minded integrity who excelled in a variety of activities, as politician, administrator, orator, playwright and poet. His address 'Elogio de Carlos III' (In Praise of Charles III, 1788), delivered at the end of the king's life, is a respectful and touchingly affectionate tribute, but includes a cautionary admonition to the king's successor on the need for a strong sense of responsibility in a monarch. Jovellanos's poetry has a certain moral strength and feeling for nature and he has a worthy play, *El delincuente honrado* (The honourable criminal, 1773), on the contradictions between law and honour. But his most characteristic writing takes the form of learned discourses over a wide range of subjects: law, economics, history, art and antiquities. *El informe sobre la ley agraria* (Report on agrarian reform, 1795), his most influential work, deals with the pressing problem of inequitable land tenure in Spain. It is a political question which remained a burning issue and was not resolved well into the twentieth century.

A distinctive voice reflecting contemporary values in an individual way is José de Cadalso (1741–1782). His posthumous *Cartas marruecas* (Moroccan letters, published 1789) is a fascinating satirical work, which uses the popular device of the imaginary traveller. The structure is uneven, uneasily poised between essay and fiction, but it allows for animated discussion among three participants, a young naïve Moorish visitor, his mentor at home and a traditionalist Spaniard, on issues pertaining to Spanish history and society: Spain has been left like the *esqueleto de un gigante* (giant's skeleton) by the Habsburgs; regional differences are described in sympathetic detail; the merits of industrial development are underlined; contemporary vices such as luxury, licentiousness and foppery (*petimetres*) are denounced in favour of military virtues and public service. The period was in fact one of a marked relaxation of morals, and there is a strong undercurrent of sensuality and eroticism in much of the writing of the time.

Cadalso's other principal work, *Noches lúgubres* (Lugubrious nights, 1789–1790), is often classified as pre-romantic, and certainly its melancholy tone and its subject-matter, the exhuming of the lover's body, gives some justification for this view. However, the structure of the dialogue, in which philosophical issues such as the purpose of life and the nature of justice are raised, places it firmly in a typical eighteenth-century mould, an intellectual discussion in which an influx of sensibility occurs.

All this is unequivocally high-culture, and we should not neglect the rise of a more everyday entertainment for ordinary people, exemplified by the *sainetes* of Ramón de la Cruz. Using standard figures of the time – *majos* (young working men from Madrid), *manolas* (their girls) and *petimetres* (fops) – these light satirical pieces serve to remind us that beneath the aristocratic intellectual veneer there existed a live folk-culture which anticipates the popular manifestations of the nineteenth century.

Spanish confidence in the future grew with the reforms, and a French encyclopaedia article by Masson de Morvilliers dismissing Spain's achievements aroused a passionate defence of the country by the king himself and by leading intellectuals, the most important being the vehement satirist

Juan Pablo Forner. But the Spanish Enlightenment was both incomplete and precarious. Several factors militated against it on Charles III's death. One was the inadequacy of his successor, Charles IV, who was speedily dominated by a favourite, Manuel Godoy, the Queen's lover. Even more important was the outbreak in 1789 of the French Revolution, a watershed in the history of the Western world. It bedazzled or appalled the whole of Europe, casting doubt on the apparently unassailable ideological presuppositions on which the *ancien régime* had rested. In Spain, it fatally interrupted a process of renewal that was far from complete, without replacing it for several generations with any viable alternative system. The Revolution was followed by the political manoeuvres of Napoleon that culminated in the French occupation of Spain and Portugal in 1808 and the disastrous Peninsular War (for the Spanish, the 'War of Independence', 1808–1814) it provoked.

THE NINETEENTH CENTURY

The Peninsular War and Spanish-American Independence

Progressive-minded Spaniards were caught in a quandary. Intellectually, they were largely in sympathy with the revolutionary reforms consolidated by Napoleon, but their patriotic pride was wounded by the blatant opportunism of the Napoleonic invasion. As a consequence they were divided. Jovellanos broke with one of his mentors, Cabarrús, who sided with the French, and supported the incipient resistance; Meléndez Valdés and Moratín became supporters of the French or *afrancesados*. An intriguing figure, José María Blanco White (1775–1841), first a priest, then a vehement revolutionary, left Spain in disgust to pursue a successful clerical career in England (Liverpool). The patriotic opposition coalesced around the constitutional assembly summoned at Cadiz in 1812, the Cortes de Cadiz, which offered a liberal but unstable alternative to autocracy. Literature, especially poetry, became increasingly nationalistic under the pressure of events, as in the patriotic rhetorical odes of the once highly esteemed Manuel José Quintana (1772–1857); the equivalent, in the context of Spanish-American independence, is the Ecuadorian José Joaquín Olmedo (1780–1847).

The war itself was characterised by spontaneous local initiatives, from which the word *guerrilla* (little war) derives, which buttressed the Duke of Wellington's more orthodox army. Perhaps the most monumental effect of the Peninsular War was the emancipation of the Spanish Empire. With the confinement of the Spanish king, Ferdinand VII, in France the colonies no longer had any ultimate authority, and speedily took political responsibility into their own hands (see Chapters 7 and 8). The daring exploits of Simón Bolívar (1783–1830) from Caracas, and José de San Martín (1778–1850) from

Buenos Aires, to emancipate the continent, between 1812 and 1824, constitute a rousing story, culminating in San Martín's withdrawal in 1822, leaving Bolívar, known as the 'Liberator', as sole leader. Bolívar failed however to inculcate much sense of unity among the new emerging Republics, which followed roughly the administrative divisions of the Spanish Empire. Mexico, after several false starts, and Central America, finally secured their independence in 1822.

After Napoleon's defeat, the restoration of the monarchy in 1814 under Ferdinand VII (reigned 1814–1833) brought back the despotism without the Enlightenment. Under his tyranny Spain became polarised; his liberal opponents went into exile, while other zealots craved for even greater absolutism as well as for local rights (*fueros*). These were the Carlists who, according to Salic law, supported the succession of Ferdinand's brother Carlos against his infant daughter Isabella II (reigned 1833–1868), in a series of ferocious civil wars. Violent dynastic, religious, and political disputes continued until the last quarter of the nineteenth century, and during this time the ultimate political arbiters were army generals.

An unequalled demonstration of the remarkable transformations the country endured is offered by the one undoubted international genius of the period, the painter Francisco de Goya (1746–1828). Not only does he provide masterly portraits of his contemporaries, but he reveals the whole gamut of artistic reaction from 1780 till 1820, passing from such bucolic canvasses as *La gallina ciega* (Blindman's buff) to the patriotic depiction of the Spanish resistance to the French in the *Dos de mayo* (2 of May). Subsequently comes the increasing disillusion of the etchings *Los desastres de la guerra* (Disasters of war) and the *Disparates* (Absurdities); and in despair the painter abandons the country to take up residence in France.

Romanticism

Romantic ideas reached Spain by fits and starts. The political turmoil interrupted the normal process of the infiltration of sensibility that occurred in the eighteenth century, and only a few manifestations of a new cultural consciousness, such as the *Europeo* group in Barcelona and the dispute over the value of the Golden Age theatre associated with Juan Nicolás Böhl von Faber and Agustín Durán, relate to general European currents. Mostly, Romanticism was affiliated with liberalism and nurtured in exile. Indeed the exodus of intellectuals in successive waves in the 1820s and 1830s was comparable to that which followed the Civil War in 1939. A series of highly theatrical dramas such as *Don Álvaro o la fuerza del sino* by the Duque de Rivas, Antonio García Gutiérrez's *El trovador*, and *Los amantes de Teruel* by Juan Eugenio Hartzenbusch followed Ferdinand VII's death in 1833. These three plays show a clear evolution as their heroes develop from the ill-starred rebellion of a Don Álvaro to a lyrical if equally incredible Don Manrique in

Map 4: Latin America in 1830

the second play, and a lachrymose and sedate Marsilla in the third. It is no accident that romantic drama formed an attractive source for operatic libretti; Verdi's *La forza del destino* and *Il trovatore* are the best-known examples.

The swashbuckling Byronic pose affected by the leading Romantic poet José de Espronceda (1808–1842) lacked the deeper subtleties of the more intimate side of the movement; though he gives an absolute priority to his emotions, they are not very closely analysed. While Espronceda consistently shows concern for the rebellious and the marginalised in his poems, women are treated with contempt and condescension. The grandiose Don Juanesque figure of Don Félix de Montemar, in the long poem *El estudiante de Salamanca* (The student from Salamanca, 1840), contrasts greatly with his victim Elvira, who is grovellingly submissive and dies of a broken heart. The well-known *Canto a Teresa* (Song for Teresa), included in his unfinished philosophical poem *El diablo mundo* (The devil's world, 1840), is an extreme example of the polarisation between unrestrained idealism and equally bitter disillusionment, ranging, in the poet's words, from a 'manantial de purísima pureza' (a spring of utmost purity) to an 'estanque . . . de aguas corrompidas, / entre fétido fango detenidas' (a pond of putrid water, stagnating in fetid mud). Espronceda's style is highly declamatory, though parts of *El diablo mundo* did show a promising satirical vein.

A forceful woman writer from Cuba (still a Spanish possession), Gertrudis Gómez de Avellaneda (1814–1873), was tolerated as a sort of female counterpart to Espronceda. Love poetry was, of course, considered a suitable subject for a woman poet, but the potent images Avellaneda uses are significant: the moth irresistibly hovering towards the deadly light; the squirrel falling victim to the serpent; clouds and dry leaves buffeted by the hurricane. In her most famous love poem, 'A . . .' (To . . .), she asserts her god-given power to eventually triumph, even if the independence thus gained is attained at a high cost of distress and loneliness. Another woman poet whose significant place in literary history has been finally restored is Carolina Coronado (1823–1911). She actively encouraged other female writers, asserting decisively the right of women to participate in literary activities and complaining at the loss of intelligent contributions women might have made throughout history. She takes up the cause of domestic violence, and in a rousing popular air, notes that calls for freedom during revolutionary periods do not encompass women's liberation. Like much of the most interesting verse of the time, Coronado's poetry has a hidden or oblique dissident tone:

Libertad

Risueños están los mozos,
gozosos están los viejos,
porque dicen, compañeras,
que hay libertad para el pueblo . . .
Mas, por nosotras, las hembras,
no lo aplaudo, ni lo siento,
pues aunque leyes se muden
para nosotras no hay fueros.
¡Libertad! ¿qué nos importa?
¿qué ganamos, qué tendremos?
¿un encierro por tribuna
y una aguja por derecho?

(The young men are laughing,
the old men are joyful,
because they say, [women] comrades,
that there is freedom for the people . . .
But for us females, I don't applaud it or regret it,
for, though the laws may change,
for us there are no customary rights.
Freedom: what does it matter to us?
What do we gain? What shall we get out of it?
Being confined is our rostrum,
and a sewing needle is our rights)

One distinctive offshoot of Romanticism is characteristic of Spain: this is referred to as *costumbrismo*. At its most superficial it is merely a complacent defence of national traditions, a Spanish counterpart of the curious phenomenon of the cult of exotic Spain, predominantly Andalusia, found in the work of Prosper Mérimée (author of the story of Carmen) and Washington Irving. At its best it demonstrates the strong local and popular roots of Spanish culture and foreshadows the observational power of the realist novel. In its urban form, *costumbrismo* embraces what was virtually a new genre for Spain, the newspaper article. Finding its form through the growth of the press, this development gives rise to acute social analysis, suave and engaging in Ramón de Mesonero Romanos, bitter and penetrating in the major writer Mariano José de Larra (1809–1837).

In his short lifetime Larra wrote in various established genres, including the historical novel and the theatre, but it is on his journalism, of an exceptionally high quality, that his reputation depends. Its strong satirical tone takes in both individual eccentricities and social, cultural and political problems, including Carlism (referred to above). Larra's outstanding humorous qualities and brilliant style do not detract from his intellectual seriousness. His essay

'¿Quién es el público y dónde se encuentra?' (Who is the public and where is it to be found? 1832) demonstrates the degree to which he creates his own audience. Spain, he ruefully concludes, is a country 'a medio hacer' (half constructed), like Penelope unweaving at night what she has done during the day. His suicide at the age of 28 was often (and unwisely) considered to be symbolic of his despair about Spain.

Forces of tradition soon reasserted themselves in the *Romances históricos* (Historical Ballads, 1841) of the Duque de Rivas, and in the poems and plays of José Zorrilla (1817–1893) where Romantic innovations are assimilated into conservative patriotism: Don Juan Tenorio, in Zorrilla's celebrated play of that name (1844), retains his macho self-assertiveness, but is incongruously saved by the selfless love of his victim. Ramón Bretón de los Herreros gives the Moratinian comedy, referred to earlier, a distinctly bourgeois form. Later developments in the theatre follow similar conventional norms: high comedy and melodrama, as practised by José Echegaray. The preferred entertainment was the opera, including a distinctively Spanish form of light opera, the *zarzuela*.

There is one phenomenon that merits special attention. In addition to the female authors mentioned earlier, unrecognised groups of women writers struggling against a hostile environment carved out a territory for themselves in the proliferating magazine culture. Yet, despite some economic advance as a result of this development, women's rights suffer a regression. A clear indication of this can be found in a poem by Pilar Sinués de Marco, editor of the influential and significantly titled magazine *El ángel del hogar* (The angel of the hearth). The poem is a dialogue between the wind and the clouds; it does not take much effort to see that they represent men and women respectively. The wind firmly puts down any attempt at pride on the clouds' part, but magnanimously respects them, provided they are properly submissive. Beneath this preposterous subjugation lies, one may suspect, a certain adroit application of the doctrine 'If you can't beat them join them'.

Only in the second half of the century do we find such qualities as the emotional subtlety and heightened imagination that we associate with European Romanticism in general. Gustavo Adolfo Bécquer (1836–1870), once treated condescendingly as a naïve, hopeless sentimental, has come to be seen as a key figure, in both his *Rimas* (Rhymes, 1870) and his *Leyendas* (Legends, between 1858 and 1864), in the development of imaginative and unforced expression. His definition of his poetry as 'natural, breve, seca, que brota del alma como una chispa eléctrica . . .' (natural, short, dry, flying from the soul like an electric spark) captures exactly the nature of his direct, concentrated verse, which has a brevity and a spontaneity reminiscent of popular poetry, and tends to eliminate all cause and circumstance. While some poems show a disconcerting ingenuousness, many others go through the whole gamut of Romantic attitudes: self-pity, recrimination, sarcasm, meditation on death, and escape into dream or the unconscious. In the images he employs, all the senses are brought into play, light being particularly prominent; they have a measure of synaesthesia or fusion of the senses that anticipates symbolism, 'con palabras que fuesen a un tiempo / suspiros y risas, colores y notas' ('with words that were at once sighs and laughter, colours and notes', Rima 1, see Urrutia, p. 509). At times, too, we find an unexpected touch of objective analysis, as when he indicates faults on both sides in amorous situations. In these respects he seems surprisingly modern.

Rosalía de Castro (1837–1885) is likewise, belatedly, recognised as one of the major poets of Spain both in the Galician language and in Spanish. These days, unlike in the past, she is regarded, not as a much admired example of self-sacrifice, abnegation and resignation, but as representing a consistent underlying current of dissent and protest about society and in particular about the condition of women. Trapped by the limitations of her environment, she is emotionally marginalised from it by language, perception and gender (see Chapter 6). Her renowned pessimism is defiant as well as resigned, while her yearning for a lost paradise is a tacit criticism of the impossibility of Galicia's becoming anything like the garden of Eden. In particular, Castro bears strong witness to the sufferings brought about by the special curse of the Galician poor: emigration, both seasonal, within Spain, and overseas. The consequences of emigration are seen in the uprooted men, the deserted fields, the orphaned children and above all the women who are left physically defenceless and spiritually alone.

HISTORICAL AND CULTURAL EVOLUTION OF SPANISH AMERICA

The national development of the newly liberated Spanish-American republics was turbulent and uneven, dominated by dictators (*caudillos*), of whom the Argentinian Juan Manuel de Rosas was a particularly long-lived and obnoxious example. The continent's literary production has the fascination of being shaped by specifically continental problems. Andrés Bello sought valiently to assert classical standards in verse and language. The Argentinian statesman Domingo Faustino Sarmiento presented in his book *Facundo* (1845) the clear-cut opposition between civilisation and barbarity, that is, Buenos Aires and Europe against the savage pampas and gauchos associated with Rosas (see Chapter 8). José Mármol's sentimental novel *Amalia* (1851–1855) is also an attack on Rosas. The other side of the picture is the exaltation of the primitive life of the gauchos in José Hernández's poem *Martín Fierro* (see Chapter 8). Ricardo Palma writes, from the 1850s onwards, nostalgic and sophisticated *Tradiciones peruanas* (Peruvian traditions) of his native land. The Chilean Alberto Blest Gana's *Martín Rivas* (1862) shows an early influence of Balzac, while the popular sentimental tradition continues in the idealised novel *María* (1867) by the Colombian Jorge Isaacs. Slavery, not abolished in Cuba until 1886, is the subject of two novels, Avellaneda's *Sab* (1841) and the more forceful *Cecilia Valdés* by Cirilo Villaverde, started in 1839 but not finally published till 1882.

Mexico survived a particularly tumultuous period. Under the ferocious general Santa Anna the country lost half its territory in 1848 to the United States; it suffered foreign intervention as a result of insolvency and the imposition by the French of the Emperor Maximilian until rescued by the patriot Benito Júarez, only to fall in the last part of the century under the cruel but stable dictatorship of Porfirio Díaz. By the late nineteenth century, Mexico City and, even more so, Buenos Aires had become large sophisticated cities, and, more generally, the new republics laid a justified claim to recognition of their differentiated personality. These growing aspirations led, by the end of the nineteenth century, to the first distinctively Spanish-American literary and cultural movement, spread over a wide range of countries, and possessing worldwide pretensions, *modernismo* (see Chapters 7 and 8).

THE RESTORATION IN SPAIN

In Spain, the so-called 'Glorious' Revolution of 1868, which expelled Queen Isabella II, promised, but did not deliver, a fresh start. It was followed by six years of unsuccessful political experiments: a new constitutional dynasty (Amadeo of Savoy), the First Republic (1874), and a period of conservative stability known as the Restoration, a political settlement established by Antonio Cánovas del Castillo from 1875 onwards. The constitutional system adopted, based on a two-party structure, was in fact an oligarchy dependent on large landowners, *caciquismo* (domination by local bosses) and electoral manipulation. By this time the demographic shift which had steadily been taking place for some two centuries had been consolidated. Castile, the heart of the country, had been constantly losing population to the more coastal areas. In these regions, moreover, industry, particularly textiles (Catalonia), metallurgy (Bilbao) and mining (Asturias), had been developing, thus shifting the economic strength of the country without greatly changing the power structure. This development was accompanied by the revival of local nationalisms in Catalonia, the Basque Country and Galicia, discussed elsewhere in this book (see Chapter 6).

THE SPANISH REALIST NOVEL

Fiction, which had not greatly flourished in the eighteenth century, had gradually come to the fore, first through a cult of the historical novel deriving from Walter Scott, and then as a result of cheap serial publications, which produced an influx of translations of pulp literature from the French. In the descriptive novels of a conservative woman writer, Cecilia Böhl de Faber (1796–1877), writing under a masculine pseudonym, Fernán Caballero, *costumbrismo* merged with regionalism. The process was continued by Pedro Antonio de Alarcón (1833–1891) whose *El sombrero de tres picos* (The three-cornered hat, 1874), made into a ballet by Manuel de Falla, owes its charm to its evocation of the *ancien régime* and folk-tradition.

The Spanish novel developed on an unprecedented scale during the Restoration. Under the umbrella of the realist novel inspired by Balzac, which set out to portray contemporary society in a credible fashion, many works were published that deserve international status and today, with the increasing number of translations available, they are belatedly recognised abroad.

In its broadest sense, realism did not exclude regionalism. Juan Valera (1821–1905), a polished diplomat and man of letters, hailed from Andalusia. His best known work is his first, *Pepita Jiménez* (1874), a charming, unpolemical but mildly subversive love story. The undesirable social realities of Spanish rural life are present but disarmed. Pepita is a poor girl obliged by circumstances to marry an elderly man. After his death she is courted by the local *cacique*, the father of Luis, the seminarist whose growing love for the young widow is revealed in his letters, and Pepita is not above seducing Luis (in the nicest possible way) in order to force the situation, which is then accepted with perfect equanimity by all concerned. It is well constructed, with excellent use of the epistolary form as Luis writes to his uncle about his growing but unconscious attraction for Pepita. Valera is a very accomplished stylist, but his characters speak with Valera's own urbanity, with the result that they appear remote, within a fairy-story setting. José María de Pereda, from Santander, was a resolute traditionalist, with a keen sense of landscape and human interaction with it; in this respect he may be compared with the Brontë sisters and Thomas Hardy. He is a good narrator, but his novels are very slow. The best two take the sea (*Sotileza*, 1884) and the mountain (*Peñas arriba*, Rocks above, 1895) as their backcloth.

Three novelists stand out for today's taste as exceptionally important. The key figure is the extraordinarily prolific writer Benito Pérez Galdós (1843–1920), now acknowledged as a major novelist of the stature of Balzac and Dickens, both of whom he greatly admired and with whom he is directly comparable. He enjoys a deservedly large following among younger scholars and students as his narrative skill (through the use of a personalised narrator), his capacity for dialogue and his idiomatic verve, are increasingly appreciated.

More than the early *Doña Perfecta* (1876), exemplifying liberal ideas, the complex social structure of his 20 *novelas contemporáneas* (1881–1897) commands attention. These novels mostly have Madrid as their urban setting, and detailed attention is paid to the rise and fall of individuals within the administrative and commercial middle class. A few examples among many are the collapse of the Bringas family with the expulsion of Isabella II, the tragedy of the redundant civil servant Villaamil, and the reluctant ascent into the aristocracy of the skinflint moneylender Torquemada. Galdós portrays a priest, Nazarín, endeavouring in vain to follow Christ's example, and a woman, Tristana, seeking independence with no greater success. In one exceptional novel, *Misericordia* (Mercy, 1897), the servant Benina, representing the increasing spirituality of his later work, cheerfully maintains her middle-class mistress by begging in a spirit of perfect charity, and the novel also brings into question purely realist criteria when a figure she invents in the novel turns up in real life. Galdós's longest and most ambitious novel, *Fortunata y Jacinta* (1886–1887), has an amazingly live world of interlocked and fully-developed characters revolving around the four central figures. The working-class Fortunata is seduced by a wealthy idler Juanito, who is subsequently married to his cousin Jacinta. After being reduced to prostitution, Fortunata reluctantly marries the deranged and impotent Maxi, and resuming her affair with Juanito, has a child by him. When she dies she leaves the boy to be adopted by her childless rival Jacinta, thus infusing new blood into the inbred aristocracy of wealth. The historical background is meticulously outlined (Juanito's behaviour is compared to the fickleness of Spain's political institutions) and the themes encompassed include precise analyses of changing financial and social status, religious exaltation and frustrated love.

Among Galdós's historical chronicles, known as *episodios nacionales*, the earliest, starting with the familiar subject of the battle of Trafalgar, are traditionally better known. Yet the fourth and truncated fifth series on near contemporary Spain have greater interest for today's reader, both for their subject-matter, the reign of Isabella II and the revolutionary period, and for their technique: the skilful intertwining of fictional and historical stories and their subtle narrative pattern. Galdós also wrote plays of considerable interest, though somewhat deficient in dramatic force; the most famous is the anti-clerical *Electra*, which caused a major scandal when it was performed in 1901.

The second major novelist of the period is Emilia Pardo Bazán (1851–1921), a woman of formidable capacities who resolutely pressed her claims to attention in a man's world. She introduced Émile Zola's doctrines of Naturalism in an attenuated form into Spain, advocating a wider range of concern for the underprivileged classes but rejecting rigid determinism. She depicted in *La tribuna* (The female tribune, 1883) the first working-class woman heroine and forcefully analysed the decadence of rural feudalism in *Los pazos de Ulloa* (The house of Ulloa, 1886) and its sequel *La madre naturaleza* (Mother nature, 1887). She also wrote scores of effective short novels and stories.

The third major novelist and writer of short narratives was Leopoldo Alas (1852–1901), known as Clarín, though he was thought of by his contemporaries mainly as an acerbic critic. *La regenta* (The magistrate's wife, 1884–1885) is widely considered the greatest nineteenth-century Spanish novel (its possible rival is *Fortunata y Jacinta*). Its implacable study of the intrigues of clerical, social and political mores in a county town based on Oviedo makes Trollope's provincial society seem trite and tame. The heroine, Ana Azores, married to an elderly dysfunctional husband, is torn between two forces: the clerical domination, full of sexual undercurrents, of her spiritual adviser and confessor, and the attentions of the local ageing Don Juan, to whom she eventually succumbs. One of a whole series of nineteenth-century novels of adultery, Clarín's novel has an intensity comparable with *Anna Karenina*. Both the start (the vision of the city seen from the cathedral tower) and the ending (the leech-like kiss implanted by a choirboy on the fainting heroine) are masterful. Alas's only other full-length novel is an intriguingly enigmatic tale revolving around the unresolved parentage of the baby the ineffectual hero desperately asserts is his only child, *Su único hijo* (1890).

The clash of ideologies is a crucial issue throughout the century. Though the conservatives had a powerful champion for traditional values in the extraordinarily erudite Marcelino Menéndez Pelayo late in the century, intransigent Catholic doctrine had been gradually undermined by a highly idealistic philosophy known as Krausism (after a German philosopher, C. F. Krause), and by the practical achievements of the great educator Francisco Giner de los Ríos. Agrarian and legal reforms were forcefully advocated by the Aragonese economist Joaquín Costa, and working-class figures, often of militant Anarchist persuasion, developed their own social philosophy. Just as it is fitting to date the beginning of the nineteenth century at the French invasion in 1808, so the Spanish-American War of 1898, in which Spain lost its remaining colonies (Cuba, Puerto Rico, the Philippine Islands), represents a convenient cut-off point for its end. The generation named after this date (the Generation of 1898), together with the complementary movement of *modernismo*, leads immediately into the cultural, aesthetic and intellectual concerns of the twentieth century.

FURTHER READING

Alborg, J. L. 1972–1999. *Historia de la literatura española*, III, IV, V i–iii. Madrid: Gredos.

Alonso, E. et al. 1989. *Goya and the spirit of Enlightenment*. Boston: Little, Brown.

Anderson-Imbert, E. 1969. *Spanish-American literature. A history*. 2 vols. Detroit: Wayne State University Press.

Carr, R. 1982. *Spain 1808–1936*. Oxford: Clarendon Press.

Flitter, D. 1992. *Spanish Romantic theory and criticism*. Cambridge: Cambridge University Press.

Franco, J. 1994. *An introduction to Spanish-American literature*, 3rd edn. Cambridge: Cambridge University Press.

Gies, D. Thatcher. 1994. *The theatre in nineteenth century Spain*. Cambridge: Cambridge University Press.

Glendinning, N. 1972. *A literary history of Spain: the eighteenth century*. London: Benn; New York: Barnes Noble.

Haidt, Rebecca. 1998. *Embodying Enlightenment. Knowing the body in eighteenth century Spanish literature and culture*. New York: St Martin's Press.

Herr, R. 1958. *The eighteenth century revolution*. Princeton: Princeton University Press.

Kirkpatrick, S. 1980. *'Las románticas': women writers and subjectivity in Spain, 1835–1850*. Berkeley: University of California Press.

Labanyi, J. (ed.) 1993. *Galdós*. London: Longman.

Llorens Castillo, V. 1968. *Liberales y románticos*. Madrid: Castalia.

Navas Ruiz, R. 1990. *El romanticismo español*. 4th edn, Madrid: Cátedra.

Oleza, J. 1984. *La novela del siglo XIX*. Barcelona: Laia.

Polt, J. H. R. 1994. *Poesía del siglo XVIII*. 4th edn, Madrid: Castalia.

Shaw, D. 1972. *A literary history of Spain: the nineteenth century*. London: Benn; New York: Barnes and Noble.

Urrutia, J. (ed.) 1995. *Poesía del siglo XIX*. Madrid: Cátedra.

5

Twentieth-century Spain

Derek Gagen

Spain in the twentieth century experienced enormous changes as it moved from being an unevenly backward society, marginalised from Europe in many ways (taking little or no part in the World Wars of 1914–1918 and 1939–1945) to a position where it has an assured role in the European Union and in world affairs. Culturally it followed a similar path, moving from a marginalised, if vibrant, position around 1900 to one where Spanish films and writing, art and architecture, pop music and sporting prowess, SEAT cars and *Hola* magazine, are instantly recognisable outside its frontiers, while within Spain previously minimally recognised social or regional groups are at the forefront of cultural life. What we study at university level is the cultural framework of the hybrid society, or set of societies, within which these developments take place and Spain assumes its contemporary identity. The space inhabited by Hispanic twentieth-century studies has considerably widened recently, as Spain itself has changed. The study of twentieth-century Spain is an interdisciplinary undertaking. Every text we read, film we view, or historical event that we study, takes its place in a context.

The century begins with a Disaster (the capital letter is obligatory); in the 1930s Spain suffered a civil war that left a festering scar throughout 36 years of dictatorship; and the century closes with Spain transformed into a dynamic, rumbustious, if at times disenchanted, society, one in which some of the old wounds remain open. At the close of the nineteenth century a leading British statesman had deemed Spain one of the dying nations. At the close of the twentieth century it is very much alive. Schubert (1990) refers to this as a century of dynamism. In some areas Spain was far from dying even as the century opened. In the literary and pictorial arts it was about to experience a *Silver Age*, in many ways one to rival the *Siglo de Oro*. And yet this incipiently vibrant culture was set in a society full of conflict, reeling in the aftermath of the Disaster.

A FAILING LIBERAL DEMOCRACY: A REVIVING CULTURE

The liberal constitution of 1875 had been a heroic attempt on the part of the conservative Prime Minister Cánovas and those about him to urge modernity upon the Spanish, impelling them towards an allegedly British *convivencia* by forging a two-party system in which by 1890 all Spanish men had the vote, and by keeping the army off the streets. However, it failed to deal with *la cuestión social* (the social question), the chronic disparities in living standards and life expectancy among the population. The tensions within society led to the failure of this experiment as some fought against the modernisers, seeking to recreate a bygone age, whilst others conjured nationalistic visions, both centralist and regional. New ideologies caused Spaniards to question the very nature of their democracy as Spain tried to regain some sort of late imperialist destiny in North Africa. Spanish culture in the first third of the century is formed by and in its turn helps to bring about the collapse of the constitutional system in the struggle for modernity, for the artists of the turn of the century, like the parliamentarians, sought initially to Europeanise Spain. We cannot neglect these matters since, if we understand what the social reformers, politicians and leaders of opinion were arguing, we are more likely to appreciate the work of the important writers of the day, Miguel de Unamuno, Pío Baroja and García Lorca, as well as the work of artist Picasso, composer Manuel de Falla and the other artists of Spain's Silver Age.

The Cuban revolt (1895–1898), the Spanish-American War of 1898, and the consequent loss of Spain's American and Pacific colonies, at a time when the other European powers had consolidated their Imperialist expansion in Africa, are subsumed as *El desastre*. They initiate a period from 1898 to 1931 that is characterised by:

1 Disaster (1898) → Dictatorship (1923–1931) → Republic (1931–1939).
2 The predominance of the so-called *fuerzas vivas* (living forces), the elite that was prioritised by the philosopher Ortega y Gasset, and which gave way to *las masas* (the masses), whose rebellion Ortega was similarly to analyse.
3 Successive attempts at revival:

1898   *Regeneración*, the motto of politicians and the modernising writers known collectively as the Generation of 98.

1917   *Renovación*, the plea of Catalan regionalists and dissident military groups seeking to have their voice heard in the crisis of parliamentary democracy.

1923   Regeneration from above, the dictatorship of General Primo de Rivera.

1931   Republican modernisation, the ultimately unsuccessful mission of Spain's Second Republic.

THE 'DISASTER' OF 1898

At the end of the nineteenth century Spain had entered the war with the United States in a mood of absurd pride in army and *patria*. The defeat brought a terrible loss of faith, reminiscent of later similar postcolonial débâcles such as Suez or Vietnam, and summed up by the *Heraldo de Madrid* in its end-of-year survey of 1898:

> El espantoso balance de este año memorable no dice sólo tantos miles de muertos, tantas colonias perdidas, tantos buques en el fondo del mar, tantos millones deshechos . . . Lo peor de este balance es lo que añade: la fe destruida, los hombres de Estado sustituidos por flamantes quirománticos

> (The shocking outcome of this memorable year is not only thousands of dead, so many lost colonies, so many ships at the bottom of the ocean, so many millions destroyed . . . The worst outcome is what we now have: a faith in tatters, and statesmen substituted by palmists.)

The psychological effect of the crisis was profound. New political leaders took the place of the assassinated Cánovas and the toppled Liberal leader Sagasta. Soon there was a new king as in 1902 Alfonso XIII came of age. In his diary he wrote:

> En este año me encargaré de las riendas del Estado, acto de mucha trascendencia tal y como están las cosas; porque de mí depende si ha de quedar en España la Monarquía Borbónica o la República.

> (This year I will take over the reins of the state, an extremely significant act as things stand, because it depends on me whether Spain is a Bourbon monarchy or a republic.)

With no Cánovas to keep him on the rails, the new king had a dangerously personal view of the constitution. The contrast between the present self-confident Spain at the start of the twenty-first century, led by a constitutional monarch, Juan Carlos I, and the psychologically fragile Spain of a century earlier, with its idiosyncratic young playboy king, is extremely marked.

The Spain of the reign of Alfonso XIII (1902–1931) is characterised by three features:

1 In the economic, social and political spheres, Spain appeared to lag behind most of the major powers of Europe. The country as a whole lacked the modernising features discernible in its most immediate neighbours France and Italy, or the most industrially advanced economies such as Britain. Significant commentators, for example Unamuno, in referring to Spain's economic backwardness, would use the term *Manchesterismo*. Spain, it was argued, lacked the sort of thriving business/industrial/cultural capitalist icon that was Manchester.

2 And yet, as in Italy, there existed a notable disparity between the regions in terms of development. Regions such as Catalonia and the Basque Country present features that are markedly 'European', in their industrial development, strong bourgeoisie and vibrant culture, whilst the more agrarian regions are decidedly pre-industrial, even though they were equally to appeal to certain groups of artists and writers.

3 There is a Manichean sense of *Las dos Españas* (the two Spains) analysed by Antonio Machado in a celebrated poem: traditional Spain, opposed to change, Catholic, authoritarian and centralist, and liberal Spain, European and progressive in outlook, the enemy of feudal Spain.

Relevant here is the comment of the economic historian Joseph Harrison as he notes that Spain's twentieth-century crisis had its roots not in short-term factors (such as the World Depression or the ideological battles of the 1930s) but in profound structural faults:

> The origins of the brutal and costly civil war of the 1930s are to be found less in the international economic depression of that era than in the frustrated efforts of a reformist regime to tackle some of the many structural problems endemic to early twentieth-century Spanish society, such as the excessive influence of the Church, the armed forces and centralising administrators.
>
> (Harrison 1978: ix)

The structural backwardness and uneven development provide a constant backcloth to the evolution of Spain in the first half of the century. It was, however, compounded by another factor. Over the previous century, between 1797 and 1900, Spain's population had increased from 10,541,000 to 18,594,000, a rise of 75 per cent. Yet this, in a European context, was a relative expansion. Only France and Ireland experienced a lower growth rate. In the twentieth century there would be periods of strong growth such as the 1960s and early 1970s. Indeed, by the mid-1990s Spain's population had risen to nearly 40 million, but it retained a low fertility rate in European terms. What particularly characterised the twentieth century was the uneven population distribution. The majority of the Spaniards live in the coastal areas and the islands or a few large cities; by the 1990s half the population of Spain lived in cities of more than 100,000 inhabitants. Thus, during the twentieth century the average Spaniard changed from a country peasant, working in an agrarian economy, to an urban dweller probably working in the service sector. We need to bear these factors constantly in mind when we study the recent literature and wider culture of the twentieth century.

Rapid change in society, such as population growth, migration into the cities, and inflation, will often lead writers and artists to contrary reactions, as it did in Spain:

1 There was a nostalgic desire to retain elements of a disappearing past, seen in the writers of both Spanish and Catalan at the turn of the century as they

depicted the spiritual and other noble virtues of rural Spain while, with rare exceptions such as Azorín in *La Andalucía trágica* (Tragic Andalusia), they ignored the hunger of the peasantry. Unamuno was characteristically to reject his early socialism and propose Don Quixote as a model for Europe, rather than Manchester, as a model for Spain.

2 Or, as in the 1920s and the final quarter of the century, there was a celebration of an avant-garde and frequently disruptive modernity that exalts the urban joys of film, mass media and popular culture. The first poems and other texts devoted to sport, the cinema and the values of modernity date from the 1920s.

THE POLITICS OF A FAILING DEMOCRACY

Politically *regeneración* came to mean finding successors to Cánovas and Sagasta, the creators of the Restoration settlement (see Chapter 4). The conservatives sought 'revolution from above' under the controversial figure of Antonio Maura but elitist reform was shattered by the events of the *Semana trágica* (tragic week) in 1909. The cry of 'Maura, no' echoes down the next decade, and is still heard in Valle-Inclán's play *Luces de Bohemia* (Bohemian lights) in the early 1920s. The dissolution of politically coherent conservatism coincided with the anticlerical onslaught of the liberals. Canalejas, potentially the Lloyd George of Spanish politics, caused offence to Spanish Catholics simply by allowing Protestant chapels to display their presence with a sign on the door. Protesters took to the streets in 1911 over this footling issue when the need for radical modernising reform was much more urgent.

Those groups who opposed the centralist parliamentary democracy of the liberals and conservatives gained strength in the first third of the century. The socialists, under their charismatic yet moralistic leader Pablo Iglesias, and their trade union, the UGT (General Workers' Union), made steady progress and attracted intellectuals with their democratic, if centralist, strand of the Marxist tradition. The anarchist movement, appealing strongly to the anti-centralism of Spaniards, founded their Union, the CGT (General Confederation of Workers) in 1911 and became increasingly syndicalist and in practice less attractive to intellectuals. The growth of strong working-class movements and the simultaneous rise of regionalist/nationalist dissidence in Catalonia and the Basque Country placed an unbearable strain on the fragile parliamentary system, above all when Spain was fighting a nasty little colonial war in her Moroccan protectorate.

It was to be the war in Morocco that triggered the final crisis. In 1917, disaffection in the army, allied to widespread demands for *renovación* coming from Catalonia, caused the regime to falter; in 1923 it was toppled when General Miguel Primo de Rivera led a military takeover to prevent publication of a report on the army's ineptitude, and Alfonso acquiesced. It was widely believed that Primo would clear the decks of corrupt politicians and walk away, but the anger when he installed a variant of Italian fascism was great. The Moroccan campaign, soaking up Spanish men (largely working-class conscripts) and a significant slice of the budget, was successfully concluded but had opened up great rifts in society. Intellectuals such as Valle-Inclán taunted the military in plays and novels, just as Lorca would pillory the behaviour and values of the Civil Guard in his best-selling *Romancero gitano* (Gypsy ballads) in 1928. The dictatorship of Primo de Rivera was to be a major step in the politicisation of Spanish culture and by the 1920s intellectuals and artists were sufficiently important for this to matter.

SPAIN'S CULTURAL RENAISSANCE

At the turn of the century Spain was already showing signs of artistic ebullience in a variety of fields. It had a flourishing popular musical theatre in the great cities, the *género chico*, and a lively tradition of parodic theatre that was to influence later artists. The lofty figures of the previous century, Pérez Galdós in the novel and Echegaray in drama, no longer dominated the scene. Nineteenth-century discourses such as Romanticism and Realism were undermined in all the arts by the exponents of International Modernism, in literature the *modernistas* and the Generation of 98. For these writers and artists the idealistic rhetoric of Romanticism and the Realists' pretence that an exact reproduction of reality was possible, and even desirable, were both rejected. In poetry *modernismo*, the Spanish version of Symbolism, would produce two towering but notably different figures, Juan Ramón Jiménez (1881–1958) and Antonio Machado (1875–1939). It is important to note that the culturally dissident *modernista* movement informed the early work of these poets. As the Bohemian *modernistas* idealised beauty and form, and explored the sensual and the erotic, they felt that they were opening up a deeper reality which had been ignored by so-called Realists. Something very similar was to occur in prose literature and the theatre.

The novel

Nowhere is the radical shift clearer than in the novel. The 'great tradition' fiction of the previous century focused on character portrayal, as the titles of the major novels suggest: *Pepita Jiménez*, *Doña Perfecta*, *La Regenta*. Novelists would now turn from psychological probing to issues, and to the very nature of fictional reality. The titles again show this: *La voluntad* (Willpower), *El mundo es así* (The way of the world), *Niebla* (Mist). The latter, the masterpiece of Miguel de Unamuno (1864–1936), illustrates how fiction becomes the space for philosophical discussion rather than a text inviting us voyeuristically to observe characters and analyse (or even rejoice in) their failures. When Augusto Pérez, the bland and socially inept protagonist of *Niebla*, confronts the allegedly omniscient author Unamuno, this draws attention to literary issues (Don Quixote, as Unamuno argued in *La vida de don Quijote y Sancho* (1905), lives on in a way that Cervantes can never do) and also to theological questions, not least whether we, God's creatures, are creating Him rather than being created by Him. Writers at this time were making Spanish readers challenge beliefs and premises exactly as dissident political groups were undermining the assumptions underpinning the Restoration state. Paradoxically those same writers, rejecting radical political reform, at times canvassed 'spiritual' solutions that in Mainer's words reflect the authors' 'profundo trauma social' (deep social trauma) (1975: 40).

The theatre

This exciting questioning of Realist discourse was soon reflected in other genres such as drama. The theatrical equivalent of mimetic-mode fiction is naturalism, associated with the middle-class psychological dramas of Galdós and Jacinto Benavente (1866–1954), the latter dominating the Spanish stage in the first half of the century. However, as early as 1905 the great actress-impressario María Guerrero launched a campaign of *teatro poético* to move theatrical evolution a step forward. By the 1920s a number of writers more associated with other genres were to achieve the breakthrough, most significantly Valle-Inclán (1866–1936), with his aesthetic of *esperpento* (shock-horror) set forth in *Luces de Bohemia* (1920), and writers originally better known as poets, such as García Lorca (1898–1936) and Rafael Alberti (1902–1999).

Here the key figure is Lorca. While some of his plays fit into the category of 'poetic theatre', they nevertheless explore significant social issues, most notably female and gay sexuality, that lay at the heart of Spanish life in the years running up to the Civil War. Yet Lorca, Alberti, Jacinto Grau (1877–1958) and others also at times employed a much more avant-garde discourse. Lorca's *El público* (The Public), never performed in his lifetime, and Alberti's *El hombre deshabitado* (Empty man, 1931) collapsed the naturalistic framework just as forcefully as had Unamuno for fiction. In Alberti's expressionist updating of the Genesis creation myth, man is born on a building site and God is a night-watchman of Pinter-like malevolence. In Grau's *El señor de Pigmalión* (Mr Pygmalion, 1921) life-size puppets, mechanical replacements for actors, murder their creator.

Poetry

By the 1920s, Spain was gripped by the dictatorship of Primo de Rivera, with the newspapers full of blank spaces where the censors had been at work. Yet in this sundered society there flourished painters such as Picasso (though he worked in Paris), Miró and Salvador Dalí, the film director Luis Buñuel, the composer Manuel de Falla, as well as the extraordinary group of poets known as the 1927 Generation. Alongside Lorca and Alberti this included major figures such as Jorge Guillén (1893–1984) and Pedro Salinas (1891–1951), following initially in Juan Ramón's footsteps, and Nobel Prizewinner Vicente Aleixandre (1898–1984) and Luis Cernuda (1902–1963), the poets most akin to surrealism. The date 1927 was a reference to their celebration of the work of the seventeenth-century poet Luis de Góngora (see Chapter 3), the tercentenary of whose death, in 1927 gave the more iconoclastic members of the group an opportunity to offend senior literary critics, urinate against the walls of the Royal Spanish Academy and pen some decent poetic jokes.

Thought

While frowning upon such activities, the Spanish philosopher and aesthetician José Ortega y Gasset (1883–1955), Spain's leading ideologue in the first half of the century, as well as establishing his own philosophical position (summed up in the lapidary 'Yo soy yo y mi circunstancia' (I am me and my circumstance)), analysed Spanish reality in essays such as *España invertebrada* (Invertebrate Spain) and *La rebelión de las masas* (Revolt of the masses). Ortega saw Spain as lacking an ideological core and a backbone of modern (middle-class) elite. But he recognised Spain's significance in the cultural field as he turned an elitist gaze on modern art in his essay *La dehumanización del arte* (The dehumanisation of art, 1925), where he considered the avant-garde as essentially unpopular, the 'higher algebra of metaphor', the purest of pure art. Ortega was one of the intellectuals whose sniping at the dictatorship and the monarchy that condoned it (a celebrated article 'Delenda est monarchia' humiliated Alfonso), in addition to the pressure from the masses whose revolt he described, were to create a Republic very different from that which he hoped for. The elitist intellectuals fled their algebraic metaphors and engaged in politically committed and decidedly impure art.

SOCIETY AND CULTURE IN CONFLICT – THE SECOND REPUBLIC (1931–1936) AND THE CIVIL WAR (1936–1939)

In the late 1920s the mood of the Spanish changed. Despite the dictatorship, the decade had been *los felices años veinte* (the happy 1920s). As elsewhere, radio, the silent cinema, dance crazes such as the Charleston, Oxford bags, and a devil-may-care attitude characterised those years until reality broke in. Maybe this was only the surface of the modernity that Ortega and forward-looking Spaniards craved. Writers such as Lorca in his nightmare-like vision of North America in *Poeta en Nueva York* (Poet in New York, 1929–1930), and Alberti in the real nightmares recounted in the apocalyptic visions of *Sobre los ángeles* (Concerning the angels, 1929), anticipated the political turmoil that Spain experienced in the 1930s as the country felt the effects of the great Depression and age-old enmities became redefined in terms of such possibly alien concepts as fascism and communism.

The republic was born in April 1931 when the monarchists lost the local elections in Spain's main cities and the king and royal family fled. The balance of political power had shifted enormously since the collapse of the old parliamentary system in 1923. The Cortes elected in 1931 to draw up a fresh constitution and reform Spain's institutions was formed by a new set of parties. Radicals and socialists, Catalan and Basque nationalists, now dominated. They were to be replaced in the 1933 elections by an ever more strident series of rightist groups, and, still further to the right, Spain's fascist party, the Falange, founded in 1933 by José Antonio Primo de Rivera, son of the late dictator. In the five years of the republic, Spain's tensions became more urgent. Attacks on the institutions of traditional Spain, the burning of churches, violence against priests and nuns, and the enfeebling of the military, abounded. The radical first parliament (1931–1933) was dominated by anticlerical and antimilitarist lobbies, but also sought to settle the Catalan question and instituted agrarian and financial reform in legislation which served only to alienate powerful interests rather than solve infrastructural weakness. The tensions were if anything further intensified as the Spanish, well aware of Mussolini's rise in Italy in the previous decade, now saw the climb to power of Hitler in Germany and the rest of German-speaking Europe. When in early 1936 a Popular Front coalition was successful in the republic's third general election, the *convivencia* sought by the liberals of the previous century had dissipated. In July 1936 a group of army generals, among whom Francisco Franco soon emerged as leader, led a coup against the democratic republic and set off a civil war that was not to be resolved until the Republican defeat at the end of March 1939.

There was little wonder, then, that the clowning light-heartedness or ivory-tower musings of the 1920s had gone. Spain's culture and art in the 1930s were politically committed, either on behalf of radical parties, such as Alberti's adherence to communism, Machado's traditional socialism and some writers' flirtation with fascism, or, as in Lorca's startling picture of a childless and loveless marriage in *Yerma* (Barren, 1934), through the representation in art of issues at the forefront of social debate. The Civil War took the lives of many writers, including Lorca who was murdered, and many were driven into exile, but it also opened the arts to a wider public. Soldiers at the battlefront wrote and published poems. Artists on both sides (at times against their better judgement) composed propaganda pieces. At the same time, of course, this civil war was a world war in miniature. The rebel forces relied heavily on support, in men and material, from Hitler and Mussolini. The foreign volunteers in the International Brigades, who ranged from Welsh miners to American union members (in the Abraham Lincoln Brigade), and unattached free spirits such as George Orwell, were to ensure that Spain's conflicts had a worldwide dimension and that the regime that emerged following the Republican defeat in 1939 would remain an international pariah. Picasso's great mural *Guernica* with its potent reminder of the German air attack on the iconic Basque town, Auden's 'Spain' and Orwell's *Homage to Catalonia*, as much as the militant wartime verse of poets more closely involved such as Miguel Hernández (1910–1942) and the Peruvian César Vallejo (1892–1938), all served to ensure that the issues of the Civil War remained alive for decades. On my first visit to Spain as a schoolboy in the Franco period I was handed a clandestine copy of poems from Hernández's *Vientos del pueblo* (Airs of my people) by a radical student at Madrid University. The product of the extraordinary cultural rebirth of Spain in the early twentieth century had gone underground.

CULTURE AND CONFLICT DURING THE FRANCO REGIME (1936–1975)

The Civil War (1936–1939) is one of the great defining moments in Spanish history. Its aftermath remained significant for decades, in a way reminiscent of earlier major upheavals such as the revolt of the *Comuneros* in 1520–1521, the siege of Barcelona in 1713–1714, or Madrid's heroic defence against Napoleon in 1808. The Civil War initiates a period of nearly four decades that now seem a kind of parenthesis in Spain's development as the regime sought to isolate itself from the democratic world. When we study this period we often take a double look at the Civil War and the workers' revolution it set off behind Republican lines. If approaching it chronologically, as we have done here, we adopt the viewpoint of a republic defending itself against insurrection. But from the standpoint of the Franco years, our stance may need to shift. We come to view Franco as a traditional Spanish military figure seeing himself as a legitimate defender of a territorial and social unity that, in his opinion and that of those who supported him, had been threatened by liberals, anticlericals, regionalists (and it should not be forgotten that Franco was a Galician) and by all who attacked a unified, centralist, God-driven Spain. For Franco and the Nationalists the Civil War had been a *cruzada* or crusade under their *caudillo* (leader) against the new infidel, against all that was un-Spanish.

The configuration of Franco's Spain was initially decided by the urgent need to reward those external and internal supporters who had contributed to the victorious crusade. Given the level of aid provided for the Nationalist cause by Germany and Italy, Franco's assistance for the Axis powers in the Second World War (1939–1945), under the euphemistic category of 'non-belligerent status', was a foregone conclusion. The main fascist legislation in Spain dates from the period of Axis victories in the early years of the war. Only the isolationist economic policy known as autarky was to remain in place until the 1950s. By 1943 when it became clear that the Axis was beginning to crumble and the USA was putting pressure on Franco, his regime began to adopt the façade of 'organic democracy'. Following the triumph of the Allies in the Second World War in 1945, Spain was initially isolated and was not admitted to the United Nations until 1955. But the Atlantic Alliance's need for support in the Cold War against communism led to a more benign view of the regime. Franco's only active role in the Second World War had been to send volunteers, the Blue Division of Falangists, to aid the Germans against the Soviet Union. Now in 1953 his regime's anti-communism led the American administration to sign an agreement allowing US military bases on Spanish soil (outside Madrid, and in Rota, Andalusia).

At home Franco's policy was similarly to reward those who had supported him, namely the military, the Church and the financial–economic oligarchy. The Falange had been weakened when in the spring of 1937 Franco had forcibly combined it with the traditionalist Carlist movement (see Chapter 4) and imprisoned the *camisas viejas* (old shirts) who resisted change. (The Falange's founder José Antonio Primo de Rivera had been executed by the Republic in 1936.) The Falange's role in Franco's Spain was to serve as a scaffolding that supported Franco's real power base until the Movement, as it came to be known, resembled those Roman gods in whom no Roman believed but who were essential to the State's well-being. The Falange was omnipresent. The only compulsory subjects in the university curriculum were religion, physical education and politics – as understood by Falangists; but in practice it was impotent. The organisation's only real power was to impose and run the censorship, the cultural equivalent of autarky, the aesthetics of isolation.

The cultural tsars of *franquismo* set agendas that clearly impacted in a number of ways. The nationalistic religiosity of the regime, its *nacional-catolicismo*, was reflected in the escapist, traditionalist cultural tone of the early 1940s. The stage and the cinema were dominated by lavish productions that focused on Spain's folklore, its imperial past, with Ferdinand and Isabella, the *Reyes Católicos*, being the major cultural icons. Yet this *bien pensant* mould was broken in the 1940s:

1 In fiction, in December 1942, came the publication of *La familia de Pascual Duarte* (Pascual Duarte's family) by Camilo José Cela (1916–2002), the diary of a mass murderer, curiously publicised by the regime's propaganda office as a Falangist novel; and in 1944 the remarkable novel *Nada* (Nothing) by Carmen Laforet (1921–). She was the first of a series of highly influential women authors who were to appear over the next few decades.

2 In verse, with the publication in 1944 of *Hijos de la ira* (Children of Anger) by Dámaso Alonso (1898–1990), the tone changes markedly: a savage

awareness of the existential anguish in the world and in Spain's newly expanded capital is projected from the memorable opening line: 'Madrid es una ciudad de más de un millón de cadáveres (según las últimas estadísticas).' (Madrid is a city of more than a million corpses (according to the latest statistics)).

3 In the autumn of 1949, *Historia de una escalera* (Story of a Staircase) by Antonio Buero Vallejo (1916–2000) brought a harsh and pitiless tone to the stage, far different from the escapist folklore and drawing-room comedies that had dominated the postwar theatre.

Relatively young writers such as Cela, Laforet, Buero Vallejo and the most significant of the young poets, Blas de Otero (1916–1979), established a relentlessly probing tone despite the censorship, and taught Spaniards at home and in exile abroad to read between the lines. Cinema and theatre audiences became very adept at reading the hidden codes. The students in Madrid cinemas would all shout 'corte' (cut) when the all too obvious scissors of the censors had snipped away at the print.

By the 1950s, in the wake of the US bases agreement of 1953, signed coincidentally with a concordat with the papacy to assuage the passions of those (above all in the armed forces) who still resented the US role in the Disaster of 1898, Spain began to change. The 1940s had been years of shortages: the *años de hambre* (hunger years) led to an inevitable questioning of the isolationist policies of autarky. The Falange lost this and every other ideological battle, and soon a group of liberal economists, often associated with the lay religious group Opus Dei, became dominant. The near collapse of the peseta in 1959 led to a series of liberalising economic plans as the siege economy of *Falangismo* gave way to a free-market agenda.

This is the background against which Spain's writers and film-makers educated and enlightened audiences that were becoming ever more sensitive to nuance and hidden agendas. Even the traditional romances of boy-meets-girl and virtue rewarded that dominated popular film and stage seem at times to have been read by audiences in an anti-regime way. Hints are found of rising levels of economic expectation. The hopes of working-class women in Buero's play *Hoy es fiesta* (Today is a holiday, 1955) centre on the acquisition of a washing-machine. Just over ten years later, Carmen in *Cinco horas con Mario* (Five hours with Mario) by Miguel Delibes (1920–) laments, over her dead husband's body, their lack of even a small car, the SEAT 600 known as the *ómbligo* (navel) 'because everybody has one'. Sporting fixtures, above all Real Madrid's feats in the European Cup, television, the fleeting triumphs in the Eurovision Song Contest, the increasing flow of tourists lured by the regime's advert 'Spain is different', all combined to widen the horizon of expectation as Spain aspired to the status of a consumer society.

Delibes's novel is characteristic of an emerging experimentation in the 1960s, seen most markedly but not exclusively in fiction and film. Even in the truncated version published in his lifetime, the novel *Tiempo de silencio* (Time of silence, 1962) by the psychiatrist Luis Martín Santos (1924–1964), with its Joycean monologues, running debate on the backwardness and class-bound nature of Spanish cultural life, backstreet abortions, and withering reconsideration of Ortega's philosophical system, made Spaniards, and foreign Hispanists, re-examine their understanding of what was going on in Spain. There was a desire for self-criticism, seen most poignantly in Buero's play *El tragaluz* (The skylight, 1967) and in the novel *Señas de identidad* (Identity marks, 1967), the early masterpiece of Juan Goytisolo (1931–). These works, together with the films of Juan Antonio Bardem, Luis Berlanga and others, had the virtue of suggesting that the self-righteousness of the anti-Franco opposition in Spain, Paris, Mexico and Moscow, was as ill-founded as the certainties of the smug supporters of Franco's organic democracy. Álvaro Mendiola, the protagonist of *Señas de identidad*, in particular, learns that by the late 1960s the Spain defeated in 1939 was long dead, that the Spanish were not going to rise up in a general strike against the *Caudillo* and the future king, Prince Juan Carlos. The people of Spain, an Americanised tourist paradise in Mendiola's view of Barcelona in the final pages of Goytisolo's novel, would seek to improve their lot economically and wait for Franco to die.

In 1969, at the age of 76, Franco formally recognised Juan Carlos, grandson of Alfonso XIII, as his successor as head of state. In truth it seemed a poisoned chalice as the Basque Terrorist group ETA was becoming increasingly active, and the communist-dominated *comisones obreras* (trade unions) were increasingly influential. More significantly, Franco was losing the wholehearted support of two of the internal pillars of the regime, the Church and the banking and business community. The 'new' Catholic Church, following the liberalising Second Vatican Council, disengaged itself from the regime. Business interests, basking in the economic miracle of the 1960s, resented the fact that entry into the European Economic Community was out of the question so long as Franco remained head of state. In truth the regime was frail some time before the death of Franco in November 1975. His close friend and Prime Minister, Admiral Carrero Blanco, had been assassinated by ETA in 1973. Student strikes, Maoist and terrorist groups, and a general feeling that the regime's day was done, left an ominous message for the *Caudillo* in his last years. The sombre mood of the million or more who filed past Franco's body in the Royal Palace in Madrid contrasted with the delirious joy of the millions celebrating his death in the rest of Spain. The right-wing hope of 'un franquismo sin Franco' (Francoism without Franco) was dashed by the new king and his supporters within months of the general's death.

THE TRANSITION AND THE CULTURE OF DEMOCRATIC SPAIN

If the political transition to democracy was in practice being prepared before Franco's death, the cultural shifts were already evident. Cultural commentators, notably the influential Catalan critic Josep Maria Castellet (1926–), had been observing in verse and other genres a new experimentation that echoed the joyous dissidence of the old avant-garde. The Beatles and their Spanish imitators, Spanish epigons of Bob Dylan such as the *cantoautores* (singer/songwriters), the increasingly influential young women writers, all served to confirm the failure of Franco's cultural agenda.

Such political and cultural phenomena now make the transition to democracy seem a certain outcome but at the time it was touch-and-go. As the King was sworn in a few days after Franco's death, struggles began within the regime. It was only when the King appointed Adolfo Suárez as *Presidente del Gobierno* in July 1976 that rapid movement began. Suárez typifies the transition; he was a man bred in Francoism and leading a cabinet of Catholics, bankers and former *franquistas* yet he took apart the edifice of centralist politics. The Suárez Cabinet persuaded the Francoist Parliament to sign the institution's own death warrant in November 1976, and Spain moved towards a democracy that accepted diversity. Political parties were recognised for the first time since 1939. Elections were held, and by December 1978 a constitution was in place that established 'un estado de derecho' (state of law), ruled by law rather than arbitrary decree, with two houses of parliament. This so-called 'constitution of consensus' was characterised by the devolution of power to the 17 autonomous regions, albeit with a greater degree of devolution to Catalonia, the Basque Country, Galicia and Andalusia. By 1986 the modernising process had taken Spain, after debate and no little heart-searching, into NATO and the European Union. It is often forgotten that 1992, the year of Spain's worldwide prominence as Barcelona hosted the Olympic Games and Seville the great Expo 92 exhibition, was also the year of the Maastricht Treaty in which Spain agreed the convergence criteria that cemented her *europeísmo*. Before the century closed the Secretary General of NATO was a Spaniard (Javier Solana), and a former Socialist minister moreover. These changes were not uncontested, however. There were attempts at a military coup, and the incursion of Colonel Tejero, a pistol-wielding Civil Guard, into Parliament on 23 February 1981, broadcast live to the nation, made the Spanish acutely aware of the fragility of their freedoms.

Spain's writers, film-makers and artists reflected these changes, at times with great relish. The tense period of rumours of coup attempts was reflected in Buero Vallejo's *Jueces en la noche* (Judges in the night, 1979), with its portrait of one of Franco's former ministers now seeking to project himself as a democrat. In general, however, the focus was on social rather than political change. Women writers such as Montserrat Roig (1946–1991) and Rosa Montero (1952–) as well as gay writers chronicled, over the last third of the century, the freedoms and rights newly available after the regressive impositions of the Franco period. Divorce, contraception, abortion, gay and lesbian relationships, indeed a whole series of behaviours and alternative lifestyles previously hidden or banned have been treated and celebrated by the artists of democratic Spain. Changes that were amazing to older Spaniards have tended to gain a higher degree of visibility in the cultural production of post-Franco Spain. Here culture was reflecting reality. Little villages where in the 1960s wearing a bikini would have led to arrest now have a drug problem and can boast of video shops that rent material that might shock many British and Americans. Yet those same villages will still have conservative inhabitants uneasy with the rapidity of change.

The celebratory tone of the arts in the long period of Felipe González's PSOE (Socialist) government from 1982 to 1996 became tempered well before the accession to power of José María Aznar's right-wing Partido Popular. A conservative neoclassicism dominated Spanish verse by the 1990s but the carnavalesque and hedonistic tone of film, novel and popular music remains the dominant note of the period following Franco's death. The Madrid *movida*, the Spanish capital's version of London's swinging sixties, produced a popular yet at times oddly literary art. The films of Pedro Almodóvar (1949–), the novels of Manuel Vázquez Montalbán (1939–) and Eduardo Mendoza (1943–), both Catalans writing in Castilian, and the host of younger writers, singers and film-makers who flourish in Spain today, all continue the mix of avant-garde and vibrant punkish modernism that most non-Spaniards associate with the democratic Spain of the end of the twentieth century. In fact the blend of *lo popular* and the cultural avant-garde was far from new. Alberti's 'Platko', a poem in praise of Barça's goalkeeper written in 1928, or the wicked parodies common in the music hall and *género chico*, suggest that the cultural elite and mass entertainment were never too far apart in the ebullient culture of twentieth-century Spain. Hispanism, generally lacking the burden of French high culture, often rejoices in cultural products of very broad appeal and therein lies its strength.

FURTHER READING

Brooksbank Jones, A. 1997. *Women in contemporary Spain*. Manchester: Manchester University Press.

Brown, G. 1972. *A literary history of Spain. The twentieth century*. London: Benn.

Carr, R. 1982. *Spain 1808–1975*. Oxford: Oxford University Press.

Davies, C. 1994. *Contemporary feminist fiction in Spain. The work of Montserrat Roig and Rosa Montero*. Oxford: Berg.

Graham, H. and Labanyi, J. (eds) 1995. *Spanish cultural studies. An introduction, the struggle for modernity.* Oxford: Oxford University Press.

Harrison, H. 1978. *An economic history of modern Spain.* Manchester: Manchester University Press.

Harrison, J. and Hoyle, A. (eds) 2000. *Spain's 1898 crisis. Regeneration, modernism, post-colonialism.* Manchester: Manchester University Press.

Hooper, J. 1995. *The new Spaniards.* Harmondsworth: Penguin.

Jordan, B. and Moragan-Tamosunas, R. 2000. *Contemporary Spanish cultural Studies.* London: Arnold.

Mainer, J-C. 1975. *La edad de plata.* Barcelona: Asenet.

Preston, P. 1986. *The triumph of democracy in Spain.* London: Methuen.

Preston, P. 1993. *The Spanish Civil War, 1936–39.* London: Weidenfield & Nicolson.

Rodgers, E. 1999. *Encyclopedia of contemporary Spanish culture.* London: Routledge.

Romero Salvadó, F. 1999. *Twentieth-century Spain. Politics and society in Spain, 1898–1998.* Basingstoke: Macmillan.

Shubert, A. 1990. *A social history of modern Spain.* London and New York: Routledge.

Stanton, E. 1991. *Handbook of Spanish popular culture.* Westwood, Connecticut: Greenwood Press.

6

Catalan, Galician, Basque

David George

The concept of Spain as a single nation has been the subject of debate and conflict for centuries. There has been tension between centralising and centrifugal forces in Spain ever since the marriage of the Catholic Monarchs, Ferdinand and Isabella, brought together the kingdoms of Castile and Aragon in 1479 (see Chapter 2). At certain periods in history the centralisation has held sway, giving Spain the trappings of a unified country, while, at other times, power has lain with the peripheral areas of the peninsula. In the twentieth century, the Franco regime (1939–1975) was an extreme example of central control, while, during the years of the Second Republic (1931–1936) which immediately preceded the Spanish Civil War and more particularly since the late 1970s, a degree of power has been devolved to the often disparate communities which make up the country. Indeed, today, the Spanish state has arguably the most devolved form of government in Europe with seventeen separate autonomous communities enjoying varying degrees of control over their own affairs. The four communities which have the most autonomy are Andalusia (the largest in area) and the three so-called historical communities: the Basque Country (Euskadi), Catalonia and Galicia.

Although Basque history and society are studied as part of Hispanic Studies in some universities, the difficulties of its language make the Basque culture inaccessible to most foreign learners. Basque is one of those few European languages whose origins are unknown, and one of the oldest. There are about half a million Basque speakers in Spain and France. Catalan and Galician, on the other hand, are Romance languages and therefore present fewer problems to the student of Spanish. You only need to look at a couple of lines of Catalan, Galician, Spanish and Basque to realise how different Basque actually *looks* from the other three. The following is a verse from a song called *Lluna de llana* (Woollen moon) by the Catalan singer Marina Rosell. The title is translated into Spanish as *Luna de lana*, and into Galician as *Lúa de lan*, which all sound and look similar. The Basque title, however, is *Artilezko hilargia*, completely different! A comparison between the last two lines of the first verse of the song further illustrates the point that Catalan and Galician (and Spanish), although they are separate languages, clearly belong to the same family whereas Basque most certainly does not:

> Lluna, cirera blanca,
> et menjarem a l'alba (Catalan original)
>
> Luna, cereza blanca,
> te comeremos al alba (Spanish)
>
> Lúa, cereixa branca
> comerémote ca ialba (Galician)
>
> Hilargia, gereizi zuria,
> jan eginen zaitugu goiztirian (Basque)
>
> (Moon, white cherry,
> We will eat you at dawn.)

CATALAN

The 6 million speakers of Catalan are to be found all over what are known as the Catalan Lands, or *Països Catalans*, which include the Valencia and Alicante regions and the Balearic Islands within the Spanish state, as well as Andorra, parts of the Roussillon area of France, and Sardinia. Catalan *looks* familiar to someone who knows French or Spanish, but it *sounds* quite different from either. It tends to have more consonant sounds than Spanish and many more words ending in a consonant, or even combinations of consonants. It is a less phonetic language than Spanish, so more difficult to pronounce. As far as Catalan grammar is concerned, it too is more complex than Spanish. Although Catalan shares many features of Romance languages, including many irregular verbs, its combination of weak object pronouns ('Give *it* to *them*', for instance) is particularly exacting for the learner.

In broad terms, the Catalan and Galician languages and cultures have had two high points in their history, the Middle Ages and the period from about 1850 to the present day. As we have stated, this latter period was punctuated by years of repression, especially during the Franco dictatorship, but a distinctive consciousness and sense of identity remained intact, especially in Catalonia. In order to understand the development of the languages, history, society and politics of Galicia and the Catalan Lands, one has to look back to the Middle Ages. But before doing that, it is necessary to contextualise them briefly within the contemporary world and to introduce some of their most salient features.

GALICIA AND CATALONIA

Geographically, and in terms of their economies, Galicia and Catalonia are really quite different areas. Galicia's position in the north-western corner of Spain, facing the Atlantic Ocean, determines its temperate, humid climate, making it a part of what is known as Green Spain, or *La España verde*. The climate of Catalonia, on the other hand, is Mediterranean, although inland regions have the hot summers and cold winters associated with the continental climate of much of central Spain. Both Galicia and Catalonia are lands of physical contrasts, with mountains alternating with plains and long coastlines. This latter feature has led to the development of fishing and shipbuilding, especially significant industries in Galicia, while the Catalan capital Barcelona's position as a leading Mediterranean port has been crucial to its growth.

Indeed, Barcelona has an international profile that no Galician (and indeed few European) cities can match, but it would be a mistake to consider Catalonia as a one-city area. There has long been a sharp contrast between sophisticated, progressive, urban Barcelona and the conservative, traditional, but relatively prosperous Catalan countryside. Such contrasts do not really exist in Galicia, lacking as it does an urban centre of the power and size of Barcelona. The early development of industry in the Greater Barcelona area has meant the existence of a large middle class and a level of prosperity that an overwhelmingly rural Galicia (and many other areas of Spain) could only dream about. Catalan prosperity was built during the nineteenth century on textiles, to such a degree that Barcelona became known as the Manchester of Spain.

Nowadays, there is little left of the textile industry, but Barcelona remains the economic powerhouse of Spain, with a diverse, often high-tech economy. One result of this situation has been several waves of mass immigration over the last century, mainly in the form of inward migration from the poorer south of Spain but increasingly from Africa and Latin America. In complete contrast, Galicia has had an endemic problem of emigration for several centuries, as *gallegos* sought a better life in other areas of Spain, especially Madrid and Barcelona, other European countries and Latin America (notably Cuba and Argentina). As with their so-called Celtic cousins in Ireland, emigration was a huge economic and human drain on Galicia, although in both areas this has been largely stemmed due to the growing prosperity of recent years, resulting in no small measure from economic support from the European Union and from the confidence which comes from a sense of independent identity, a characteristic they share with Catalonia.

Historical importance

During their cultural and political heyday in the Middle Ages, both Galicia and Catalonia were also firmly plugged into Europe. Galicia's splendour came rather earlier than Catalonia's, and was due largely to the emergence of

Santiago de Compostela as a major destination for Europe's pilgrims from the eleventh century onwards. Thirteenth- and fourteenth-century Galician poetry is among the earliest lyrical poetry written in the Iberian Peninsula.

Catalan culture's high point came later. Barcelona's development between the thirteenth and the fifteenth centuries owed much to the fact that it was the major centre of power and influence in the Kingdom of Aragon and Catalonia, in whose domain lay Valencia, the Balearic Islands and Sardinia. The Gothic Quarter, with the narrow streets and squares, churches, including the famous Gothic cathedral, and commercial and government buildings which are still a tourist attraction today, was built with remarkable speed and is the most complete collection of buildings from that era still in existence in Europe.

The growth of Catalan as a commercial and literary language also belongs to this period. As in Galicia, poetry was the most potent literary form in medieval Catalonia. The most remarkable scholar and writer was a Mallorcan, Ramon Llull (1232/33–c.1316), while the first poet to write entirely in Catalan was the greatest of all Catalan poets and one of Spain's leading writers, Ausiàs March (1397–1459). March hailed from Valencia, whose literary scene in the fifteenth century was more varied and creative than that of Barcelona. The significance of the Valencian school of writers reminds us that one should refer to the Catalan Lands rather than Catalonia, at least as far as language and culture are concerned. Cultural identity can transcend political boundaries, and can come into conflict with them. Valencia, the Balearic Islands and Catalonia are separate political entities today, but a common linguistic and cultural heritage cannot be denied.

The decline of Galician and Catalan

The concept of languages straddling regional and national boundaries is also relevant to Galician. In the Middle Ages, Galician and Portuguese were one and the same language, although the former was dominant, especially culturally. However, by the fifteenth century, Galician was becoming an increasingly fragmented minority language as its society suffered changes brought about by the shift of cultural and political power to Castile. Following Columbus's discovery of the New World, whose gold and silver enriched the newly centralised and ever more powerful Castile-dominated Spain, peripheral areas such as Galicia and Catalonia lost importance, wealth and power (see Chapters 2 and 3).

A result of this newly-imposed 'unity' was a period of long decline in the Catalan and Galician languages and cultures, a trend which was not reversed until the nineteenth century. Catalonia's low point, at least as far as its linguistic and cultural identity are concerned, was in the early eighteenth century under the Bourbon dynasty. The Catalans backed the wrong side in the War of the Spanish Succession, for which the Bourbons exacted a severe revenge (see Chapters 1 and 4). However, although such actions affected cultural life, the language continued to be used by the majority of the people. As one critic graphically puts it, 'most Catalans [. . .] cared no more about what was going on in literary circles than Joe Sixpack cares about Jacques Derrida today. They just got on with speaking their vernacular' (Hughes 1993).

Cultural revival

The long road to the recovery of their language and literary tradition began in the early to mid-nineteenth century. As in other European countries, this was bound up with a growing sense of nationalism linked to Romanticism. The cultural movement was known as the *Rexurdimento* in Galicia. Galician was gradually reinstated as a serious literary language by the poet Rosalía de Castro (1837–1885) (see Chapter 4). In Catalonia, the cultural renaissance was known as the *Renaixença*. The two basic aims of the movement were to dignify the Catalan language and to create a national literature, which led to a great increase in the number of books published in Catalan from about the 1830s onwards. *Renaixença* writers evoked the Middle Ages with nostalgia, with an emphasis on localism and picturesque rural environments, the most representative figure being the poet-priest Jacint Verdaguer (1845–1902). Although the *Renaixença* stemmed largely from the growing confidence associated with a developing Catalan bourgeoisie, in many ways its values were rural rather than urban, and more concerned with timeless myths than the contemporary world. Rural Catalonia shares with Galicia the conservatism which typifies country areas. However, their social structure and their farming traditions have traditionally been quite different. In Catalonia, property passed to the eldest son, or *hereu*, who had the responsibility of using his wealth to look after his family. The Catalan system was different from that of the large *latifundios* of southern Spain with their absentee landlords and landless peasants, but also from the small-plot system of the Galician *minifundios*, in which each child received a plot of land which was too small for efficient farming.

CATALONIA IN THE TWENTIETH CENTURY

By the late nineteenth century, the society of Greater Barcelona, which absorbed the rural exodus from Catalonia and from other parts of Spain, had been transformed by industrial development. A dynamic entrepreneurial spirit characterised Catalan economic life, and Catalan industrialists saw themselves as the economic powerhouse of Spain. This was accompanied by a growing frustration with the Spanish state, which the Catalans felt was hampering rather than aiding the new capitalism. Frustration with the Spanish political process, combined with a growing sense of self-confidence in their business ability and Catalan-language based cultural life, led to the development of autonomy movements.

Unlike other large centres of minority cultures in Spain, such as Bilbao or Valencia or even Galicia, where the economic elite have traditionally spoken Spanish, the mother tongue of many members of the Catalan bourgeoisie was Catalan, and there was a strong conservative slant to Catalan nationalism. Conservative Catalanism had its greatest success with the establishment in 1913 of a limited form of self-government in the form of the *Mancomunitat*, or 'commonwealth' of the four Catalan provinces, which attempted to modernise Catalonia through the introduction of technical education and the development of road and telephone systems. The Institute of Catalan Studies (1907) and the National Library of Catalonia (1914) were built during this period. However, Catalan nationalism was complex and constantly shifting, and crossed the social divide. A result of the unfettered growth of capitalism in Barcelona was exploitation of workers and low wages, which led to an increase in working-class militancy. Barcelona suffered a rapid growth in population, with migration from the countryside of the centre and the south of Spain by far its largest source. No similar phenomenon occurred in Galicia. In the early twentieth century, Barcelona became one of the most radical cities in Europe, and there were regular episodes of Anarchist direct action from the late 1880s onwards, accompanied by the corresponding police repression.

It was during the Second Republic that both Catalonia and Galicia acquired more autonomy than they had had for centuries. Catalonia's autonomy was channelled through the *Generalitat*, or autonomous parliament, which was re-established in the 1930s, and took over most central government services and the running of the war effort during the early part of the Spanish Civil War. The Left was the main political force in Catalonia during the early 1930s and, during the early years of the Civil War, the radical, chiefly Anarchist sectors of Barcelona held considerable power, and hierarchical social structures were disrupted. However, as the war progressed, the Republic relied more and more on Russian military support, in return for which Stalin demanded the suppression of the libertarian Left and the imposition of greater central control. The consequence for Barcelona was a war-within-a-war when, in May 1937, the Anarchists and the Catalan Marxist group the POUM clashed with communists and socialists. The latter group won, and many libertarian socialists were killed or imprisoned, or fled. This is the situation so graphically described by George Orwell in *Homage to Catalonia* (1938).

The turbulence which characterised Barcelona society between the late nineteenth century and the Civil War was reflected in Catalan cultural life. This was the most brilliant phase in its history and permeated all branches of the arts, including prose writing, poetry and theatre, but more particularly the visual arts of painting and architecture. It is in these latter two areas that Catalan art is internationally known, although how many people outside Spain know that Antoni Gaudí, Salvador Dalí and Joan Miró were Catalan?

Catalan art

The architect Gaudí, who was responsible for a number of Barcelona's best-known tourist attractions, cannot be understood outside the cultural movement known as *modernisme*, which embraced literature as well as architecture, the visual arts and music. In international terms, *modernisme* is the rough equivalent of Art Nouveau or the English Arts and Crafts Movement and Pre-Raphaelites. Some of the *modernistes* were defenders of an arts-for-art's-sake philosophy, but there was a socially-critical edge to the work of others. The meeting place of the *modernistes* was the bohemian Els Quatre Gats café (which still exists), where the young Picasso hung out around the turn of the century. The *modernistes* were strong defenders of Catalan culture and used traditional Catalan motifs in their work, but they found the regionalism of the *Renaixença* stultifying and looked to the north of Europe for their artistic inspiration. Gaudí and his contemporaries aimed to beautify Barcelona, in a style which was at once traditional and modern. An excellent example of this blend is Gaudí's best known building, the church of the Sagrada Família.

The *modernistes* were succeeded by the *noucentistes*, who rejected what they saw as the former's decadence and who defended a kind of Mediterranean neoclassicism. The avant garde, too, was always a major force in Barcelona, as one would expect with artists like Picasso, Dalí and Miró. The first Cubist exhibition outside Paris was held in Barcelona in 1912.

Catalonia and Franco

This creative, dynamic environment was all but destroyed by Franco. Although Dalí supported the regime in his own eccentric way, the exile which was Miró's fate for a short time was typical of the fate of many Catalans who opposed the regime and who survived the Civil War and the repression of the early Franco years. Franco was determined to suppress expressions of linguistic and cultural variety and unleashed a particularly savage campaign against the Basques and the Catalans. This led directly to the formation of the Basque terrorist movement ETA, but there were no groups of comparable activity and influence in either Catalonia or Galicia. Nevertheless, it has to be said that Franco was supported by large sections of the Catalan bourgeoisie and landowners, as well as by devout Catalan Roman Catholics.

The decade following the Civil War (1940s) was a black one as far as the language and culture of Catalonia were concerned. Books in Catalan were burnt and street and town names Castilianised (hence Girona becomes Gerona, and Lleida, Lérida). The use of the spoken language was restricted to family life, and many Catalans were fined for using their language in public. Franco repeated the attempts of the monarchs of earlier centuries (with an equal lack of success) to Castilianise Catalonia by appointing reliable non-Catalan supporters as teachers and to posts in the civil service, the armed forces and the police, and dispatching Catalan teachers and other professionals to areas of Spain well away from their native Catalonia. Like Galicia and the Basque Country, Catalonia suffered from a double censorship, which was linguistic as well as content-based. Catalan writers either wrote in Spanish, or maintained a self-imposed silence. The best Catalan writer since the Civil War, the poet and playwright Salvador Espriu (1913–1985), did not publish anything between 1939 and 1946.

Gradually, some semblance of normality returned to Catalan civic and cultural life, although this was not fully achieved until the return of democracy at all levels of government, enshrined in the 1978 Constitution. Opposition to the Franco regime grew, particularly among the younger generation of the 1960s and 1970s, and Barcelona was a key Spanish centre of opposition to Franco, which embraced Catalan and Spanish speakers. The young Catalans of the 1960s and 1970s were naturally influenced by the new pop music and other youth cultures which were transforming Western society. This interest gelled into the peculiarly Catalan phenomenon known as the *Nova Cançó*, or 'new song', a phenomenon in which protest music was combined with the rediscovery of the folklore of regions like the Balearic Islands. Exponents of the *Nova Cançó* include the Valencian Raimon, the Catalan Lluís Llach and the Mallorcan Maria del Mar Bonet, who has frequently sung traditional Mallorcan songs that she has adapted herself. Another *Nova Cançó* stalwart is Joan-Manuel Serrat, who sings in both Spanish and Catalan and has a large following in Catalonia, the rest of Spain and Latin America. Renewed interest in popular and folk music led to a rediscovery of Catalan popular music during the 1970s.

The Catalan publishing industry is thriving, although it should be noted that more Spanish-language books are published in Barcelona than in Madrid. This links with another important point to be considered when discussing Catalan literature, namely the presence of writers who were born in Catalonia but who write in Spanish. Indeed, some of the best Spanish literature of the postwar period has been written by Catalans, who often come from immigrant families. Several novelists stand out, including Juan Goytisolo. A similar phenomenon occurred in Galicia in the late nineteenth and early twentieth centuries with the novelist Emilia Pardo Bazán and the poet, playwright and novelist Ramón del Valle-Inclán, two Galicians who wrote in Spanish and who, along with their fellow Galician Rosalía de Castro, are considered to be among the greatest writers in modern Spanish literature. One of the best-known Spanish novelists of the post-Civil War period, Camilo José Cela, was also a Galician (see Chapter 5).

CATALONIA TODAY

The recovery of popular culture in late Francoism and during the transition to democracy is reflected in a surge of interest in festivals such as the Lent carnival and annual local festivals, which had been suppressed by the Franco regime. Such festivals, as well as mime and dance, inspired internationally-known Catalan performance groups like Els Joglars and Comediants, while the stars of the so-called second generation of performance groups, La Fura dels Baus, were heavily influenced by rock music. Two other flourishing forms of entertainment in Catalonia as in most other Western countries are television and football. The Catalan television channel TV3 is noted for the quality of its programmes and plays an important role in the diffusion of the Catalan language. Barcelona Football Club, one of the best-supported and richest clubs in the world, is much more than a football club. It became the focus of anti-Franco, and more generally anti-Spanish, sentiments during the Franco regime, and, even in today's democratic Spain, Barcelona v. Real Madrid matches encapsulate a rivalry that has as much to do with questions of nationalism and identity as it has about football.

Following the re-establishment of the Generalitat in the late 1970s, the Catalan language has been consolidated. Since 1980, the ruling group in the autonomous parliament has been the right-of-centre nationalist party Convergence and Unity (CiU), under its charismatic leader, Jordi Pujol. The study of Catalan is compulsory in schools, and university classes are conducted more and more in Catalan, while holders of public administration posts are normally required to have a knowledge of Catalan. Its language policy has sometimes brought the Generalitat into conflict with the central Spanish government and provoked resentment outside Catalonia. However, within Catalonia itself, although tensions do exist, the Spanish and Catalan languages normally manage to co-exist peacefully in what is a genuinely bilingual society. Such co-existence is much less in evidence in another of the so-called Catalan Lands, Valencia.

BASQUE AND GALICIAN NATIONALISM

Whereas Catalan nationalism was often seen as progressive, rejecting the backwardness of the Spanish state, Basque nationalism is conservative and anti-modernist. One possible reason for this is the fact that Basque is not as widely spoken as Catalan, and the language cannot be called upon to represent a distinctive national identity (see Conversi 1997). Thus Basque nationalism has relied more heavily on notions of religion, race, and ancient privileges (*fueros*). In the 1960s the younger Basque nationalists broke away from these racialist theories and advocated direct action instead. Their organisation, ETA (*Euzkadi ta Askatasuna*, Basque land and freedom), split from the traditionalist Basque Nationalist Party (PNV). Subsequent splits in ETA itself stemmed from debates regarding the role of culture, or direct action. Since the 1982 Linguistic Normalisation Act, central government has encouraged and subsidised writing and publishing in Basque, while Basque film-makers (such as Víctor Erice, Julio Medem and Imanol Uribe) are among the most well known and productive in Spain.

Unlike Catalonia and the Basque country, there was little demand for autonomy in Galicia during the period following Franco's death. However, as the whole devolution process has been consolidated and accepted, a growing self-confidence in Galician identity has accompanied increased prosperity. The Galician language continues to be very widely spoken (possibly even more than Catalan), although only just over a quarter of the population are able to write it while just under 50 per cent can read it. There is a division between defenders of Galician as a separate language, and those who claim it is a sub-division of Portuguese. Nevertheless, it is losing its tag as a language of rural backwardness as it passes from a spoken language of the countryside to become a language of commerce and public institutions. Over the last decade, the President of the Galician government, or *Xunta de Galicia*, has been Manuel Fraga Iribarne, Minister of Information under Franco, founder of the right-wing Allianza Popular (AP) Party (later to become the Partido Popular (PP)), and originally a strong (Spanish) centralist. However, he has undertaken his task with relish, and has proved a highly effective leader.

A key element in economic progress in the autonomous regions has been the European Union. Galicia in particular, as one of the poorest regions in the Union, has benefited greatly from European regional funds, which have helped it to improve its infrastructure and encouraged industry. The regions have partnerships with others in Europe and these have led to trans-European projects, such as Galicia's membership of the Atlantic Arc and Catalonia's role as one of the four motor regions of Europe. For the Catalans, the links with Europe are an extension of their historic internationalism. A particularly important event in this regard was Barcelona's staging of the 1992 Olympic Games, in which Barcelona and Catalonia showed themselves off to the world and which led to significant infrastructure developments.

In short, autonomy and Spain's membership of the EU have been highly influential in the recent development of Catalonia, Galicia and the Basque Country. They have contributed to economic development and have helped to reaffirm a sense of identity which brings its own self-confidence. This chapter has demonstrated that a sense of separateness is not a new phenomenon, but, culturally and politically, pre-dates the existence of a recognisable Spanish state.

FURTHER READING

Balcells, A. 1996. *Catalan nationalism past and present*. Trans. by J. Hall. London: Macmillan.

Boyd, A. 1988. *The essence of Catalonia*. London: André Deutsch.

Burns, J. 1999. *Barça*. London: Bloomsbury.

Conversi, D. 1997. *The Basques, the Catalans and Spain: alternative routes to nationalist mobilisation*. London: Hurst and Company.

George, D. and London, J. (eds) 1996. *Contemporary Catalan theatre: an introduction*. Sheffield: Anglo-Catalan Society.

Giner, S. 1980 (reprinted 1984). *The social structure of Catalonia*. Sheffield: Anglo-Catalan Society.

Hughes, R. 1993. *Barcelona*. New York: Vintage Books.

Mackay, D. 1985. *Modern architecture in Barcelona*. Sheffield: Anglo-Catalan Society.

Terry, A. 1972. *A literary history of Spain: Catalan literature*. London: Ernest Benn, and New York: Barnes and Noble.

Webber, J. and Strubell i Trueta, M. 1991. *The Catalan language: progress towards normalisation*. Sheffield: Anglo-Catalan Society.

Wheeler, M. W., Yates, A. and Dols, N. (eds) 1999. *Catalan: a comprehensive grammar*. London and New York: Routledge.

7

Mexico, Central America, the Caribbean and the Andes

Peter Standish

During his first voyage, Columbus established a colony on an island he dubbed 'Hispaniola', an island that was to become the home of present-day Haiti and the Dominican Republic. Soon afterwards the Spaniards set up their first vice-royalties, the principal administrative centres of colonial power, in Mexico and Peru. So it is that the areas that concern us in this chapter were the places colonised first, and have been the ones subject to the longest Spanish influence. They have also been much affected by the proximity of the USA. In all, some fifteen countries are involved and as a result it will only be possible to characterise briefly some of the features that make the areas culturally interesting today.

UNDERLYING FACTORS

Ethnic variety and social stratification

Apart from the peoples of European (largely Spanish) descent there are still considerable indigenous communities in several areas, particularly Mayan peoples in southern Mexico, Guatemala and Honduras, and descendants of the Incas who live in Peru, Bolivia and Ecuador. In the Caribbean islands, and along the coastal fringe of the isthmus and northern South America, we find a significant African presence, the result of the importation of slaves into the Caribbean and their later migration out towards the other shores. In those same coastal areas and some other places there are people of middle-eastern origin, twentieth-century immigrants from places like Syria, Lebanon and Palestine. And a Chinese element is noticeable in one or two countries (Cuba and Peru in particular).

Map 5: South America

Power has traditionally been concentrated in the hands of people of Spanish descent, and located in the larger cities, most of which are on the coast. Society remains patriarchal. Women may have had considerable authority at home, but their wider role in society has been proscribed. Illiteracy has been widespread, especially outside privileged creole communities. Racial prejudices undoubtedly exist, but from the earliest days of conquest there was a great deal of mixing of races, far more than occurred in the USA, for example, and as a result a majority of today's Latin Americans are of mixed ancestry. The Dominican Republic is a good illustration of this sort of diversity. It is estimated that as many as half a million indigenous people may have been on the island Columbus named Hispaniola, and that was later to become two countries, the Dominican Republic and Haiti. All those people were wiped out in early colonial times by conflict or illnesses imported by the Spanish. Later, especially in the nineteenth century when sugar became an important commodity and there was a pressing need for a workforce, slaves were imported, largely from West Africa. Nowadays there are a great many mulattos (people of mixed black and white race) in the Dominican Republic; skin colour there can be a touchy topic, bearing in mind that privilege and prestige have traditionally been associated with whiteness and the idea of 'pureza de sangre' (purity of blood).

Politics

Most countries achieved independence from Spain in the early to mid-nineteenth century, but it happens that there are two in the region that concern us here, Puerto Rico and Cuba, that proved to be Spain's last possessions on the continent, and have had rather special histories since. Cuba was the last of all, lost by Spain in 1898. Not long before, Puerto Rico had come under the wing of the USA. Puerto Rico came to occupy a unique position, its relationship with the USA giving it a number of benefits but also generating a somewhat schizophrenic attitude among its people. The ambiguities of that relationship underlie much of Puerto Rico's cultural activity today. As for Cuba, it went from being a corrupt playground for the Americans of the USA to being their arch enemy, almost the cause of a third world war; and it is still a thorn in their side. Also much affected by its relationship with the USA is Mexico, which was at war with the USA in the mid-nineteenth century, when it lost a good deal of its former territory (Arizona, California, New Mexico, Texas). For years Mexico has been the source of a constant influx of immigrants into the richer neighbouring country (see Chapter 10). These three countries, Puerto Rico, Cuba and Mexico, provide the core of the thriving and growing Hispanic community in the USA itself, though every Latin American country contributes to some degree. Finally, it should be noted that there is a long, sad tradition of authoritarian regimes in Latin America, and only in the late twentieth century did democracy become a generalised phenomenon in the continent. Since questioning the *status quo* is an essential part of artistic creativity, the many dictatorial regimes tended to repress or attempt to control cultural production, and creative artists often found themselves protesting from abroad, or compromised, censored or persecuted if they stayed to work in their native countries.

Cultural dependence

For a long time creative artists and craftsmen in colonial Spanish America were trained to be skilled practitioners of forms that were essentially defined by Spain, or Europe. For example, one can find composers of music from colonial America whose works are barely distinguishable from those of their European masters. Some people argue that such a dependent mentality is still in evidence. To a number of intellectuals the revolution that freed the USA from British rule suggested a way towards a new independence for Latin America, one that would be both political and creative; but others were at best ambivalent about it, regarding the people to the north as philistines and fearing that their dominance would only replace Spain's. Nowadays, there still is much ambivalence in that the influence of the big brother to the north is undoubtedly strong, yet while US culture is enthusiastically embraced in some circles there is also a marked sensitivity to what many believe is a new form of imperialism.

Isolation

Lastly, we must consider the role isolation has played. Quite simply, those outside Latin America have on the whole been ignorant about it, or misinformed. Within the continent there has also been mutual ignorance and suspicion, of one economic class or racial group vis-à-vis another, or of one country vis-à-vis its neighbours. Communications between nations have not always been easy, due both to geographical factors and to political rivalries and economic protectionism among the emergent republics.

CULTURAL ILLUSTRATIONS

The above are some of the essential elements underlying the range of artistic activity that I shall attempt to exemplify in the following pages. As my starting point I shall take a short story, a choice that may at first seem surprising, but one that is symptomatic of the importance that Latin American writers have accorded the short story as a genre, cultivating and perfecting it to a remarkable degree. *El advenimiento del águila* (The advent of the eagle) is by Rosario Castellanos (Mexico, 1925–1974).

The name of the protagonist, Héctor Villafuerte, brings to mind the Hector of classical times, but the Héctor of the Mexican story is hardly a brave leader.

Rather, he is a perfect example of a *criollo*, a Latin American person of European lineage and consequently a member of a part of society that sees itself as superior, regardless of its economic circumstances. The story tells how, after a youth of self-indulgence and minimal achievement, our hero, who comes equipped with aquiline physical features, turns to preying on society in the hope of securing a comfortable life for himself. Having bankrupted his widowed mother, he tries to marry his way into affluence; then, when those plans go awry and he has no choice but to work, he uses his personal contacts to secure a minor civil service job. This job is a sinecure, but for Héctor it has two disadvantages: it takes him away from the capital to a remote rural location and makes it necessary for him to deal with that awful substratum of society, the indigenous people. The eagle of the title refers not only to the preying of the bird-like Héctor, but also to a government stamp (the eagle is one of Mexico's national symbols) that must grace all documents if they are to be officially recognised. But in the eyes of the Indians who come to Héctor to ask for that seal of approval the bird represents something that is part of nature and that has supernatural powers; in other words their way of looking at the world is radically different. Yet they have no choice but to work within the system imposed upon them, and because they are illiterate and ignorant of the workings of bureaucracy, it is easy for Héctor to abuse their trust and take advantage of them. He despises them, but the opportunist in him sees that they may be a means of ensuring that he has a good living.

Héctor is part of the strong and perhaps unassailable tradition of privilege associated with the location of power, that is to say the capital city and *criollo* society; his name, Villafuerte ('strong town'), seems to hint as much. Castellanos's story speaks volumes about the culture of Mexico and is also quite relevant to other parts of Latin America. From it we can extrapolate a number of key issues. In the first place, it demonstrates how the colonial heritage persists, how one culture is superimposed on another. Secondly, in its own way it is a small example of the artistic phenomenon known as *indigenismo*, which is the representation, especially in visual art or via the written word, of the condition and worldview of indigenous peoples.

Indigenism

However well-intentioned they may have been, many of the works associated with the rise of indigenism during the nineteenth and early twentieth century tend to give picturesque and sometimes patronising accounts, and in one or two cases these were produced by people who lacked any real experience or knowledge of the indigenous peoples whom they sought to represent. In later years efforts were made to portray indigenous people more authentically, and there are even some attempts by members of the indigenous communities to speak for themselves. Although indigenism is often thought of as a nineteenth- and early twentieth-century phenomenon, its roots can be traced back to early colonial Mexico, to an account by one of the earliest chroniclers, the friar Bartolomé de Las Casas, *Brevíssima relación de la destruyción de las Indias* (Most brief account of the destruction of the Indies, 1542), that detailed the plight of the Indians after conquest. Another early artistic milestone in this vein was the account of Peru's pre-colonial history written by 'el inca' Garcilaso de la Vega, *Comentarios reales* (Royal commentaries, 1609); he was a man whose mother had been an Inca princess, a man who came to be accepted and respected in cultural circles in Spain, and one who wrote from the heart about his native country. More exotic and picturesque portrayals of indigenous people can be found throughout the years of discovery and colonisation, but, as I have suggested already, indigenism came to the fore in the nineteenth century, with the onset of independence, and took on a new life in the early twentieth century, when nationalist sentiment was strong. Few things then seemed as good, to distinguish one country from another, as the specificity of its indigenous traditions. Sometimes, the term *indianismo* is used to refer to the sort of romanticised account that predominated in the nineteenth century, and the term *indigenismo* is used primarily for the later manifestations, and especially with reference to the 'Andean republics' (Ecuador, Peru and Bolivia) during the 1930s. But whatever the niceties of definition, obviously both terms are relevant to areas with strong, surviving indigenous populations.

In Mexico, it was not until 1921, the date of an important exhibition in Mexico City, that the arts and crafts of the indigenous people began to receive recognition in their own right. Prior to that time the attitude had been that native culture must be assimilated to the Hispanic, if not suppressed. To be sure, there had been Indian artists and musicians beforehand, but they had distinguished themselves largely by their ability to copy the prevailing European style, and they had expressed their own traditions by incorporating elements from them into what was basically a European context. It is often said that church architecture, images and rituals in Latin America provide clear evidence of such a fusion.

The new interest in indigenous culture in Mexico followed on it's war with the USA (1846–1847) and especially the Mexican Revolution (1910–1920). One important result was the rise of the muralist painters, the most famous amongst them being Diego Rivera, José Clemente Orozco, and David Alfaro Siqueiros, who together won recognition well beyond the confines of Latin America. There had long been a tradition of mural painting in Mexico. Now, in the wake of the Mexican Revolution, a government minister invited artists to decorate the walls of public buildings in Mexico City with images of national culture. Perhaps the most monumental example of such a mural is Rivera's vision of Mexican history, which he painted at the Palacio Nacional; another famous but later example is the mosaic by Juan O'Gorman covering the exterior of the library building of the Universidad Nacional Autónoma. The muralists portrayed national heroes and events, but increasingly they highlighted the glories of the common people, of peasants and indigenous people. Influenced by Expressionism and Cubism, the muralists nonetheless produced accessible, figurative images. As the status of the leaders of the movement grew, so did their left-wing political agenda.

As for the Andean countries, they, too, used indigenous traits as a means of affirming their national identities. It was a left-wing Peruvian intellectual, José Carlos Mariátegui, who in 1928 drew attention to the difference between exotic portrayals and authentic representation, and advocated more of the latter. An example of indianist writing from Peru is the novel *Aves sin nido* (Birds without a nest, 1889) by Clorinda Matto de Turner. She came from a landowning family and was raised in the Andes, near Cuzco, the ancient Inca capital, but that did not stop her idealising both the people and the land. A later, indigenist writer, José María Arguedas, also Peruvian, made great strides in conveying the Indian worldview in *Los ríos profundos* (Deep rivers, 1958), even to the extent of structuring his Spanish along the lines of Quechua syntax. Arguedas, who became an anthropologist by profession, had also been born and raised in an Andean region, speaking Spanish at home but spending a great deal of time amongst Quechua speakers in the fields as well, so he was in an unusually good position to understand and represent the Indian viewpoint. *Los ríos profundos* is largely autobiographical, about a boy growing up and undergoing a painful transition from a childhood spent communally amongst indigenous people to life on a ranch where they were treated almost like slaves. Nostalgia for the lost life gives way to indignation in the face of injustice, and the novel ends on a rebellious note. While this is clearly a novel with a message to convey, it is interesting for the ways in which it is structured and narrated; it is not wholly successful but quite innovative.

In artwork Andean indigenism came into its own in the 1920s and 1930s. The artists were inclined to reject the avant-garde techniques of that time since these were felt to be foreign to Latin America; instead the style tended to be conservative and descriptive, sometimes driven by a Marxist agenda. José Sabogal promoted the movement in Peru from his important position as director of the Escuela Nacional de Bellas Artes. The principal indigenist painters of Ecuador were Camilo Egas (1899–1963), Oswaldo Guayasamín (1919–2001) and Eduardo Kingman (1913–). Inspired by the writings of Mariátegui and much influenced by the Mexican muralists, Kingman left Quito to live for a while among the indigenous people. A painting that is illustrative of his work is called *Los guandos* (Freight loads), which portrays the suffering of indigenous people who are forced to carry heavy loads between the coast and the mountains, supervised by an overseer on horseback who is armed with a whip.

That powerful image links conveniently back to the story by Rosario Castellanos, in which, near the end of the tale, Héctor has the indigenous people carry him back towards the capital, in search of a new eagle, a new symbol of his authority over them. Clearly, Castellanos is making a very precise cultural allusion here, deliberately echoing the experience of Hernán Cortés, the sixteenth-century conqueror of Mexico, who is known to have had some of his indigenous allies carry him along to Tenochtitlan, the Aztec capital over which Mexico City was later built.

African heritage

How might a country that lacked a strong indigenous culture assert its national identity? In the other lands that concern us in this chapter either there had never been strong indigenous communities, or they had long since disappeared as a result of violence or disease. So it is that the Caribbean nations, into which large numbers of slaves were imported to work on the plantations, have tended to look to their African heritage as a means of signalling their national and cultural difference. African images, cultural traditions, rhythms and instruments characterise the artistic activities of those countries. Nicolás Guillén (Cuba) and Luis Palés Matos (Puerto Rico) were poets who exploited the African tradition for themes, sounds and rhythms in their poetry. Both were influenced by *Négritude*, a movement with Caribbean and African roots (though its main proponents were based in Paris) that reacted against the traditional dominance by whites and emphasised African cultural contributions.

The Cuban painter Wifredo Lam fused African elements with surrealist techniques in his paintings. Part African, part European and part Chinese (and in Cuba that mixture is not uncommon), Lam grew up in contact with all three traditions, and was familiar with *santería*, a religious practice that draws on Yoruba and Catholic elements. After studying art in Havana he moved first to Madrid then to Paris, where he came under the influence of Picasso; not surprisingly, Picasso introduced him to avant-garde styles in art, but ironically he also introduced Lam to African art. It was not necessary to have African blood to realise the importance of the African contribution to Caribbean cultural identities.

Turning now to music, another Cuban, Alejandro García Caturla, was a *criollo* who, like Lam, also spent time in Paris. He came into contact with adventurous composers such as Milhaud and Stravinsky, and managed to achieve a synthesis of African and European traditions in works with evocative titles such as *Bembe* and *Yamba-O*. In popular music Cuban *son* is a type that draws heavily on Africa, for example in its use of the call-and-response format and of various drums. *Merengue*, a hybrid song and dance form most closely associated with the Dominican Republic, has an interesting and revealing history. Like many popular art forms it was regarded for a long time as a lascivious and undignified practice of the poor and 'unsophisticated', yet after the Dominican Republic's war with Haiti in the middle of the nineteenth century *merengue* was adopted by the country's ruling class and transformed into a national symbol. Both *son* and *merengue* were subsequently taken under the wing of *salsa*, which is a product of Hispanic musicians living in New York. A significant contribution to understanding the diversity of cultural influences came from the work of a Cuban intellectual named Fernando Ortiz, who in 1940 published a book in which he famously used the term *transculturación* (transculturation) to describe the process by which African and other cultures had influenced those of Latin America.

Landscape and Nature

Another option for creating a sense of a distinctively national culture was to highlight the flora and fauna of one's homeland, to emphasise the ways in which nature was special. In Venezuela, for example, the jungle areas deep along the Orinoco, or the flatlands known as the 'llanos', became symbolic in this way. Venezuela gave us one of the most famous Latin American 'novelas de tesis' (novels with a message), *Doña Bárbara*, written by the country's sometime president, Rómulo Gallegos. It is a novel about the experience of an enlightened, civilised man from the coast who ventures into the interior, where he finds a wild world dominated by a barbarous woman. In addition to highlighting the role of the environment in determining human life, this novel exemplifies the stock Latin American theme of *civilización y barbarie* (civilisation and barbarism); that is, the urbane, Europeanised, predominantly white culture of the city confronts an unbridled, natural lawlessness in the backlands. Like Héctor, Santos Luzardo, the hero of Gallegos', novel, has a heavily suggestive name: ostensibly he is the bringer of light (*luz*) and holiness (*santo*), while Bárbara, of course, is a barbarian. A moment's thought will show that the Castellanos story also has some relevance to the theme of civilisation and barbarism.

Exploration of historical and cultural roots

Delving into one's cultural origins is widespread among Latin American creative artists. An interesting exploration of natural forces in relation to cultural roots (though not, this time, in a nationalistic vein) was undertaken by the most famous of all Cuban novelists, Alejo Carpentier. Carpentier was also a musicologist (author of *La música en Cuba*, 1956), and this is quite apparent in his work. Some of his literary works are structured around musical motifs and forms, and are peppered with musical terminology. In his best-known novel, *Los pasos perdidos* (The lost steps), Carpentier sends a musicologist into the jungle of the Orinoco in search of ancient musical instruments. This man becomes enchanted with the ways of a primitive group of natives whom he views as original and authentic, but on a subsequent visit he discovers that nature has taken over and that he cannot regain access to that world; his only option is return to the modern one. Carpentier indulges in baroque, symbol-laden prose that can seem as dense as the jungle he is portraying, but the civilised, technological world is skilfully set in contrast to the timeless exuberance of nature.

POLITICAL INFLUENCE ON ARTISTIC ACTIVITY

The influence of politics on art has been significant. As we saw earlier, national interest, especially in the case of Mexico, accounts for a large part of the promotion and recognition of indigenous cultures. Partly that search for national identity was (and still is, to a degree) a reaction against European domination and exploitation. But in the twentieth century it was not Europe that was at issue so much as the USA; the Latin-America-is-our-back-yard mentality that encouraged the USA to interfere so frequently in the affairs of countries to the south, and economic exploitation of those countries by the USA, which takes several forms, have generated countless artistic expressions of protest. Nicolás Guillén, the mulatto Cuban poet already mentioned, has a book of poems significantly entitled *West Indies Ltd*, in which one of his complaints is about the tourist who 'viene a comerse el cielo azul, / regándolo con Bacardí' (comes and gobbles up the blue sky, washing it down with Bacardi). Another illustrative short story will serve us here: Augusto Monterroso's *Mr Taylor*. Mr Taylor, lost in the jungle one day, bumps into a native who offers to sell him a shrunken head. Within a few ironically written pages, the American has set up a thriving business, a sort of perversion of the 'brain drain', which involves exporting the heads to New York, where they become fashionable items. In return, the producing country is tempted with the promise of the revelation of the secret formula for a drink that sounds suspiciously like Coca-Cola, while its leaders are regaled with new bicycles. Meanwhile the demand for heads gets out of hand, and in order to satisfy it the government introduces measures designed to encourage an increase in the national death rate. This story was written at a time when Monterroso, a Guatemalan, was in exile in Chile, because the democratically elected government of his country had recently been overthrown by a CIA-backed coup.

There were quite enough political and social problems at home, without further help from foreigners. The revolutions in Mexico and Nicaragua, the activities of guerrilla movements in Peru, the period in Colombia known as 'La violencia', and the drug trade of more recent years – these are all examples of political situations that in some way encouraged cultural activity. The Mexican Revolution inspired a cluster of novels, not all of great quality. Late among them came *Pedro Páramo*, by Juan Rulfo, who sets his work against the background of a political rebellion (the Cristero Rebellion) that has merely trapped the poor; they find themselves abused by ruthless landowners and bandits, and abandoned by the church. The Mexican Revolution itself did little to better the lot of the poor, and until 2000 the country found itself in the stranglehold of a single political party called, contradictorily, the *Partido*

Revolucionario Institucional (the Institutional Revolutionary Party). Rulfo wrote his novel in the 1950s, looking back to the last years of the revolution. Its spare, dry prose captures the harshness of rural existence, and the Mexican obsession with death, but Rulfo's work is most important because it is boldly experimental; for that reason it is generally regarded as a precursor of the 'Boom' in Latin American fiction (see below).

The Cuban Revolution and its opponents account for a great deal of cultural activity too, some no better than propaganda. The many right-wing dictators spawned by Latin America have inspired a whole subgenre of novels of protest. Although this subgenre dates back to the nineteenth century, it underwent a revival in the 1970s with works by novelists such as Alejo Carpentier and Gabriel García Márquez (Colombia). One of the most famous of the dictatorship novels, which will serve as an example, was by another Nobel Prize winner, the Guatemalan Miguel Angel Asturias. Asturias bases his most famous work, *El señor presidente* (Mr President), on the rule of the dictator Manuel Estrada Cabrera, who took power in Guatemala after the assassination of the previous president. His rule, which coincided with the heyday of exploitation of Latin America by the United Fruit Company, saw a marked deterioration in the lot of the indigenous people. Asturias portrays Estrada as a devilish, mythical figure who inspires fear and sows corruption; his narrative techniques draw both on native myths and on surrealism.

And here we come to a significant fact: somewhat as in the case of Wilfredo Lam, Asturias learnt his surrealism in Paris, and even did his research into the myths of his native country while in that city. Asturias was, in short, an example of yet another particularly distinctive Latin American phenomenon, the creative artist who lives abroad. Even when artists have not been exiled by political circumstances, they very frequently have chosen to engage in a personal *viaje iniciático* (journey of initiation), an extended period abroad, usually in Europe, and usually in Paris. The idea of Paris as the place where one would come of age as an artist was always partly mythical, but there is no doubt that exile, whether voluntary or enforced, has been the driving force behind much artistic activity. Being abroad provides a new perspective on one's home country, and it also stimulates the creative artist by bringing him or her into contact with new ideas and techniques. Most of the great writers who brought Latin American literature to world prominence in the 1960s wrote while living abroad. But exile has also become a matter of controversy, leading some Latin Americans to argue that a person who is abroad can become out of touch with reality at home, and even to accuse such people of being traitors, culturally subservient or at least escapists.

Latin American artists as leaders

What exactly is the role of the Latin American creative artist to be? Broadly speaking there are two prevailing views regarding the purposes of artistic activity: some believe that it should be a vehicle for social change; others see it as a personal vocation, and its ends as aesthetic. In this connection it is interesting to note that the first truly Latin American artistic movement (that is, the first movement that was not simply imitative of something elsewhere, though it was certainly influenced by French poetry) was an aesthetic movement. Spearheaded by Rubén Darío (1876–1916), a Nicaraguan, *modernismo* was primarily a poetic movement of the early twentieth century (the *belle époque*) that pursued elegant and beautiful forms, and dealt with exotic themes that had very little to do with Latin American reality. Yet as time went by even Darío felt the need to come closer to real life and to speak of politics: in *Oda a Roosevelt* (Ode to Theodore Roosevelt) he described the USA as the new invader of an innocent America, one that had indigenous blood and spoke Spanish. The airy-fairyness of early Latin American *modernismo* could not last, and the time came when poets had had enough of the elitist aestheticism and were calling for the swan's neck to be wrung (the swan being one of the prime symbols of the movement). As we have seen, *modernismo* was above all an aesthetic movement; by contrast, and somewhat paradoxically, Mexican muralism, the first movement in art to be noticed internationally, was driven by national and political interests, not aesthetic ones.

Not that the decline of *modernismo* was to herald the death of poetry. On the contrary, in Latin America poetry has always flourished and been highly valued. Poetry has also been written by several politicians. Poetry was in fact the pre-eminent genre in the nineteenth and early twentieth century. Essay writing also has a strong tradition, with practitioners such as Mariátegui, José Vasconcelos (Mexico) and José Martí (Cuba). Although both genres have persisted (two outstanding writers are the Peruvian poet César Vallejo and the Mexican poet, essayist, and Nobel Prize winner, Octavio Paz) they have been somewhat eclipsed by prose fiction. As for theatre, that has been something of a Cinderella, Mexico City being one of few places able to support a theatre establishment. Among the other countries, only Cuba can boast more than the odd, isolated dramatist. Two Mexican dramatists who dealt with specifically Latin American issues are Rodolfo Usigli (1905–1979), whose theatre is somewhat subversive and focuses on socio-political themes, and Salvador Novo (1904–1974) who often deals with the pre-Hispanic world. Cuba has produced several notable dramatists, such as Virgilio Piñera (1912–1979) and José Triana (1932–); post-revolutionary Cuban drama tends to be either absurd or propagandistic, and sometimes both! The outstanding dramatist of Puerto Rico is René Marqués, a writer of social protest most often concerned with the fraught relationship between his country and the USA.

The 'Boom' and 'Post-boom'

Above, I referred to the refined aestheticism that characterised *modernismo*. Another sort of aestheticism is found in a group of novels that came to prominence in the 1960s. Although these books treated Latin American issues they were ambitious in scope, all-embracing in their implications, and technically adventurous. There was soon talk of a 'Boom' in Latin American literature. Prior to that time, literature by Latin Americans had been largely unknown outside the continent, and even within Latin America the readers and writers of one country had tended to be unaware of those in another. Happy coincidence, astute marketing, and the undoubted quality of many works of the 1960s led to Latin American writing becoming more widely distributed over the continent and translated for foreign readers. All of a sudden Latin America was no longer a backwater: people the world over became aware of its artistic products and were influenced by them. The books most commonly associated with the onset of the Boom are all novels: Carlos Fuentes's *La muerte de Artemio Cruz* (The death of Artemio Cruz, Mexico, 1962), Julio Cortázar's *Rayuela* (Hopscotch, Argentina, 1963), Mario Vargas Llosa's *La ciudad y los perros* (published in English as *The time of the hero*, Peru, 1963) and Gabriel García Márquez's *Cien años de soledad* (One hundred years of solitude, Colombia, 1967). One common feature of these novels, particularly the first three, was their complex, difficult and technical sophistication. Gone were the days when a writer told a simple story, with a clear message, in a straightforward linear manner. Not only were these novelists effecting a conscious break with the indigenist and regionalist writing of earlier times, they were admirers of novelists such as Faulkner, Proust and Woolf. They no longer attempted only to create an illusion of reality, and to encourage their readers credulously to enter into this illusion, forgetting their own; instead, in a very self-conscious and sometimes playful way they called attention to their own trickery and often expected their readers to work hard at deciphering meaning.

To get some flavour of the works of this time, I shall look briefly at Vargas Llosa's first novel, *La ciudad y los perros* (literally, 'The city and the dogs'). Inspired in part by the work of his compatriot, Arguedas, and drawing on his own education, Vargas Llosa invents a *Bildungsroman* (a novel of coming of age) about a group of cadets, representing a cross-section of Peruvian social types, who attend a secondary school run by the army. The school has a brutalising effect on everyone. The cadets form alliances and rivalries in their dog-eat-dog society, although beneath their façade of macho behaviour one can sometimes discover a surprising vulnerability; for example, the most ruthless of them turns out to be sensitive and insecure, a fact that is cleverly masked throughout the novel by narrative strategy. In fact this social novel, which is disturbing, distasteful, violent and yet touching by turns, is most distinguished by its great technical polish. The mindset of each of the main cadet characters, it turns out, can be related to different narrative styles; furthermore, the author influences the reader's perspective by intermingling conversations from different places and times. The results are somewhat challenging, but immensely rewarding.

The Boom novelists, having learnt from the work of the great Argentine writer, Jorge Luis Borges, had a refreshing habit of avoiding the self-indulgent rhetoric, the dead weight of words that marred the works of many earlier Latin American writers. Yet, fine as many of the works of the Boom period are, one or two reached a degree of conceptual and organisational complexity that is sufficient to try even the most devoted reader. At all events, most of their works were (and are) out of reach for a portion of the literate Latin American populace, and for that reason the writers were criticised as elitist. In time, there were increasing demands for art that was within reach of the masses, and above all for art that would change the realities of everyday living in poor and oppressed conditions. The writers mentioned responded to such demands in various ways, but in any case, by the late 1960s and 1970s there were other writers who were moving in a different direction, writing less demanding books. Thus we arrive at what came to be known as the 'Post-boom', a period in which narrative fiction grew more linear, more transparent, thematically less ambitious, structurally less complex. Also evident in the Post-boom is the incorporation into literature of elements drawn from other forms of culture, such as film and popular music. A good example is a novel by a Puerto Rican, Luis Rafael Sánchez, entitled *La guaracha del macho Camacho* (Macho Camacho's beat, 1976). This book's playful title is symptomatic of its humorous and irreverent style; it is a celebration of Puerto Rican popular culture, and another exploration of this particular national identity, so overshadowed by the relationship with the superpower to the north. ('Guaracha' is a song and dance form of mixed Hispanic and African roots, originating in Cuba.)

The Cuban Revolution

One vital force in the development of modern Latin America has been the Cuban Revolution, which brought Fidel Castro to power in 1959. The overthrow of the corrupt dictator Batista, the empowerment of the Cuban people, the snub to the USA, and the inspiration to be had in the ideas of Che Guevara, the 'brains' behind the revolution, captured the imagination of a great number of Latin Americans, including intellectuals and artists, many of whom enthusiastically backed Cuba. For a while after the revolutionary forces came to power there was considerable cultural freedom on the island, and at that time significant initiatives were taken to promote artistic activity: the establishment of the publishing house called Casa de las Américas and the founding of the Cuban Film Institute (ICAIC), a major producer of quality feature films. Shortly after the triumph of the revolution many major Latin American writers went to Cuba, and many were published there. Poster art flourished. Popular music took on a new life. A new generation of dramatists came to light. A new subgenre of 'testimonial literature' (of which more below) was recognised when the Casa de las Américas established a prize for it.

However, with time the revolution grew more stiff-jointed, insisting increasingly that artistic activity should reflect or promote its own socio-political aims. Increased repression meant that many foreigners who had actively supported Cuba now broke with it. In the 1970s, controls on artistic activities became more strict, and many artists left the island. One example is Guillermo Cabrera Infante, a writer who had once actually represented the revolutionary regime as a diplomat, and who now became its bitter enemy, leaving to live in London. All this, however, does not change the fact that, next to Mexico, Cuba is the most important powerhouse of cultural productivity in the region that concerns us in this chapter.

Testimonio

Testimonial writing was given formal recognition in 1971. The rules established by the Casa de las Américas for the prize have an ideological and a regional basis, requiring that entries document some aspect of Latin American or Caribbean reality, draw directly upon it, and also demonstrate literary merit. In fact, writing of such a kind already existed in abundance. Generally, the adjective 'testimonial' is now applied by critics to writing that deals with marginalised, 'voiceless' groups, such as ethnic minorities, women and the illiterate. There is usually a first-person narrator, or informant, who gives an account of personal or collective experience, and that account is then committed to paper by a mediating writer. The Cuban Miguel Barnet's *Biografía de un cimarrón* (The autobiography of a runaway slave, 1966), for example, is a transcription of interviews with a former slave. The most famous piece of testimonial writing is *Me llamo Rigoberta Menchú* (I, Rigoberta Menchú, 1983) by, of course, Rigoberta Menchú, a Guatemalan; Menchú, a Mayan woman, had her account of life in her community written for her by another woman, a Venzuelan/French journalist, and the account documents the ways of the Quiché Mayans, telling of the political oppression and violence to which they were subject. Rigoberta Menchú won the Nobel Peace Prize in 1992. Testimonial accounts such as hers do, however, raise interesting questions about the role of the mediator, the veracity of her account, and the documentary status of the endeavour (see Chapter 10).

Women writers

I began this chapter by considering a story by a Mexican writer, Rosario Castellanos, in which she creates a self-centred man who uses women. Writing in a society dominated by men, Castellanos was an early feminist, and for her day she was somewhat exceptional (although she was not without precedent: one of the greatest of colonial writers was a seventeenth-century Mexican nun, Sor Juana Inés de la Cruz, who was not averse to criticising men in her poetry). The increased recognition afforded to Castellanos in recent decades is a result of a deliberate agenda on the part of critics and teachers, particularly in the USA, to bring more women writers to readers' attention. By now, the days have long passed when women could be said to be lacking recognition or in need of special treatment. If anything, the tables have turned, and among Latin American writers of the Post-boom, women constitute probably the most forceful and notable contingent; Angeles Mastretta and Elena Poniatowska (Mexico), Nancy Morejón and Lydia Cabrera (Cuba), Rosario Ferré and Ana Lydia Vega (Puerto Rico), Claribel Alegría (El Salvador), and Carmen Naranjo (Costa Rica) are just some of the women gaining international status today.

NATIONAL, CONTINENTAL OR INTERNATIONAL CULTURE?

As our world becomes increasingly well communicated, so literature moves more in step with the performing and the visual arts, becoming more international. In general, it is increasingly difficult to talk meaningfully of cultural products in national terms. Music knows no frontiers. Turning to art, consider the example of Fernando Botero, a painter and sculptor of engaging, bulbous, parodic images, who may be Colombian by birth but who works in Italy and whose art is universal. Somewhat similarly, Vargas Llosa, in whose works Peru is almost always a presence and who was even a candidate for the presidency of Peru, lives much of the time in London and has taken Spanish nationality; García Márquez writes in Spanish of a world that is obviously Latin American, usually evocative of coastal Colombia, but he has lived for many years in Mexico and Spain. Both men write in the knowledge that their books will be read across the Hispanic world and immediately translated into many languages.

A final consideration is the fact that the migration of significant numbers of Hispanics to the USA (now the country with the largest Hispanic population in the world after Mexico, Spain, Argentina and Colombia) has generated an extraordinarily vibrant cultural activity there, sometimes protest activity against Cuba, but more often related to the Hispanic-Americans' quest for acceptance. Can the Hispanic be part of the wider community in the USA, a country notorious for its homogenising tendencies, without having to jettison the Hispanic tradition? Yet even at home in the Latin American countries, where the influence of the USA is also strong, comparable questions apply. How are Latin Americans to define themselves without on the one hand seeming to be culturally subservient or on the other withdrawing into isolation? What does being a Latin American creative artist entail? Does it mean stressing Latin American issues, rather than universal ones, or staying in the home country in order to remain in touch with its realities, or writing in a particular variety of Spanish or Portuguese, or drawing consciously on the Iberian cultural heritage? Because surely it is that common heritage that most strongly binds these nations together, however concerned they may be to assert their separate identities.

FURTHER READING

Ades, D. 1989. *Art in Latin America: the modern era, 1820–1980*. New Haven and London: Yale University Press.

Balderston, D., González, M. and López, A. 2000. *Encyclopaedia of contemporary Latin American and Caribbean cultures*. London: Routledge.

Béhague, G. 1979. *Music in Latin America: an introduction*. Englewood Cliffs, NJ: Prentice-Hall.

Collier, S. et al. 1985. *The Cambridge encyclopaedia of Latin America and the Caribbean*. Cambridge: Cambridge University Press.

Foster, D. W. 1992. *Handbook of Latin American literature*. New York and London: Garland.

Smith, V. 1997. *Encyclopaedia of Latin American literature*. Chicago and London: Fitzroy Dearborn.

Standish, P. 1995. *The Hispanic culture of South America*. Detroit and London: Gale Research.

Standish, P. 1996. *The Hispanic culture of Mexico, Central America and the Caribbean*. Detroit and London: Gale Research.

8

The Southern Cone

Philip Swanson

The Southern Cone of Spanish America comprises Argentina and Chile, as well as the smaller countries of Uruguay and Paraguay. The term 'Southern Cone' is a technical and geographical one. However, in recent years the term has taken on a conceptual quality as academics have sought to identify a sense of shared consciousness typical of the region. There are probably two reasons for this growth of a conceptual notion of the Southern Cone. One is the common experience of military dictatorship, torture and 'disappearance', particularly in the 1970s and 1980s in Argentina and Chile; the other is the rise of Cultural Studies in universities, which has refocused attention away from a cosmopolitan and 'universal' literary culture towards a more localised yet more embracing idea of culture as experienced in specific contexts. However, it would be a mistake to over-emphasise either the cohesiveness of the region's culture or its distinctiveness from other parts of Latin America. The isolationist history of landlocked Paraguay with its *mestizo* (mixed-race) population of overwhelmingly indigenous descent, for example, makes it a very different proposition from Argentina, with its long trading history, its port capital Buenos Aires and route to the Atlantic, and its lengthy tradition of European immigration and technological investment. On the other hand, the political, intellectual and cultural battles of Argentina after winning independence from Spain in the nineteenth century did more than merely influence the thinking and development of Latin America as a whole. They came to shape and underpin its entire discourse up to the present day. In a sense it is the relationship between Buenos Aires and the Argentine interior that provides the key to understanding Latin American culture as a whole. Thus it is the Argentine experience with which we must begin and which must remain pivotal to any reading of the Southern Cone and its relation to the rest of the Latin American continent.

ARGENTINA

Argentina is different from, say, Peru or Mexico, because of the relative absence of a significant indigenous population or tradition (Paraguay is the major exception to this rule in the Southern Cone). The elimination of the indigenous question and the effective eradication of most of the indigenous population give a clue to the significance of Argentina in the development of a notion of Latin American identity. For it was essentially here that, after independence, the main debates began about what the relatively newly emergent Latin American nation states should be. There was an anxiety in the period that these new nations were only precarious constructs, with pockets of civilisation in the (often coastal or near-coastal) cities threatened by the barbaric primitiveness of the vast, untamed interior. The thought began to grow amongst intellectuals of the time that Latin America must break with its primitive (and, by implication, indigenous) past and develop an advanced or modern ethos based on the example of great nations such as Great Britain, France and the USA. This apparently simple position was, in fact, rather complex and contradictory. For a start, independence from Spain marked an obvious break, yet the new elites remained obsessed with purity of blood and the model of European civilisation. In a sense, 'independence' was an idea as much as anything else, a means not so much of freeing the people as of legitimising the aspirations of the ruling *criollo* elites (that is, of Spanish descent but born in the Americas) to run and control the wealth of their own territories. Hence, there was a tension between the implicit liberalism of independence philosophy and the need to control huge and fragmented societies, between the urge to create free and prosperous nations and the deep fear of lawlessness and social collapse.

'Civilisation and barbarism'

The work which encapsulated this dilemma and cast its shadow or influence over not only the whole of the Southern Cone but the whole future development of Latin American thought was Domingo Faustino Sarmiento's *Facundo* (as it has come to be popularly known) published in 1845. Its subtitle is commonly known as *Civilización y barbarie* (see Chapter 7). Though dealing specifically with the wars of the 1820s to the 1870s between Unitarians and Federalists, in a crude reading the book more generally opposes the unifying forces of city-based and European-influenced civilisation with the dangerously destructive native barbarism of the Latin American countryside. Sarmiento is, in fact, much more subtle or at least ambiguous, but 'civilisation-versus-barbarism' was nonetheless taken up as the central dichotomy in Latin America's quest for identity and a fair social order, a dichotomy that has been endlessly asserted, challenged, denied and reversed throughout the subcontinent's subsequent history. In terms of cultural production it spawned in Argentina a whole series of texts on national identity focusing in particular on the figure of the gaucho. It provided more widely the intellectual basis for the great novels of the land in the early twentieth century such as the Venezuelan Rómulo Gallegos's 1929 classic *Doña Bárbara* (see Chapter 7) and even of the Mexican Revolution such as Mariano Azuela's *Los de abajo* (The underdogs) (1916), and it continued to inspire the key themes of later twentieth-century works by writers such as Colombia's Gabriel García Márquez or Peru's Mario Vargas Llosa.

In the specific context of the Southern Cone, a major focus of Sarmiento's criticism was the dictator Juan Manuel de Rosas, a provincial rabble-rousing *caudillo* or boss-figure who came to power on the back of a vicious anti-liberalism and a populist personality-cult campaign aimed at the dispossessed masses (though conspicuously failing to bring them real practical benefit). Students wishing to get a flavour of this criticism would do well to look at the story *El matadero* (The Slaughterhouse, 1838) by Sarmiento's harsher but perhaps more readable contemporary Esteban Echeverría, in which the nation under Rosas is allegorically depicted as a gruesome slaughterhouse populated by degraded butchers and enemies of civilised values. Despite the ideological limitations of Sarmiento and Echeverría, there was a prophetic quality to their warnings given the emergence in the twentieth century of the cult of Peronism, a bloody dictatorship against the background of a fanatically-enjoyed football World Cup victory on home turf and the misguided patriotic populism of the Falklands or Malvinas War.

Gauchos and 'gauchesque' literature

More problematically in the shorter term, the attack on Rosas was linked with a perceived attack on his natural supporters, the gauchos. They were the descendants of the indigenous people via their unions with early settlers, but as the indigenous peoples were gradually wiped out or marginalised, the gaucho became a central cultural icon, representing paradoxically both the barbaric outlaw of the interior and the soul of the nation. The early gauchos led a nomadic existence, riding freely across the vast Argentine pampa or grasslands. However, their numbers began to decline in the nineteenth century as they became embroiled in frontier disputes, independence and civil wars, the latter emphasising their barbaric nature in the eyes of intellectuals who sympathised with Sarmiento and the liberal rulers who followed Rosas from the 1860s onwards. For many in the elite, the gauchos were emblematic of the barrier to progress, and their status and traditions were undermined further during the massive process of economic modernisation in the later nineteenth century. The pampa was transformed by the construction of railway networks, refrigeration plants and large ranches or *estancias* which absorbed the once free-roaming gauchos as farm labourers. Moreover, the money, expertise and labour for the new economy were provided increasingly by massive European immigration, which swelled the population enormously. The traditional culture of the pampa was dying on its feet.

It is against this background that the phenomenon of the 'gauchesque' grew. As the gauchos began to disappear, writers began to produce literature, particularly poetry, which sought to capture and preserve the culture of these formerly nomadic cowboys. These writers were educated and often urban-born, but were essentially seeking to recreate the style of the *payadores*, the old folksingers who preserved their gaucho stories in song form. The most famous example of this recuperative writing and the classic of Argentine literature is José Hernández's *Martín Fierro*, published in two volumes in 1872 and 1879 respectively. This book, through the story of its eponymous gaucho hero, attempts to rescue the gaucho from the image of lawless barbarian and reverse the civilisation-versus-barbarism ethic by presenting the gaucho as the innocent victim of cruel or unsympathetic central authorities. Indeed, in romanticising the gaucho as the essence of all things Argentine, the book basically portrays Sarmiento's idea of 'civilisation' as the force that destroys authentic national identity. This was the beginning of an intellectual backlash against the idea of *civilización y barbarie*. The truth is, though, that both Sarmiento and Hernández were a good deal more ambivalent than they are often given credit for. The former betrays awe and admiration for the gauchos' rugged authenticity, while the latter ends up counselling them to give up and reach an accommodation with the forces of change.

Don Segundo Sombra

This ambiguous cultural fascination with the gaucho reaches a climax early in the twentieth-century with Argentina's first great novel, *Don Segundo Sombra* (Don Second Shadow), written in 1926 by Ricardo Güiraldes. Here the gaucho is elevated to the status of representative of the true Argentine nation. The novel is essentially a portrayal of the life and customs of the gaucho, and the reader is treated to scenes of herding, horse-breaking, lassooing and so forth, mixed in with colourful accounts of their guitar-playing, dancing, jokes and story-telling, as well as some elucidation of their basic values: courage, stoicism, caution, loyalty, and indifference to misfortune. The title character, Don Segundo Sombra, is the gaucho par excellence, a sort of super-gaucho representing the very best of cowboy qualities. However, his idealisation suggests there is something unreal about him and he is famously described as 'más una idea que un ser' (more an idea than a human being). The point is that by the time the novel was written, the gauchos had more or less vanished as a social group and the novel is neither an accurate portrayal of the gauchos of old, nor of rural Argentina of the 1920s, but rather a mixture of both. Güiraldes's book is nostalgically preserving the past as a lesson for the present and the future. Towards the end of the novel Don Segundo's young apprentice, Fabio, inherits a large *estancia* (ranch) and the older man rides off into the sunset. The future is safe, it seems, because the new generation of leaders will build the nation on authentically Argentine values and traditions.

The gaucho thus seems to have been totally rehabilitated. But, once again, things are not so straightforward. Don Segundo embodies the gaucho cults of the knife-fighter and of honour. Following his, for Fabio, astonishing intervention, a peaceful young man is provoked by a grudge-bearing stranger into a fight. The outcome is the gory death of the stranger and the ruining of the youngster's life. The implication surely is that the gaucho code of machismo is in fact a rather dangerous basis for a national identity. By the end of the novel, Fabio is no longer a gaucho in any real sense, but is on his way to becoming an educated and sophisticated landowner with his very own *estancia*, presumably full of ex-gaucho employees. This could be taken constructively as a modification of Sarmiento's alleged notion of 'civilisation'. Progress and modernisation along European lines are absolutely essential, but the process must be modified or balanced by an awareness of the traditional national values associated with the past. But perhaps what Güiraldes's novel really reveals is a desperate anxiety about social change (as immigration and modernisation threaten to break down the accustomed privileged position of the *estanciero*) and a subsequent clinging to the values of the past. The cultural effect of this may actually be quite damaging as it risks casting the shadow of violence and machismo over the project of progress. Later events in Argentine history may lead some to feel that this danger was not avoided.

The past in the present

Don Segundo Sombra is by and large a piece of conventional realism. The dominant prose literary form of the early twentieth century in Latin America was a form of realism known as Regionalism (or autochthonous fiction, or the *novela de la tierra*, novel of the land), which sought to document realistically regional conditions in order to explore issues of regional, national or continental identity. *Don Segundo Sombra* is the Southern Cone's great example of the genre. The general view is that the more modern, adventurous or experimental fiction, the so-called *nueva narrativa* (new narrative) which, later in the twentieth century, gave Latin America an international literary reputation, was a reaction against the simplistic black-and-white realism of the earlier period. However, if we look briefly at one of the most famous stories of a key figure in the development of the new narrative, Argentina's greatest writer Jorge Luis Borges, we will see that despite the dramatic changes in style and tone, the same dilemma regarding the gaucho, the past and Argentine identity remains.

'El Sur' was a short story written in the early 1950s and appears in the collection *Ficciones* (1944, 1956). The story concerns a librarian, Juan Dahlmann, who lives in Buenos Aires. Following an accident, he travels south to the interior to convalesce in an old estancia, which evokes memories of his ancestors' historic *criollo* past and the gaucho legend. On arriving in the south, he is hassled by a bunch of unruly youths in a bar. An old gaucho, who seems to exist *fuera del tiempo* (outside of time), reminds him of the traditional male honour code of defending one's name and reputation. When one of the young toughs challenges Dahlmann directly, the gaucho tosses the city man a knife. The story ends with Dahlmann stepping out onto the grasslands apparently to die in a knife-fight. The most commented upon feature of this story is a technical one in keeping with the new narrative's penchant for novelty, experimentation and play. A close reading of the story suggests that it is possible that Dahlmann never went south at all, but died on an operating table. The heroic death scene is a compensatory fantasy in which the dying man feverishly fashions a death that is more exciting than his humdrum life in the modern city. This clever double narrative is a sign of the text's sophistication and modernity, but its values are deeply ingrained in the past. Dahlmann obsessively cultivates a fascination with the nation's past, with his collection of memorabilia and love of the romance of *Martín Fierro*. Indeed his journey south is presented explicitly as a journey back in time. Dahlmann's lifestyle and the double narrative suggest, however, that the past survives into the present. Hence the 'timeless' gaucho. When he throws Dahlmann the knife, the city man feels that the entire tradition represented by the south is forcing him to fight. The 'barbarism' of the interior and the past still infects the 'civilisation' of the city and the present. Yet the bookish librarian naively romanticises the past.

The implication may be that the myth of a pure and heroic national tradition cultivated by the likes of Güiraldes has had a dangerously destructive effect on Argentine identity (which would manifest itself in the future in the fanaticism of Peronism and the Malvinas débâcle).

Urban culture and the tango

The interplay of city and countryside is obviously important in the above story. In a sense, the gaucho mythology was exported to the cities. Buenos Aires grew enormously as its population was swelled by immigration from Europe and migration from the countryside. A new urban culture developed and the macho tradition of the gaucho was translated into the image of a new figure, the *compadrito*. *Compadrito* was originally a term for peasants recently arrived in the city, but soon came to refer to the knife-packing wise guys who populated the *conventillos* or tenements of the *orillas*, the dodgy suburbs on the edge of town. (Borges's story 'Hombre de la esquina rosada' (Streetcorner man) is a good introduction to the type.) Whereas the music of the gaucho was the song of the *payadores*, the music associated with the *compadrito* was the tango.

The romantic view of the tango is that it captures the mood of the night-time Buenos Aires streets where recently arrived gaucho-types met European immigrants in the bars and brothels of the expanding port area, the music expressing both the melancholy nostalgia of lonely men and the thrill of dominant masculine sexuality. An approximate equivalent would be the early days of the New Orleans jazz or Chicago blues scene. The music of the tango is a mixture of the rural Argentine *payada* or *milonga* and the *habanera* of Cuba, with other European and black African influences. It typically combined the Spanish guitar with the Italian violin and was given a distinctive edge with the sound of the *bandoneón*, a kind of concertina or accordion imported by German sailors (piano and flute were also introduced). It was music to dance to, dances which jettisoned polite group-dances for sexually charged dancing by couples. By the 1920s, as workers began to own their own homes, residential areas grew and a café, bar and club culture thrived, the tango had become mainstream. Though shunned at first by the social elite, it became thoroughly popular once validated by Europe. It was a huge hit in Paris in particular before the First World War and went on to become a *succès de scandale* as it was slammed by the Pope, forbidden in the German military, and declared by the English aristocracy a slight to good breeding.

A further development in the cementing of tango's national status was its transition to song form. Tango records became popular from the 1920s onwards and the biggest recording artist of the time was Carlos Gardel. Gardel became a legend, a Glenn Miller, Buddy Holly or Elvis of tango. With his smooth image, slicked-back hair and trademark trilby and white scarf he easily made the transition to the cinema, and – like Miller and Holly – took on the status of a near-mythical idol following his death in a plane crash in 1935. Even though one of his biggest hits was called *Mi Buenos Aires querido* (My beloved Buenos Aires), his songs are permeated by a sense of nostalgia for what many take to be Europe (Gardel himself was born in France and came to Argentina via Uruguay). This sense of loss became even stronger as the boom of the 1920s gave way to the Depression and military rule in the 1930s, and the electrifying dancing of the tango was eclipsed by the melancholy of the sung version.

The lyrics of these songs were strongly *porteño* in flavour (*porteño* being the adjective used to refer to the traditional culture of the port of Buenos Aires), with their mix of *lunfardo*, a sort of immigrant Italian slang, and Argentine Spanish. Moreover, the songs came to be seen to reflect the wide-boy identity of the *compadrito*. The tango, then, represents the same ambiguity as *civilización y barbarie* and the gauchesque: stylish yet rooted in the world of the underdog, frenetic yet gloomy, urban yet country, full of European longing yet quintessentially Argentine. As with the gaucho many were keen to embrace tango as a national symbol. Peronist nationalism pushed it as the authentic sound of Argentina in the 1940s and 1950s and it saturated the airwaves.

Though its appeal waned from the later 1950s onwards, the tango was later revitalised by the anti-Peronist and Brooklyn-raised Astor Piazzolla, who created a new cerebral style of tango which was less sentimental and more jazz-influenced. Today, tango still thrives, although, like flamenco in Spain, it has become touristified in some areas and exported as a globalised package in the form of Broadway shows such as *Tango Argentino* or *Forever Tango*, the *Riverdance* of the River Plate.

Borges's poem 'El tango' (from *El otro, el mismo*, The other, the same, 1964) captures well the mood of the tango and its cultural significance. The poem complains that 'una mitología de puñales . . . se ha perdido / En sórdidas noticias policiales', that a romantic machista heroism (a mythology of knives) has been replaced by the sordid realities of crime reports. But these long gone 'heroes' survive:

> Hoy, más allá del tiempo y de la aciaga
> Muerte, esos muertos viven en el tango.
>
> En la música están, en el cordaje
> De la terca guitarra trabajosa,
> Que trama en la milonga venturosa
> La fiesta y la inocencia del coraje.

(Today, beyond time and fateful / death, those dead men live on in the tango. // They are in the music, in the strings / of the obstinate, labouring guitar, / which insinuates into a spirited milonga / the celebration and the innocence of courage.)

The *compadrito* lives on in the music of the tango and his violent deeds are celebrated as authentic and pure. The tango transcends time and allows the listener to identify with the 'heroic' act: 'El recuerdo imposible de haber muerto / Peleando, en una esquina del suburbio' (the impossible memory of having died / fighting, on a street corner in the slums).

This, of course, is a metaphor for Borges's own poetic philosophy, but just as his poetry seeks to extract what is essential from the flux of human experience, so too does the tango grasp what is essential and immortal about Argentinian life. But the danger is all too apparent, behind the veneer of 'civilisation' lies the haunting spectre of a creed of mindlessly idealised machismo and violence.

Perón and Evita

Such contradictions perhaps explain Borges's distaste for Peronism yet his turning a blind eye to the excesses of later military dictatorships. Yet Borges's 'blind eye' was a literal one. He was isolated, ageing and without sight in the period of military terror. Even so, the bitter criticisms of him (in the 1970s and 1980s) show just how volatile the mixed cocktail of European elitism and rugged Argentine tradition was. Peronism was to bring out this tension.

Juan Domingo Perón was an army colonel who used his positions in the Ministries of War, and Labour and Social Welfare, to build up a power base, particularly amongst organised labour. When the nation's worried leaders jailed him in 1945, the trade unions' mass demonstrations forced his release, and he went on to win easily the presidential elections the following year. Already backed by the workers' movement, he secured his position in the military via a programme of sackings, rewards and cronyism. In many ways, he became the urban equivalent of Rosas. Though happy to exploit the rhetoric of gaucho mythology, he was essentially positioned against the rural farming elites and his natural constituency was that of the industrial workers, to whom he often appealed via frenzied rallies in Buenos Aires's main square. What he depended on was a near fascistic cult of the personality, and in this he was profoundly aided by his wife Eva Duarte, popularly to be known as Evita.

Eva was an illegitimate village girl who moved to the big city and through her liaisons with wealthy older men came to be an actress with her own radio show and to be close to the military elite. She caught the eye of Perón and married him at 25, when she was nearly half his age. It was really through Evita that the Peróns earned the almost fanatical devotion of the workers he had dubbed the *descamisados* (shirtless ones). The welfare works of her charitable foundation firmed up her image as the saviour of the poor. It is hard for those on the outside to understand the appeal of Evita. She was venerated in a quasi-religious way, like the Virgin Mary; her antics often aped those of royalty or film stars, yet she was seen as a down-to-earth woman of the people who embodied the possibility of the underprivileged 'making it' to the top. The mystique was only increased by her tragically young death from cancer in 1952. There was even a campaign to beatify her. The upper classes saw her as an upstart who simply mirrored the vulgarity of the Perón regime, and her potential to unleash mob power was much feared. After Perón's fall, the military had her body removed to Europe lest her grave became a rallying point. Her appeal continued long after death. The inscription on her tomb, roughly translated as 'Don't cry for me, Argentina, the truth is I shall not leave you', became the words of the most famous song from Tim Rice and Andrew Lloyd Webber's hit musical *Evita*.

The musical *Evita* caused an outrage in Argentina as did the casting of Madonna in Alan Parker's 1996 film version. Such a perceived slur on Evita's saintly image (despite her real-life background) prompted the rapid commissioning of a supposedly more authentic 'Argentine' version of her life. Tomás Eloy Martínez's novels *La novela de Perón* (The Perón novel, 1985) and *Santa Evita* (1995) give a good flavour of the Juan and Evita phenomenon. The point is, though, that the populism of the Peróns was by its nature doomed to failure in real terms. The touchy-feely code of so-called *justicialismo* made economically unsustainable promises to the workers while reducing competitiveness, and the wooing of the *descamisados* alienated both the middle and upper classes and the countryside. Short-term growth based on exports to struggling postwar Europe brought some good times back home, but a downturn soon followed and by the early 1950s the economy was in crisis. Crackdowns on freedoms and social disorder quickly followed.

Oddly, it was the Catholic Church that really finished off Perón. The two forces had been in conflict over the sacrilegious cult of Evita, the attempts to canonise her, the Peronisation of the school system and the introduction of divorce. Once the Church began organising bigger demos than the Peronists, there was an upsurge of church burnings, and the army eventually intervened to oust Perón in 1955. Peronism as a force did not disappear. The Peronist Carlos Saúl Menem became President of Argentina as late as 1989 (and again in 1995), moving orthodox Peronism to the right of centre. But back in the 1960s Peronism had even taken on the quality of a leftist, nationalist discourse reminiscent of Castro's Cuba, and in the 1970s guerrilla groups such as the Montoneros were its heirs.

Traditionalist Perón supporters got their way when their man was brought back from exile in Spain to power in 1973, but he died a year later and by the time his new wife Isabelita took over, the country was in chaos. As the situation declined further, a military coup seemed inevitable. It came in March 1976 and one of the darkest periods in modern Argentine history was ushered in (discussed below).

Military or similar forms of dictatorship had become a shared heritage of the Southern Cone as a whole. Before examining their social and cultural impact from the 1970s onwards, it is important to sketch other developments elsewhere in the region to flesh out this cultural survey up to the end of the 1960s. Though culturally Argentina was dominant up to the mid-twentieth century, similar concerns were often shared, especially in the *Río de la Plata* (River Plate) area.

URUGUAY

Uruguay's José Enrique Rodó influenced a whole generation of Latin American intellectuals with his anti-materialist appeal to spiritual growth and inner freedom in *Ariel* (1900), while Horacio Quiroga, for example, if not explicitly enunciating a civilisation-versus-barbarism conflict, wrote stories in the first decades of the century dealing with the pioneer's relationship with the interior. His tales, often focusing on men of immigrant stock who seek to make a living in the jungle around Misiones (a remote part of north-east Argentina), emphasise both the arrogance and puniness of these men in the face of the wild, untamable power of native nature, and at the same time the bravery and heroism of their progressive plans ('El hombre muerto' (The dead man) or 'A la deriva' (Adrift) would be good examples of the former, and 'Los fabricantes de carbón' (The charcoal burners) of the latter). Yet Quiroga also wrote stories of the imagination and the macabre, pointing to another literary trend in the region associated increasingly with fantasy and experimentation (and echoed too in the near anarchic vision of modern city life, back in Buenos Aires, by Argentine writers such as Roberto Arlt or in the plotless anti-novels of Macedonio Fernández).

POETRY

In a sense, it was in poetry above all that early twentieth-century excitement over experimentation was manifested. Writers such as Leopoldo Lugones (Argentina) were already associated with *modernismo* (see Chapter 5) and its exoticising, aestheticising (if, later, Americanising) tendencies. Other writers such as Chile's rather more eclectic Gabriela Mistral (Spanish America's first Nobel laureate) showed the mark of the movement's founder, Nicaragua's Rubén Darío. The influence of the European avant garde was huge in the Argentine capital, and was translated into the notion of the *vanguardia*, while a more general notion of cultural fashion was later promoted by influential magazines such as *Sur* (South). Borges's early flirtation with *ultraísmo* or, in Chile, Vicente Huidobro's *creacionismo* were examples of the region's fascination with the promotion of a flashy vanguard aesthetic.

Pablo Neruda

It was Chile's Pablo Neruda who would become the truly great poet of the Southern Cone and of Latin America as a whole. Though it was during his avant-garde phase that his reputation grew, his fame (culminating in a Nobel Prize in 1971) is really based on his more earthy poetry of love and his (both portentous and plain) social poetry. His *Residencia* or 'Residence' cycle (written between 1925 and 1945) is the turning point, marking as it does a transition from a rather obscure and anguished avant-garde hermeticism to a more 'oral' style of near propagandistic political poetry. The climax to this process comes in 1950 with the *Canto general* (General song), a grandiosely prophetic-sounding piece of third-worldism that tries to re-present the epic saga of Latin American history from the people's perspective and set up the poet, especially in the celebrated 'Alturas de Machu Picchu' (The heights of Machu Picchu) section, as a spokesperson for the continent. Neruda's left-wing political career reinforced his popular perception, and works such as his later *Odas elementales* (Elemental odes, 1954), with its simple celebration of wood, suits, the onion, and the traditional Chilean dish of eel soup, a celebration, that is, of the ordinary things in life and the ordinary people who use them, consolidated his position as a man-of-the-people poet.

His early love poetry (despite some recent lambasting by feminists) did not do his popular reputation any harm. *Veinte poemas de amor y una canción desesperada* (Twenty poems of love and a song of despair, 1924) is still a bestseller, whose bitter-sweet appeal was widened further after Michael Radford's international hit film fictionalisation of an episode from Neruda's life, *Il postino* (1995). But Neruda's death brings us back to the 1970s. He died shortly after the Pinochet coup in 1973. His funeral procession became a symbolic event, and his house at Isla Negra virtually a place of pilgrimage.

THE 'NEW NOVEL' AND THE 'BOOM'

The key literary development in the Southern Cone, as in the rest of Latin America, was the rise of the *nueva narrativa* culminating in the so-called Boom of the 1960s. This phenomenon has been fairly comprehensively documented and analysed (see Chapter 7), so will be considered sparingly here. Essentially, it is the culmination of the long process sketched above of reaction against conventional ways of depicting reality, particularly social realism with its tendency to oversimplify and to forget that 'reality' was about perception or limited comprehension as much as external observation, and could therefore not be copied or represented confidently or coherently in writing.

The massively influential Borges encapsulated this attitude in a range of stories that questioned the human mind's ability to make any sense of the universe. 'La muerte y la brújula' (Death and the compass) is the classic example of one of his favourite devices: the logical investigation of a mystery by a rational detective leads to no resolution and merely confirms the vanity of the human quest for knowledge and understanding. Ernesto Sábato (Argentina) wrote in 1948 the short novel *El túnel* (The tunnel). Here the narrator's version of the crime he has committed turns out to be completely unreliable as his vision is partial and totally subjective, yet his madness may be closer to the true nature of reality than the reader's own smugly rational understanding of the world. Uruguay's great precursor of the Boom is Juan Carlos Onetti. The moment in his 1950 novel *La vida breve* (A brief life) when the protagonist Brausen flees a real city to take refuge in the imaginary town of Santa María is a defining one, anticipating the later invented worlds of Mexican Juan Rulfo's Comala or García Márquez's Macondo. It announces the fictional rather than realist status of narrative while suggesting that what is thought to be real life may itself be no more than a fiction. Increasingly, then, the experience of reading fiction was made to parallel the sense of confusion and disorientation experienced by human beings in a modern world that no longer seemed to make sense. This was the hallmark of the Boom in the 1960s, when confusing or complex narrative forms were used to reflect the confusing or complex nature of existence.

One of the major figures of the Boom was Argentina's Julio Cortázar. His weighty 1963 novel *Rayuela* (Hopscotch) is emblematic of the Boom and the heady experimentalism of the 1960s. As its title suggests, the novel's form is like a game of hopscotch. It has 56 chapters, but with an extra 99 which the reader can add in to form a second book; moreover, a chart is provided to suggest an alternative method of reading the text other than the traditional one of reading chapters in their numerical sequence. The climax to the Boom came at the end of the decade, with the Chilean José Donoso's *El obsceno pájaro de la noche* (The obscene bird of night, 1970), the last word in tortuous narrative complexity. Its 'narrator' of shifting multiple, even inanimate, identities reflects a near complete disintegration of the idea of a cohesive human identity or a comprehensible external environment.

In a sense the Boom took place in Europe. Many of the new novelists were or had been living over there and a major motor of the Boom was the Barcelona publishing house Seix Barral. *Rayuela*, set in Paris and Buenos Aires, embodies this tension. Those daunted by the prospects of the book might try Cortázar's short story 'El otro cielo' (The other sky) where the protagonist seeks, but ultimately fails, to escape the humdrum world of 1940s Buenos Aires by transporting himself mentally to the mysterious Parisian underworld of the 1860s. Not only does this reveal the ever present European consciousness imbricated in Argentine or Southern Cone identity, but curiously, despite Cortázar's Latin-Americanist leftism, it also inverts Sarmiento's dichotomy, presenting the New World as the location of conservatism, and the Old as a zone of liberation and discovery.

THE 'POST-BOOM'

By the 1970s a variation of the new narrative was beginning to emerge, now usually referred to as the Post-boom. This rejected extreme narrative complexity (which was now so familiar that it could no longer jolt the reader into any new state of awareness) and turned instead to more direct forms of narrative, employing elements from popular or mass culture and dealing more head-on with the social and political realities of Latin America (see Chapter 7). The Argentine novelist Manuel Puig is sometimes credited with marking the start of this trend: his *Boquitas pintadas* (Painted lips translated as *Heartbreak tango*) from 1969, though still a sophisticated narrative construction, was based around popular songs and soap operas, and dealt with the aspirations and limitations of ordinary small-town people. Established writers followed suit, most notably the Chilean José Donoso. A new generation of accessible novelists breathed fresh air into the region's narrative. Some of the new names to emerge were, in Chile, Isabel Allende and Antonio Skármeta, and in Argentina, Luisa Valenzuela and Mempo Giardinelli (amongst many others).

An important point is that the Post-boom cannot just be seen as a literary reaction to the perceived exhaustion of the new narrative. It must also be seen as a reaction to the shocking political events of the 1970s, which reminded writers of material reality and a particularly Latin American kind of trauma. Before turning to the military dictatorships of Argentina and Chile, it is worth mentioning the case of Paraguay and one of the forerunners of the Post-boom, Augusto Roa Bastos.

PARAGUAY

Paraguay is unusual because of its indigenous tradition and its astounding isolationist history. About 90 per cent of the population speak the Indian language Guaraní, while the small percentage monolingual in Spanish mainly inhabit the capital Asunción. The roots of this remarkable survival of the indigenous language go back to the Jesuit missionaries' radical decision to use the native language to Christianise the indigenous people in colonial times (see Roland Joffe's film *The Mission* (1986)). Though the missionaries were later expelled and the minority Spanish language and its related interests became dominant, this Jesuit protectionism was the first in a long series of isolationist episodes, just as the consequences of the Jesuit expulsion were, for the natives, part of a long series of tragic disasters.

The most extraordinary period in Paraguayan history was the dictatorship, assumed shortly after an early Independence, of Dr José Gaspar Rodríguez de Francia, the subject of Roa Bastos's *Yo el supremo* (I the Supreme, 1974). His staggering 26-year rule as protective father of a kind of hermit republic, cemented a tradition of tyranny (albeit pseudo-benevolent in this case) mixed with resistance to outside influence. A history of war and suffering followed. After the grim and futile Chaco War of 1932–1935 against Bolivia, military interference in government became the norm, culminating in the dictatorship from 1954 to 1989 of another isolationist, the notorious General Alfredo Stroessner. Roa Bastos's opposition to Stroessner is reflected in his book on Francia.

Much admired by critics and intellectuals and often linked to the Post-boom, *Yo el supremo*'s extremely complex and demanding exploration of authoritarianism and authorship will nonetheless prove unreadable for many. A much easier and more moving read is Roa Bastos's earlier *Hijo de hombre* (Son of man, 1960), a sweeping overview of Paraguayan history as an ongoing process of suffering and resistance. The novel is about the preservation of popular memory and this was to become a key idea elsewhere in the Southern Cone as military dictators wiped out opposition, silencing truth in favour of official versions of history.

MILITARY DICTATORSHIPS IN CHILE AND ARGENTINA

Violent coups took place in Chile in 1973 and Argentina in 1976. In 1970 the Socialist leader Salvador Allende was democratically elected President of Chile. Allende's attempted socialist experiment was always likely to fail and was not helped by massive opposition from the outset and US destabilisation of a country it saw as a 'communist' threat. The inevitable disorder that followed climaxed in a coup d'état led by General Augusto Pinochet. Allende died in the siege of the presidential palace, becoming a martyr figure for the Left, while in the brutal aftermath of the coup thousands of individuals were tortured and killed and many more went into exile. Another martyr figure was the popular musician Víctor Jara, one of the founders of the *nueva canción* movement closely identified with Allende's coalition: he was murdered by the military police shortly after the coup, his hands were amputated, and his music was banned as subversive.

The euphemistically-termed *proceso* in Argentina involved a long-term 'dirty war', the details of which have emerged very slowly. It is reckoned that some 9,000 (mostly young) Argentines 'disappeared' as the military junta (government) set out to systematically destroy all opposition with thinly-disguised death squads. Extraordinarily, the football World Cup took place in Argentina during this process in 1978. This was part of the junta's near-fascistic nationalist project and, despite runaway inflation, money was pumped into the plan. (The equally discreditable Uruguayan junta followed suit in 1980 with a tournament of former winners.) There were rumours of corruption and some obvious gamesmanship, but Argentina won the competition in front of frenzied supporters who were then treated to a lengthy speech by President Jorge Videla attempting to cash in on the feverish spirit of national unity.

The junta funded groups of hooligans or *barras bravas* to 'discourage' protests when the national team played abroad. This was precisely the mixture of populism, control, violence and fanaticism which had been feared and fomented since Sarmiento. The final awful outcome was General Galtieri's disastrously misjudged invasion of the Falkland/Malvinas Islands in 1982 in order to distract the population from economic chaos with the allure of a national crusade. At least the abject humiliation that followed finally exposed the illegitimacy of the military regime and a return to democracy was programmed for the following year. Pinochet's withdrawal was more gradual and reluctant, but democracy was restored in Chile in 1989 and consolidated over the next decade. Civilian rule returned to Uruguay in 1985.

Literature and dictatorship

There were cultural responses to the horror of the dictatorships. Independent theatre in Chile, for example, articulated a public if indirect critique of the Pinochet regime and similar plays were written in Argentina and Uruguay. Also, several Post-boom novels capture the tone of the times. Many (often oblique) forms of cultural expression were from Argentina, though Chile probably produced the more effective mainstream literature. One of the more successful novels was Puig's *El beso de la mujer araña* (Kiss of the spider woman, 1976), where the imprisonment of its two central characters (a homosexual for indecency charges, and a political activist) extends the notion of repression to the very bases of social organisation. Luisa Valenzuela's *Novela negra con argentinos* (Black novel with Argentines, 1990) uses New

York to explore the themes of denial and the disappeared, with exile and the detritus of the city emerging as images of the repressed memory of violence in the Dirty War. José Donoso's *Casa de campo* (Country house, 1978) is a mordant allegory of the events surrounding the Pinochet coup in Chile, and his *La desesperanza* (1986), though less satisfactory as a novel, deals with life under the dictatorship.

Isabel Allende's *La casa de los espíritus* (The house of the spirits, 1983) is the most readable novel on the Chile coup. A seemingly consciously more straightforward echo of García Márquez's *Cien años de soledad* (One hundred years of solitude), it uses a family history to give an indirect though clear portrait of Chilean history and society. The shocking transition to torture and violence in the coup sequence is genuinely affecting, though some readers have found the moving liberal emphasis on love and forgiveness at the end too hard to take. Intellectual mistrust of Allende is interesting. She has brought Latin American literature into the mainstream and pricked the awareness of many ordinary readers, as well as accessibly giving voice to women's issues and debates in feminism. Yet many academics seem to prefer more theoretically radical female or political writers such as Luisa Valenzuela or Chile's Diamela Eltit, the perceived significance of whose rather heavy-going novels might be seen as something of a critical fabrication.

A CULTURAL CONCLUSION

While many people across the world will have got to know about human rights abuses in Chile through Isabel Allende, others will have learnt about the Southern Cone by means of other forms of more direct, popular action such as that of the collective testimonial production of *arpilleras* or patchwork quilts depicting harrowing Chilean scenes, or of the Madres de la Plaza de Mayo in Argentina whose occupation of Buenos Aires' main public square forced the remembering of their disappeared sons and daughters. There can be no doubt that it was the Boom of the sophisticated and cosmopolitan *nueva novela* that brought Latin American literature to the attention of the world, helping change the direction of fiction globally, but Evita, Maradona, tango, New Song, Inti-Illimani, gauchos, Isabel Allende, colourful quilts and stubbornly defiant mothers have done their bit too. The vigour of Southern Cone culture, the popular as well as the more elite variety, means it continues to have an impact within the region and beyond it, at both continental and global level. But, despite democracy, modernisation and relative stability (now under threat from economic chaos in Argentina), that culture still encapsulates the great battles of periphery and centre, marginalisation and integration, national pride and global awareness, history and future that so vexed the region's post-Independence philosophers over a century ago.

FURTHER READING

Alonso, C. 1990. *The Spanish American regional novel*. Cambridge: Cambridge University Press.

Bethell, L. (ed.) 1993. *Argentina since independence*. Cambridge: Cambridge University Press.

Colás, S. 1994. *Postmodernity in Latin America: the Argentine paradigm*. Durham and London: Duke University Press.

Da Costa, R. 1982. *The poetry of Pablo Neruda*. New Haven: Yale University Press.

Hart, S. 1999. *A companion to Spanish-American literature*. London: Tamesis.

Hickman, J. 1998. *News from the end of the earth: a portrait of Chile*. London: Hurst and Co.

Masiello, F. 1992. *Between civilization and barbarism: women, nature and literary culture in modern Argentina*. Lincoln: University of Nebraska Press.

Sarlo, B. 1993. *Jorge Luis Borges: a writer on the edge*. London and New York: Verso.

Swanson, P. 1995. *The new novel in Latin America: politics and popular culture after the Boom*. Manchester and New York: Manchester University Press.

Williamson, E. 1992. *The Penguin history of Latin America*. Harmondsworth: Penguin.

'Lavandería', Santiago de Chile, July 2001.
Photo by John D. Perivolaris.

'Gardel', Santiago de Chile, July 2001.
Photo by John D. Perivolaris.

'Evita', Buenos Aires, July 2001.
Photo by John D. Perivolaris.

'Hacemos lo imposible'.
Photo by John D. Perivolaris.

9

Spanish and Latin American cinema

Rob Rix

In recent times Spain's film industry has become increasingly admired in the UK, USA and elsewhere as classy and original, bursting with acting and directorial talent, and very much in touch with contemporary lifestyles. Film festivals and special events dedicated to Spanish cinema have sprung up in all kinds of venues, both national and local (for example at Manchester's Cornerhouse Cinema), and they attract full houses of fans who are desperate to keep up with the latest releases and to review earlier classics.

SPANISH CINEMA

Pedro Almodóvar

International film audiences have come to associate Spanish cinema with the sexy, camp, outlandish comedies and melodramas of Pedro Almodóvar. His unconventional talent, emerging in the aftermath of a nearly 40-year-long dictatorship that ended effectively with the death of General Franco in 1975, became a standard-bearer of Spain's cultural renaissance in the early 1980s, the brief but vibrant period of innovation, celebration and liberation known as *la movida* (see Chapter 5). Almodóvar's early films were not only free from the constraints of censorship but also free of obsession with the traumatic effects of the Franco era that had haunted film-makers before him. The young self-taught director mixed a heady brew of pop, rock and punk styles applied to traditional clichés of Spanish culture, whipping up frenzied farces and burlesque fantasies based in the everyday realities of a society in transition. His garish, highly cosmeticised sets, characters and situations proclaimed the triumph of the artificial, transsexual, neurotic and psychotic demons that were finally let out of the closet of Spain's repressed past. The young man from La Mancha courted scandal with his drug-peddling nuns, pederast priests, vulnerable rapists and incestuous maids, and wove perverse plots riddled with comic sketches and visual kitsch to create a heightened expectation and fresh sense of cinematic delight in film-goers who were ready for something new. He also turned Spain's capital city into a new filmic landscape which would be used and reinvented by a new generation of film-makers following in his footsteps; as Guillermo Cabrera Infante (1995) remarked: 'Si Roma era de Fellini y Nueva York es de Woody Allen, Madrid le pertenece a Almodóvar.' (If Rome was Fellini's and New York is Woody Allen's, Madrid belongs to Almodóvar.)

Almodóvar's first international success came with *Mujeres al borde de un ataque de nervios* (Women on the edge of a nervous breakdown, 1988), the biggest box-office hit of the 1980s in Spain. Carmen Maura, whose acting career blossomed through her work with Almodóvar, played the independent career woman Pepa, whose world is shattered when her lover abandons her. As she stumbles through a series of mishaps in her attempts to locate him and inform him that she is pregnant, her apartment fills up with an assortment of characters whose problems and obsessions clash with her own. Laced with gags, coincidences and misunderstandings, the farcical unfolding of her struggle to come to terms with her predicament ends with her settling for an artificial view of Madrid and of life, high up above the bustling city in her flat-with-a-farmyard-on-the-balcony. Many of Almodóvar's characters yearn for a simpler life as they are swept along in the frenzied pace of modern living, and as in the case of Carmen Maura's Gloria in *¿Qué he hecho yo para merecer esto?* (What have I done to deserve this?, 1984) they often turn for solace to the backwaters of rural Spain, where only their ageing parents or grandparents remain, sitting it out in an ambience of eternal tranquillity.

The Oscar-winning *Todo sobre mi madre* (All about my mother, 1998) sounds a requiem for the exuberant, experimental lifestyles of the millennium, with AIDS and addiction taking their toll of the innocent, the vulnerable and the reckless alike. At the same time, the film is a tribute to motherhood, not now as a selfless sacrifice to the macho values of traditional Spain and Francoism, but in the guise of the caring, tolerant but self-validating and self-asserting new woman who emerges from a chrysalis of pain and loss to rediscover her nurturing strengths. Along with many other Spanish films at the end of the 1990s *Todo sobre mi madre* critically reappraises the lives and roles of women as mothers in post-feminist times. Younger film-makers such as the Basque Icíar Bollaín, with *Hola, ¿Estás sola?* (Hi, are you alone?, 1995), Chus Gutiérrez, with *Insomnio* (Insomnia, 1997) and Benito Zambrano with his first feature, *Solas* (Women alone, 1999) have all turned a spotlight on femininity and motherhood in crisis, through films which examine everyday lives in rather less melodramatic but perhaps also less radical forms than Almodóvar in his powerful and moving *tour de force.*

Famous as a director of some of Spain's best actresses (often referred to as 'las chicas Almodóvar') including Victoria Abril, Marisa Paredes, Penelope Cruz, and Rossy de Palma as well as Carmen Maura and many others, Almodóvar also gave Antonio Banderas his breakthrough in films. As the great showman of Spanish cinema in the 1980s and 1990s, Almodóvar continues to set the pace in a country where the film industry seems always to be in creative turmoil, despite the challenge of competing with Hollywood's blockbusters for an audience. While he has often been linked to big names in Hollywood (including actresses Jodie Foster, Glenn Close and Madonna) who have declared a desire to work with him, Almodóvar's relationship with the US film business has been a love–hate one. His fiercely independent approach to film-making, and his encouragement of other young Spanish directors through his production company El Deseo SA (Desire Limited), have kept his credentials intact as a major European film-maker capable of stunning if not always seducing the fickle world of Hollywood, and of captivating film audiences around the world. His love of the 'show-business' side of cinema makes for spectacular opening nights and merchandising. The following is a description of the street advertisement for ¡Atame! (Tie me up! Tie me down!, 1989) on show at the Berlin Film Festival:

> . . . near the centre of the western part of the city, a giant cube has been erected, thrusting 30 feet into the air and painted on all four sides with scenes from ¡Atame! . . . On one side a gargantuan masked bodybuilder wearing a leather doublet stares out in challenge; on another a battered young man holds his hand over the mouth of a bewildered young woman; on still another the same young woman, dressed in a slight, clingy shift, poses sensually, catlike, on all fours.
>
> (David Leavitt, 1990. 'Almodóvar on the verge', *Weekend Guardian*, 23–24 June 1990: 12–16, p. 12)

Luis Buñuel

Before Almodóvar, the one Spanish film-maker to achieve lasting international notoriety was Luis Buñuel (1900–1983). A close friend of the poet Federico García Lorca and artist Salvador Dalí in his youth, Buñuel made his first film, the short surrealist classic *Un chien andalou* (An Andalusian dog), in 1929, co-writing it with Dalí, and basing its violent and baffling scenes on images fresh from both of their dreams. This scandalous début was followed by *L'Age d'Or* (The Golden Age, 1930), another outrageous and deeply poetic work that satirises bourgeois propriety and subverts good taste with violent celebrations of desire and depravity.

Buñuel's involvement with the Spanish and French artistic vanguards in the 1920s and 1930s was to mark the rest of his cinematic career. After a brief spell in Hollywood at the end of the Spanish Civil War Buñuel moved to Mexico, where he lived until his death in 1983. For over a decade he made films which were marked indelibly by his chosen country of exile, including the grim drama of street children in Mexico City, *Los olvidados* (named in English *The Young and the Damned*, 1950). Condemned by the Mexican government for painting a distorted picture of life in the city, the film gained international recognition at the Cannes Film Festival. The convulsive violence which dogs the lives of the Mexican poor, the orphaned and the mutilated beggars who people this world, leads inevitably to the rubbish dump where the bodies of the forgotten ones are disposed of. Scenes of raw poverty and cruelty (for example, the stoning of a blind beggar by street children) leave the spectator no comfortable space from which to judge the victims and perpetrators of this cruelty. Alongside harrowing scenes from their daily lives are the dream sequences in which their vulnerability and fears are even more terrible; not even in sleep do they find respite from the nightmare of their lives. Liberal consciences are tormented by the images and the moral quandaries posed by Buñuel in his savage indictment of the mid-twentieth-century urban jungle.

Later in his Mexican films Buñuel turned his eye to the ambiguities of piety and perversity, as religious obsession and sexual desire both find expression in fetishism (sexual stimulation derived from contemplating objects that replace the desired person, e.g. shoes) and adoration, in *El* (translated as *This strange passion*, 1952), *Ensayo de un crimen* (named in English *The criminal life of Archibaldo de la Cruz*, 1955) and *Nazarín* (1958). The latter, based on a novel by the nineteenth-century Spanish novelist Benito Pérez Galdós (see Chapter 4), links closely with the notorious *Viridiana* (1961), Buñuel's first Spanish film since the controversial documentary *Las Hurdes (Tierra sin pan) (*Land without bread, 1933). Whereas in *Nazarín* a priest is compromised by his own goodness, discovering that by following Christ's teaching he fails to cure the ills of society, in *Viridiana* the heroine (played by Silvia Pinal), an ex-novice who attempts to rehabilitate beggars, suffers in her own flesh the failure of her Christian experiment. Betrayed by her guardian (played by Fernando Rey), who hangs himself after simulating her rape, Viridiana leaves her convent and sets up a commune of the homeless on the run-down estate where he had lived as a recluse.

Viridiana was denounced by the Vatican mouthpiece *L'Osservatore Romano* as blasphemous after it won the Palme d'Or at the Cannes Film Festival. It brought down the Director General of Cinema in Franco's Spain, who had given it official approval. Banned until the return of democracy, *Viridiana* shocked with its parody of religious iconology, as in the Last Supper scene (the beggars' banquet which freezes into a grotesque copy of the famous fresco by Leonardo), and with its typically Buñuelesque mordant moral critique of misguided piety.

It was to be several years before the Aragonese director returned to film in Spain, this time using Toledo as the setting for his version of Pérez Galdós's *Tristana*. As in *Viridiana*, the young girl Tristana (Catherine Deneuve) is the object of the lustful desires of an older man (this time, her uncle, Don Lope, once again played by Fernando Rey). After she runs away with a bohemian artist (Francesco Neri) Tristana is afflicted by a tumour which leads to the amputation of her leg. Thus punished, she chooses to return to the seclusion of her *ménage* with Don Lope. Here she freezes into a cruel image of perverse male desire, becoming an imperfect object (as she sits at the piano with its leg modestly covered by a cloth, while her own is simply missing) and a castrating monster (as she bares her mutilated body to the voyeuristic gaze of the deaf and dumb son of Saturna the servant). Her revenge on the male is completed when she opens the windows in Don Lope's bedroom as he lies dying, chilling him before calling too late for a doctor. Tristana's subverting fetishising of the male gaze is made profoundly disturbing by Buñuel's use of surrealist techniques throughout the film, as in the dream image of Don Lope's head as a bell clapper, which exemplifies the phallic imposition of his power over her innocence.

While his 'French' films, especially *Le Charme Discret de la Bourgeoisie* (The discreet charm of the bourgeoisie, 1972) and *Belle de Jour* (1967), strip bare the hypocrisy, decadence, frustration and unhappiness of the bourgeoisie, the two films made in Spain in the 1960s depict less sophisticated but no less perverse human beings, caught in moral and spiritual contradictions rather than social and ideological traps. In his Spanish scenarios repression struggles with primitive desires, and Buñuel the film-maker, like Goya before him, paints humanity in all its abject self-delusion.

Carlos Saura

Buñuel's unique contribution to international cinema was forged from his constant commitment to a surrealist vein throughout half a century of film-making. As a near-legendary but absent figure in Spanish cinema under the Franco dictatorship, his influence on other Spanish directors was rather oblique, despite his fame. However, his return to Spain to make *Viridiana* was partly due to the persuasion of a young director, Carlos Saura, whose first feature, *Los golfos* (The hooligans, 1959*)*, has strong parallels with *Los olvidados*, although Saura had not seen Buñuel's Mexican film when he made his own story of delinquents in Madrid.

Saura's début followed the adventures of a group of youngsters who dream of winning fame and fortune through the bullfighting talents of one of their number, Juan. Turning to petty crime to finance his training and secure his big chance, they suffer various setbacks and are eventually defeated by the odds stacked against them in the urban wasteland of 1950s Spain. Not only does Juan prove to be a failure in the bullring, but his pal Paco dies a ghastly death in the city sewers following a bungled attempt at a robbery. There is no way out of the poverty trap for these youths, as the repressive society they inhabit drives them to destruction.

In *La caza* (The hunt, 1965) Saura turned to the rugged Castilian landscape, where three Civil War veterans and a younger man act out an ultimately murderous ritual of macho posturing, as they slaughter rabbits for sport and then turn their guns on each other. An indictment of the underlying violence in the psyche of the Civil War victors, Saura's parable of repressed malice blatantly contradicted the Francoist slogan '25 years of peace'. A director whose range of themes and styles is very broad, Saura also analysed the baneful effects of the regime on the Spanish family, notably in the intense study of childhood trauma *Cría cuervos* (Raise ravens, 1975). In response to the perverse and malicious ways of the adult world, 8-year-old Ana (played by Ana Torrent) decides to settle scores for her dead mother by poisoning first her unfaithful father and later her repressive aunt. John Hopewell (1986) quotes another significant director, Manuel Gutiérrez Aragón, referring to the family in Spanish films of the time as 'a microscopic state . . . a summary of the tensions and structures of the nation'. In this context *Cría cuervos* is a dark warning of the damage done to the generation of Spaniards born in the middle years of the dictatorship. In his earlier *La prima Angélica* (Cousin Angelica, 1973) Saura presents this generation as 'emotionally and politically stunted children' (Jordan and Morgan-Tamosunas, 1998). Many film directors born after the Civil War presented the past through the eyes of children.

After the death of Franco, Saura abandoned his dark musings on tyranny and made a number of films based on dance, notably *Bodas de sangre* (Blood wedding, 1981), *Carmen* (1983) and later *Sevillanas* (1992). *Carmen* unravels the tale of a soldier's love for a gypsy girl through the rehearsals for a ballet (based on the novel by Mérimée and on Bizet's opera). The film is a dramatic and colourful feast of flamenco dancing, but with a sombre heart of danger, jealousy and violence, which erupt in a cruel climax with the stabbing of the dancer playing Carmen (Laura del Sol) by her leading man and dance mentor (Antonio Gades).

Víctor Erice

One of the most enigmatic masterpieces of modern Spanish cinema is Víctor Erice's *El espíritu de la colmena* (The spirit of the beehive, 1973). Set in a remote village in Castile in the early 1940s, it explores the bewilderment of a young child, Ana (also played by Ana Torrent), who is intrigued by the monster in James Whale's *Frankenstein* movie, which she watches with her sister at the village film show. In a physical and moral landscape scarred by the Civil War, and in the silence of a house whose occupants, her family, seem deadened by the recent past, Ana goes in quest for the truth about the monster. She discovers a wounded Republican fugitive and keeps his presence secret, taking him food and her father's pocket watch, which plays a wistful tune from the war period, but the fugitive is discovered and summarily executed. Ana experiences a traumatic revelation as, exhausted by her flight from her family, she sees the monster's face reflected in a moonlit stream. She is brought home to convalescence, but continues to assert her own identity and to conjure the spirit.

Beautifully filmed in the stark, austere Castilian landscape which reflects the emptiness and harshness of life for Spaniards who were the losers in the Civil

War, this film is emblematic of Spanish cinema in the later years of the dictatorship, using figurative and metaphorical subtleties in settings of realistic simplicity to provoke the audience into an interpretation not only of the film but also, and more importantly, of the traumatic past which has conditioned their present.

The Civil War on film

In a different vein, Saura's ¡Ay, Carmela! (1990) traces a musical and theatrical journey through the chaos and destruction of the Spanish Civil War. With its indirect and tragi-comic take on the war, ¡Ay, Carmela! is fairly representative of the post-Franco cinema's reworkings of the traumatic events of the 1930s in Spain. Berlanga's 1985 comedy La vaquilla (The heifer) took much of the horror out of the war with its farcical adventures at the front line, and in 1992 Fernando Trueba directed the Oscar-winning Belle Époque, a romantic fantasy set in the early 1930s at the dawn of the Second Republic. Fernando, a young army deserter (Jorge Sanz), finds refuge in the home of free-thinker Manolo (Fernando Fernán Gómez), whose four daughters take it in turn to seduce the ex-seminarian who fled both church and barracks in search of liberty. With its wry humour and light-hearted exploration of the joys of sex, Belle Époque is only in the loosest sense a film about history. Instead it is a celebration of originality and difference in an idyllic rural summer setting, a quiet, quirky, compelling story of a time when the impending civil war is almost unimaginable, although its shadow is ready to be cast over the lives of Manolo and his eccentric family. As Barry Jordan (1999: 304) writes, by portraying the troubled Spanish Republic 'into an oasis of freedom, pleasure and sexual experimentation, Trueba assigns a universality to Belle Époque which is highly attractive to the spectator just as it is highly misleading historically'.

The Pilar Miró era

This type of lushly-filmed cinema has flourished in democratic Spain, partly in response to the 1980s Socialist government's promotion of high-quality historical films and literary adaptations during the era of Pilar Miró as Director General of Cinema (1982–1985).

With a strong flavour of glossy nostalgia, the films associated with Miró's aesthetic lead also capitalised on a new generation of film stars in combination with the older favourites such as Fernando Fernán Gómez and Paco Rabal. The 1990s especially saw a new kind of star system emerge, with a substantial number of Spanish (and Latin American) actors and actresses becoming as well known in the home market as many Hollywood stars. Some were mentioned above. Others include Javier Bardem, Carmelo Gómez and Emma Suárez who have worked with new generations of innovative directors led by Bigas Luna, Juanma Bajo Ulloa, and Julio Medem, to give new impetus to the film industry in Spain by bringing back audiences (especially young spectators) to home-produced films. With a huge range of film styles and genres, and a consciousness that cinema can be entertaining as well as thought-provoking and moving, Spain's film-makers today are among the leading talents in the European if not the world film scene.

Miró herself had made a significant impact during the post-Franco years, especially with *El crimen de Cuenca* (The crime of Cuenca, 1979), for which she was put on trial by a military court for defaming the Civil Guard. Her last two films, made shortly before her untimely death in 1997, are good examples of the type of cinema she promoted in her official role. *El perro del hortelano* (Dog in the manger, 1995) is an adaptation of Lope de Vega's Golden Age play (see Chapter 3), while *Tu nombre envenena mis sueños* (Your name poisons my dreams, 1996) takes the Civil War as the background to a dark and enigmatic thriller.

Co-productions

Spanish cinema has recently led a spate of co-productions with Latin American countries, notably Mexico, Argentina, Cuba, Colombia and Peru, which combine Spanish with 'local' finance, scriptwriters, actors and technicians to produce films for the Spanish-language market. Sometimes blurring nationalities to produce Latin-flavour films, they also often examine the human and social relationships between the former colonies and the mother country. These collaborations have nurtured directorial, scriptwriting and acting talents in challenging projects; without Spanish or European input many Latin American countries would find it hard to sustain substantial film production, which is precarious at the best of times. Examples of successful co-productions during the 1990s include Argentinian Adolfo Aristarain's *Martín (Hache)* (Martin (H), 1996), which builds on previous successes in Spain to capitalise on the star ratings of Federico Luppi and Cecilia Roth, and Peruvian Francisco Lombardi's *Bajo la piel* (Beneath the skin, 1996), and *No se lo digas a nadie* (Don't tell anyone about it, 1999), based on the novel by Jaime Bayly.

Looking back over the last 40 years, cinema in Latin America has taken a very different direction from the Spanish experience of a move from complex and sometimes cryptic anti-Franco films to a cinema that is more accessible and entertaining if still socially aware. The virtual collapse of the once burgeoning film industries of Argentina and Mexico in the 1950s, as Hollywood outstripped them in terms of technical sophistication, capitalisation and distribution, left most of Latin America with only US imports to watch. However, following the Cuban Revolution of 1959, a new kind of cinema was developed with a particularly Latin American stamp. By turning the camera on 'the people' and then showing them their own condition as part of the broader picture of class (and often racial) domination and exploitation, the pioneers of what became known as the New Latin American Cinema or Third Cinema created a cinema of reflection and action which would contribute to the development of revolutionary change in the continent.

LATIN AMERICAN CINEMA

Cuban cinema

In this pessimistic context, new generations of Latin American film-makers, often inspired by postwar Italian neorealism, which also had an impact in Spain, discovered a revolutionary potential in film. This coincided with political unrest in a number of countries and with Fidel Castro's successful 1959 revolution in Cuba. Beginning with short experimental documentaries denouncing poverty and hardship among marginalised populations, and often running the risk not only of censorship but also of arrest and imprisonment by repressive governments, these film-makers took their lead from revolutionary Cuba by developing theories and practices based on the idea that the medium of film, through its accessibility to social groups excluded by their illiteracy and lack of education from other forms of communication, could have an important consciousness-raising role in terms of social and political issues.

A huge impulse was given to this movement by the creation of a new film institute (*ICAIC – Instituto Cubano de Artes e Industrias Cinematográficas*) in Havana in 1959, to promote film-making there and in other parts of Latin America. Documentaries, historical reconstructions and feature films were produced both as instruments of revolutionary struggle and as forms of critical reflection on the possibilities and limitations of cinema in contributing to social and political change. Starting almost from scratch in terms of equipment and technical experience, Cuba's film institute gave new film-makers the opportunity to experiment with and invent techniques appropriate to the task of documenting 'reality' rather than creating film fantasy for entertainment. Hand-held camera work, rough-cut editing, collage, and so on, gave these early films a shocking and breath-taking immediacy.

Of all the films produced in Cuba during the first decade of the Revolution, perhaps the most significant was one that dealt principally with the role of the middle-classes and intellectuals in Cuba, whose understanding of and commitment to the Revolution was problematic. Tomás Gutiérrez Alea's *Memorias del subdesarrollo* (Memories of underdevelopment, 1968) is set in the first few years of the Revolution, specifically between the abortive US-backed invasion by counter-revolutionaries at the Bay of Pigs (April 1961) and the October missile crisis of 1962 when Cuba was at the centre of a nuclear weapons showdown between the Soviet Union and the USA, when for almost a fortnight the world was on the edge of a nuclear war. Sergio, the protagonist, stays behind in Cuba when his well-off family flees to Miami in fear of communism; he has remained not because he supports the Revolution, but because he is sick of his former life, and of his wife, and wants to be free of all responsibilities. Despising his own class for its slavish imitation of US lifestyles, yet sceptical about the potential of revolution in such an underdeveloped country, he drifts through a sordid affair with a young girl, Elena (Daisy Granados). Having seduced her and cast her off, he is brought before a revolutionary court by her family and accused of rape, but is absolved when it is discovered that Elena had previously been arrested for prostitution.

The film is cut through with documentary footage testifying to poverty, injustice, torture, and the mercenary egotism of the Cuban bourgeoisie, all with Sergio's voice-over analysing his country's past. The unfolding missile crisis finally leaves him silent, pathetically vulnerable as he realises that he is trapped in an island which may be nuked at any moment, and that he will die just like any of Castro's revolutionaries, just like any of Cuba's underdeveloped people. His intelligence, his sophistication and his superiority cannot save him.

Gutiérrez Alea was always a supporter of the Revolution, albeit a critical one. His 1966 farce *Muerte de un burócrata* (Death of a bureaucrat) combined slapstick with a denunciation of the worst practices of revolutionary officialdom. He returned to this mordant critical vein in his internationally successful *Fresa y chocolate* (Strawberry and chocolate, 1993). In this film Diego (Jorge Perugorría), a cultured homosexual estranged from the Revolution, befriends a naïve young student (Vladimir Cruz) who wants to be an exemplary revolutionary. As their friendship unfolds, the bigotry which has infiltrated revolutionary ideology in Cuba is revealed through a humorous and intimate portrait of individuals whose lives do not fit official views of society. A huge success both in Cuba and abroad, *Fresa y chocolate* helped to re-define the cinematic relationship between social comment and popular entertainment in a way which helped to open further paths for Latin American cinema in the 1990s.

Bolivia and Chile

In the late 1960s, the surge of experimental revolutionary cinema which began in Cuba and Argentina led to the formation of other small film groups in countries such as Chile and Bolivia, neither with any consistent history of film culture behind them. In Bolivia the *Ukamau* group led by Jorge Sanjinés made films such as *Yawar Mallku* (*La sangre del cóndor*, Blood of the condor, 1968), using indigenous communities in their own environment and language. Powerful and effective, *Yawar Mallku* led to the expulsion from Bolivia of the US Peace Corps, which the film indicted for sterilising native women without their knowledge or consent. *Ukamau*'s projects ultimately struggled to bridge the cultural abyss between marginalised ethnic groups and the keen revolutionary film-makers wanting to denounce neo-colonialism with the help of its victims.

In Chile, the late 1960s saw electoral conflict between centre-right Christian Democrats who had been in power for over a decade, and the Popular Unity coalition of left-wing parties including the Communists under Salvador Allende (see Chapter 8). This period, and the three years of Popular Front rule from 1970 to 1973, was accompanied by a flourishing of the arts as writers, singers, dramatists and film-makers turned their efforts towards creating socially useful works which would express ideas and momentum for change. Miguel Littín's 1969 film *El Chacal de Nahueltoro* (The jackal of Nahueltoro) is representative of a new urgency to expose the underbelly of a supposedly prosperous society, and to give a voice to the hitherto silent and invisible masses of rural poor in Chile. Based on a notorious real-life case, the film presents the saga of one of society's outsiders, who brutally murders a widow and her five children. Using a variety of techniques including a documentary style, hand-held camera work, simulated news reportage and reconstructions, the film challenges the audience to confront issues of poverty, justice, the role of the media and of the authorities. While not overtly political, it had a powerful impact on audiences in the run-up to the elections of 1970, when socialist policies on economic and social problems were pitted against the divided forces of the right-wing and centre parties.

Littín's shocking and moving film challenged many of the assumptions and attitudes of social conservatism, and threw an uncompromising light on the sordid and violent reality of poverty and deprivation in a country that was rapidly waking up to the realities of social and economic underdevelopment. When Allende's government fell to the military coup led by General Augusto Pinochet in September 1973, many film-makers, and others involved in cultural work, suffered persecution and exile. Indeed, it can be said that Chilean cinema itself went into exile, with directors like Littín and Patricio Guzmán continuing to make films in other countries (both in Latin America and further afield). It was only in the late 1980s, after the plebiscite of 1988 and the elections of 1989 which returned democracy to Chile, that significant films such as Ricardo Larraín's *La frontera* (The frontier, 1990) were able to address the injustices of the Pinochet years from within the country itself.

Argentina

In Argentina a similar fate had overtaken radical film-makers after the coup of 1976, with censorship, persecution, disappearances and exile decimating the productive cultural forces of the nation. After the restoration of democracy in 1983 Argentine cinema came to be dominated by examinations of the years of dictatorship, known as *el proceso* (the process) (see Chapter 8). The most renowned example internationally is Luis Puenzo's Oscar-winning *La historia oficial* (The official version, 1986), in which the wife of a senior army officer discovers that her adopted daughter is really the child of a political prisoner who was 'disappeared' after giving birth. Puenzo's film was the first to raise the spectre of human-rights abuses in a society which at the first light of restored democracy seemed to want to erase the memory of the dictatorship. Although many films on the tyranny followed, the issue of the horrors of military rule has found no lasting resolution to date through the medium of film.

Fernando Solanas

From exile in Europe, Fernando Solanas made the poetic-nostalgic dance movie *Tangos: El exilio de Gardel* (Tangos, 1985), which sets out to preserve and to reinvent the national culture from which he and his fellow exiles had been distanced by force. On his return to a democratic Argentina Solanas continued in this way with the hauntingly evocative *Sur* (South, 1987), in which a released political prisoner journeys through his past to a home which has changed irrevocably; the sense of loss, sadness, and dignity is conveyed through a musical theatre of dreams and memories, in which the survivor of the military death squads and torture camps returns to the mythical working-class suburbs of Buenos Aires (the 'South' of the title) to find that freedom brings as many problems as solutions.

María Luisa Bemberg

Highly successful in coming to terms with Argentina's history and national psyche were the films of María Luisa Bemberg, notably *Camila* (1984) and *De esto no se habla* (We don't talk about that, 1983). *Camila* tells the story of a young aristocratic woman who, in the time of the tyrant Rosas (mid-nineteenth century), eloped with a young priest (played by the Spanish actor Imanol Arias); the couple are hunted down and executed by a merciless patriarchy, represented both by Camila's father and by the tyrant who presaged the dirty war carried out by the generals over a century later. In *De esto no se habla* a young child's growth is stunted, to her mother's shame, and after years of concealment she finds freedom in running away with a circus. This was Bemberg's last film (released posthumously); it is a poetic fable of the triumph of imagination over provincial hypocrisy and repression. Far from the cinema of social action, denunciation and testimony that characterised the New Latin American Cinema, Bemberg's films were, however, typical of a new *cine de autor* (films with an individual directorial style) which emerged in Argentina during the late 1980s and 1990s, with directors like Aristaraín and Subiela making captivating films that had an international impact, with, for example, *Un lugar en el mundo* (A place in the world, 1992) and *Hombre mirando al Sudeste* (Man gazing south-east, 1987) respectively.

Mexico

Mexico and Brazil are the only other two Latin American countries with long-established national film industries. Although Brazil lies outside the scope of this volume, it should be noted that the role played by Cinema Novo and Brazilian film-makers such as Glauber Rocha and Hector Babenco are crucial for a full understanding of Latin American film. Cinema in Mexico has followed a rather different trajectory over the last forty years, with far less overt political commitment than most of the New Latin American Cinema/Cinema Novo. In Mexico the struggle has been to try to reclaim national audiences from the Hollywood domination. While Mexican successes have been sporadic, there were brief moments of revival, particularly during the 1990s, when experienced film-makers such as Arturo Ripstein (a disciple of Buñuel) were supplemented by younger talents such as Paul Leduc in making high-quality features across a range of genres and styles, and with diverse approaches to social comment and critique. In 1991 veteran Alfonso Arau struck gold with the international hit *Como agua para chocolate* (Like water for chocolate, based on a novel by Laura Esquivel), which projected a sensuous and exotic chronicle of a Mexican family, using elements of magic and melodrama to weave a romantic story in a period setting (appealing perhaps to the same taste as Trueba's *Belle Époque* in Spain).

María Novaro

In more of a realist mode, María Novaro's *Danzón* (1991) follows an ordinary Mexican woman's journey in search of her regular dancing partner who has mysteriously disappeared. Determined to recover the only part of her life that gave her any respite from the demands of a routine job and mundane existence, Julia (María Rojo) discovers new dimensions to her own personality, as well as real-life romance in an extended holiday in Veracruz. Although less dramatic and less explicit in its social analysis than most Latin American films, *Danzón* broke new ground by portraying everyday popular culture in a positive way, without either idealisation or denigration, and by telling stories of ordinary people's lives which are just as engaging as the melodramatic *culebrones* (television soaps), the major media products consumed in the continent. As the cinema in Latin America faces a new millennium with chronic uncertainty and vulnerability, films like Novaro's offer an example of honesty and clearmindedness which avoids the distortions of exoticism and magical realism, yet discovers the authentic cultural dimension of lives which otherwise seem condemned to humdrum poverty.

In reaffirming the positive values of Latin American culture and history, as well as denouncing social ills and political oppression, Latin American cinema continues to awaken consciousness and create images of hope and solidarity, of genuine individual and collective identities rather than stereotypes imposed from above or from abroad.

FURTHER READING

Spanish cinema

Cabrera Infante, G. 1995. El indiscreto secreto de Pedro Almodóvar. *El País, Babelia*, 26 de agosto, 14–15, p.15.

Evans, P. W. 1995. *Films of Luis Buñuel*. Oxford: Oxford Hispanic Studies.

Evans, P. W. 1996. *Women on the verge of a nervous breakdown*. London: BFI.

Fiddian, R. F. and Evans, P. W. 1988. *Challenges to authority: fiction and film in contemporary Spain*. London: Tamesis.

Hopewell, J. 1986. *Out of the past: Spanish cinema after Franco*. London: BFI.

Jordan, B. 1999. Promiscuity, pleasure, and girl power: Fernando Trueba's *Belle Époque*, in P. W. Evans (ed.) *Spanish cinema: the auterist tradition*. Oxford: Oxford University Press, pp. 286–309.

Jordan, B. and Morgan-Tamosunas, R. 1998. *Contemporary Spanish cinema*. Manchester: Manchester University Press.

Kinder, M. 1993. *Blood cinema: the reconstruction of national identity in Spain*. Los Angeles: University of California Press.

Rix, R. and Rodríguez-Saona, R. (eds) 1999. *Spanish cinema: calling the shots*. Leeds: Trinity and All Saints.

Smith, P. J. 1994. *Desire unlimited: the cinema of Pedro Almodóvar*. London: Verso.

Smith, P. J. 1996. *Vision machines: cinema, literature and sexuality in Spain and Cuba 1983–1993*. London: Verso.

Latin American cinema

Burton, J. 1968. *Cinema and social change in Latin America*. Austin: University of Texas Press.

Chanan, M. 1976. *Chilean cinema*. London: BFI.

Chanan, M. 1985. *The Cuban image*. London: BFI.

Foster, D. W. 1992. *Contemporary Argentine cinema*. Columbia: University of Missouri Press.

King, J. 1990. *Magical reels: a history of cinema in Latin America*. London: Verso.

Martin, M. T. 1997. *New Latin American cinema*. Wayne State University Press.

Paranaguá, P. A. (ed.) 1996. *Mexican cinema*. London: BFI.

Pick, Z. M. 1993. *The new Latin American cinema*. Austin: University of Texas Press.

Rix, R. and Rodríguez-Saona, R. (eds) 1998. *Changing reels: Latin American cinema against the odds*. Leeds: Trinity and All Saints.

10

Beyond Hispanic Studies? Interdisciplinary approaches to Spain and Latin America

Jon Beasley-Murray

Globalisation challenges us all to rethink current disciplinary arrangements: as capital, commodities, ideas, and people cross borders on a world scale and at an accelerated rate, this disrupts the ordered categorisation intended by disciplinarity. Perhaps more visibly than ever before, our world is one characterised by hybridity, flux, cross-pollination, and mixtures of all kinds, giving rise both to new forms of difference unimagined by the old disciplines, and to new homogeneities that no single discipline is equipped to handle. Globalisation demands interdisciplinary approaches and signals the end of the old university order. Nowhere is this truer than in Hispanic Studies. This chapter therefore maps out what I term 'post'-Hispanism, which I compare to traffic around the ruins of Hispanic Studies.[1]

INTERDISCIPLINARY TRAFFIC

As an example and metaphor for interdisciplinary post-Hispanism, take the recent film *Traffic* (Steven Soderbergh, 2000), which concerns the interlinked drug trade and drug war as they ebb and flow across the US/Mexico border. The film accentuates the generic hybridity of cinema (which incarnates the apparent paradox of a mass cultural aesthetic). *Traffic* bridges the worlds of

[1] My thanks to Susan Brook and Catherine Davies and, especially, to students and former students Eva Langlands and Anna Shanes, for their comments on earlier drafts of this chapter.

Hollywood and independent cinema (of popular and 'legitimate' culture): it has a Hollywood budget ($49 million) and mainstream stars (Catherine Zeta Jones, Michael Douglas), but is shot with a self-conscious idiosyncrasy (above all in the use of coloured filters and extremely grainy film) and stylistic nods to avant-garde and *nouvelle vague* directors (Richard Lester, Jean-Luc Godard). Further, it straddles the linguistic border between Spanish and English: the dialogue is more or less evenly divided between the two languages. Is it then a fit object of study for Hispanic Studies?

The film's plot points to the difficulty of distinguishing between *hispanidad* and (in this case) Americanism. The flow of drugs makes a mockery of border controls and class insularity: newly appointed US drug czar Robert Wakefield (Michael Douglas) soon finds that what he has regarded as a Mexican problem of supply and a lower-class, black problem of consumption threatens to blow apart his own, comfortably well-heeled, family. As his teenage daughter Caroline (Erika Christensen) descends into addiction, Wakefield traces the network that joins Tijuana, Mexico, to downtown Cincinnati, Ohio, and the privileged suburbs. Meanwhile, Helena Ayala (Catherine Zeta Jones) discovers that her all-American lifestyle in Southern California is bankrolled by drug money; to maintain the round of picnics and parties, and to keep her family intact, she too has to follow the drugs trail back south of the border. In initiating a new form of drugs transportation, using dolls made out of moulded cocaine, Helena signals a shift whereby this illegal traffic is no longer hidden *within* other commodities: rather, the flow of drugs now permeates the very fabric of mass culture.

In tracing Helena's crossing from a California rendered in idealised Technicolor to a Mexico portrayed cinematographically through a tobacco-coloured filter, *Traffic* reveals that what makes Mexico apparently distant in its Latin American exoticism and corruption is, precisely, a filter in the viewer's (camera) eye, rather than an essential difference between 'Anglo' and 'Latino'. 'No one gets away clean,' as the film's advance publicity had it, however much the First World may wish to insulate itself from the Third. *Traffic* highlights simultaneously the way in which we see things differently according to our own context and presuppositions, and also the invisible but all too evident threads that form ever-shifting transnational networks. These new networks undermine one set of differences only to construct new and more unstable hierarchies of power; above all, the power to determine characters' life and death is exercised in almost random and unpredictable ways. Interdisciplinary approaches follow this traffic to map these contexts, networks, and hierarchies.

Traffic can stand still (or be jammed), but its essence is motion and the drive to circumvent obstacles. Negotiating traffic successfully requires an awareness of its (changing) direction and its rhythms. By contrast, the traditional image of disciplinarity, and so of Hispanic Studies, has been that of a series of discrete edifices to learning, incarnated in the neo-Gothic campuses and neo-classical façades of university architecture. In Bill Readings's memorable phrase, that university is now in ruins (Readings 1996). But although interdisciplinary approaches such as cultural studies, postcolonial studies, and the new Latin Americanism entail getting stuck into the traffic of a globalised world, it is still worth examining the edifices we are leaving behind.

THE EDIFICE OF HISPANIC STUDIES

Hispanic Studies does not quite have the symmetry or order that the neoclassical façades would suggest. Indeed, and as this volume as a whole has shown, Hispanic Studies is an anomalous discipline. It is hard to pin down what unites the various undertakings that are carried out in its name – or rather, in the various unwieldy names that include 'Hispanic Studies', 'Iberian', 'Spanish and Spanish American', or 'Spanish and Latin American' Studies. Precisely the lack of any single satisfactory label indicates the disorder that lurks within Hispanic Studies. But, in essence, the construction of the discipline is along the lines of that of the Languages studies with which Hispanic Studies tends to be aligned, and in some ways its architecture is archetypical, as befits Spain's position as the first modern European imperial state. Any anomalies in Hispanic Studies, anomalies exploited and heightened by current interdisciplinary approaches, are merely accentuations of cracks that also affect the architecture of other, similar disciplines; it is just that Hispanists are in the vanguard by being among the first to vacate the fragile comforts of disciplinarity.

Hispanic Studies is usually identified with the Spanish language and taught alongside languages such as French, German, Italian, Russian, Portuguese, and so on, all of which are often designated 'modern' and 'European'. Although much time (and increasingly so) is devoted to instruction of the relevant languages and linguistic skills, such Languages departments have been traditionally devoted above all to the teaching and research of the literatures written in those languages, and to the study of those languages' literary canons and that literature's historical context. With the discipline's ties to a constellation of Languages departments, then, and with its organisation around canonicity and chronology, the three pillars that sustain the edifice of Hispanic Studies are language, literature, and history. Yet each of these pillars crumbles slightly upon closer inspection.

The element that both binds and rests upon these three pillars, the edifice's pediment, is the nation state. French, German, Italian, Hispanic Studies and so on are all constructed similarly: supported by the pillars of a national language, a national literature, and a national history while, reciprocally, language, literature, and history are taken to define and sustain the idea of the nation. In the countries in which those languages are spoken, this reciprocal relationship is channelled through the schooling system, in which future citizens learn to perfect (or standardise) the language of state, and learn the history of their national community in part through the cultural heritage that the literary canon conveys. This national idea is then projected on a world scale via the teaching of language to non-nationals, often under the banner of national literary greatness. The Instituto Cervantes, the Goethe-Institut, and the Instituto Camões, for instance, are the state-financed arms (for Spain, Germany, and Portugal) of national self-projection, offering language classes and cultural events branded with the names of canonical literary greatness.

Yet it is clear that Hispanic Studies, and this is its apparent anomalousness, has no neat fit between pillars and pediment; the pediment is split, and its supposed supports out of kilter. As is manifested by the various, contorted efforts to name the discipline, there is no single nation state to which it refers; nor is there any single (national) language, literature, or history. Even the fiction that Spanish is a 'European' language is clearly unsustainable. Hispanic Studies is necessarily transnational, postcolonial, border-crossing, multiethnic, and multilingual. As we have seen, within the edifice of Hispanic Studies may variously be found: not only Spanish but a whole range of languages (Catalan, Galician, Basque, Ladino, Quechua, and Guaraní, not to mention English, among others); myriad national literatures (of Argentina, Peru, Brazil and so on); and diverse, often unrelated, historical chronologies (before the expulsion of the Jews, from Conquest to Independence, the origins of the Spanish Civil War, California's Proposition 187 and so on). This diversity is only accentuated by contemporary interest in marginality, fragmentation, dispossession, diaspora, autonomy, and local identities, and by the advent of globalisation, which dooms any attempts to reterritorialise the discipline within fixed boundaries. But arguably, the edifice of Hispanic Studies never had any centre or a cohering principle; it is just that we only now see through the façade.

Of course, the same forces that compel Hispanists to look beyond the nation-state are acting also on other, neighbouring, disciplines. Lusophonists have long recognised that Brazilian culture is at least as important as Portuguese, and are showing increasing interest in the cultures of the former Portuguese colonies in Africa. The vibrancy of Francophone Studies (research on the literatures and cultures of, for instance, the French Caribbean, Québec, and French West Africa) demonstrates that French Studies cannot rest on the laurels of France's traditional cultural capital as a prime incarnation of European high culture. Even some Germanists have pioneered work on the literature and culture of the millions of Turkish *gastarbeiter* (migrant workers) living in the Deutsche Republik. Similar changes have also been taking place in English Studies – and as the nation-state wanes, it becomes increasingly clear that English is simply another 'modern' language. But so long as other disciplines lag behind, Hispanic Studies (or post-Hispanism) can lead the way in negotiating the traffic of interdisciplinarity, while being most prepared for the surprises and excitement to be found in the ruins of traditional disciplines. Let us explore those ruins, to see what becomes of the three pillars that once sheltered beneath the national pediment.

EXPLORING THE RUINS

Language

In some forecasts, the collapse of the edifice as a whole leaves only the pillar of language still standing. The rationale here is that, as a film such as *Traffic* demonstrates, globalisation means not so much the triumph of English as the increased intermingling of languages, such that those who are bilingual or even trilingual will have a comparative advantage in a world of ever more ruthless international competition. With Spanish recently declared the world's second language (after Mandarin Chinese but above English), Hispanists should break out of their discipline and disperse throughout the curriculum to teach Spanish to all. This, essentially, is the conclusion of the influential Nuffield Languages Inquiry (2000). Hence, in the UK at least, the proliferation of undergraduate programmes in 'Management and Spanish', 'Business Studies and Spanish', and so on: here, language is detached from culture and becomes simply *technique* – a means to an end, a way of 'getting to "sí"' in your Mexico City business meeting. This fits well with the concept of transparency promoted by the neoliberal version of globalisation, which argues that there should be no visible barriers to capital's expansion, and that technocracy has now dispensed with ideology.

The problems with this approach (beyond what many would regard as the political perniciousness of subordinating university teaching so wholly to market priorities) are that technocracy is itself ideology, that linguistic transparency is only ever illusory (a proposition that is key to almost all twentieth-century theoretical reflection), and so translation only ever provisional, and that, while critique may be suppressed, the thickness of culture can only be repressed or ignored for so long. Post-Hispanism should pay *more* attention to language, not less – to language in itself, not simply as the means to an end. And, as speakers of so-called minority languages (from Catalan or Aymara, to Welsh or Maori) would be the first to argue, culture also inheres in language, a conclusion reached too by the traditional imperialism that tried to impose the culture of the dominant state by forcing an imperial language on conquered peoples. As the advertising industry's turn against global marketing campaigns (and towards the packaging of products according to local cultural sensibilities) also demonstrates, culture still demands attention, if only as a source of resistance to commodity flows.

Literature

The form of culture historically privileged by Hispanic Studies and other Languages departments has been literature. Indeed, traditionally, language-teaching has been almost incidental to Languages departments, at best a necessary nuisance. In the most traditional of all, the spoken language used not to be taught at all, as it was assumed that students were already fluent upon arrival at university. What language was taught, was not for conversation, but (following the paradigm of 'ancient' languages) so that students would be able to read. The main order of business for Hispanic Studies, its central pillar, has always been the study of literature (with language seen not as technique but as style). Yet a succession of assaults has undermined and toppled this centrepiece of the disciplinary façade.

Above all, the literary canon has been criticised for the fact that it has tended to exclude the voices of women, the working class, gays and lesbians, native Americans, and so on. In Hispanic Studies, as in other disciplines, the literary values that the canon instantiated were seen to convey a series of political values giving priority to white, European, middle-class or upper-class men. As well as a critique of those values (and the literary and political institutions promoting them), the task has been either to revalue works otherwise omitted from the canon or to re-assess the contribution made by dominated groups to the canon as currently constituted. The first and still most successful instance of this was the promotion of Latin American literature in the face of Castilian Eurocentrism, though even here it was only in the 1960s and 1970s, with the success of the so-called 'Boom' writers (such as Gabriel García Márquez and Mario Vargas Llosa), that Latin Americanism became academically respectable. Thereafter, earlier Latin American writers (such as Jorge Luis Borges), women writers (Isabel Allende or, for peninsular literature, Emilia Pardo Bazán), gay and lesbian authors (Reinaldo Arenas), among others, have gradually been admitted to the Hispanic Studies canon. At the same time, already canonical authors (such as Federico García Lorca, now often read in terms of his sexuality) have been re-assessed in the light of the canon's expansion.

These changes have almost always brought with them the introduction of approaches derived from disciplines such as political and economic theory, sociology, Women's Studies, or queer theory. Literature in languages other than Castilian Spanish (Joan Maragall or José María Arguedas) has also been revalued for similar reasons and in similar ways, as has literature influenced by mass culture (Roberto Arlt or Concha Espina) plus, most recently, works written by US Latinos/as or Chicanos/as (such as Sandra Cisneros). Finally, non-literary genres, above all film (with classic directors such as Luis Buñuel or Victor Erice) and photography (Tina Modotti), have further pushed the boundaries of Hispanic Studies' aesthetic canon and forged new connections to non-Hispanic disciplines.

The Fall and Rise of Literature: *Testimonio*

The limit case of questioning the canon in Hispanic Studies has probably been the debate around Latin American *testimonio*. *Testimonios* are accounts produced by those at the very bottom of the social hierarchy, or even outside it (so-called 'subalterns'), telling of the struggle to survive and, perhaps, change an unjust social order. Typically those producing these life stories come from oral cultures or have not had the opportunity to achieve full literacy, and so their account is mediated by an anthropologist or other intellectual, who records the narrative and then edits and publishes it to reach the widest possible audience. The genre became popular (and controversial) in the 1980s, and its most famous example is Rigoberta Menchú's *Me llamo Rigoberta Menchú* (My name is Rigoberta Menchú; edited by Elisabeth Burgos-Debray, 1983), by an indigenous woman in Guatemala, but other (earlier) *testimonios* include Miguel Barnet's *Biografía de un cimarrón* (Story of a runaway slave, 1966), about a former Cuban slave, or Domitila Barrios de Chungara's *Si me permiten hablar* (If I am permitted to speak, 1977), from Bolivia. *Testimonio* is a limit case not only because, almost by definition, it is written by those furthest from the privileged standpoint of the traditional literary canon. It also appears resolutely non-literary: as its primary function is to bear witness, it shares with journalism or autobiography a premium on non-fictionality; while, unlike many other non-fictional texts, it makes a virtue out of plainness and the refusal of literary style. Those who championed the genre did so not out of the desire to expand the ranks of consecrated authors, but as a gesture 'against literature' itself (Beverley 1993).

Literature and its study, in disciplines such as Hispanic Studies, was seen as degraded and inherently conservative. This judgement was made in the context of a turn against the success of Boom authors whose worldwide marketing under the exoticising label of 'magical realism' served to compensate for and even occlude ordinary people's struggles for self-determination and justice: with 'magical realism', Latin American difference was aestheticised, rather than politicised. Especially in the 1980s, during the US President Ronald Reagan's campaign against the Sandinista revolution in Nicaragua, and his support of murderous or genocidal regimes elsewhere in the region, *testimonio*, product of an alliance between a subaltern subject and a mediating intellectual, seemed to model an ethic of solidarity and so to bring a new, engaged dimension to Hispanic Studies.

Many critics of *testimonio* dismissed the popularity of the genre as a 'politically correct' substitution of political use for literary value. As such, *testimonio* became an important symbol of the so-called 'culture wars' in the United States, which pitted liberal or left-wing academics against populist figures who claimed to speak for the 'eternal values' of Western Civilisation. Yet the fact that the right wing put culture so high up the agenda, in itself shows that they also saw the canon in political terms.

More interestingly, the anti-literary stance that marked *testimonio*'s initial reception also occasioned criticism from some who were generally politically aligned with anti-imperialist and subaltern struggles. Their argument was that attention to *testimonio*'s literariness was essential if readers were not naïvely to imagine such texts to be providing 'the real thing' (Gugelberger 1996), that is, reality in its unadorned truth. They showed how Menchú, for instance, inevitably adopted strategies and techniques that should best be understood as literary, not least in the silences and absences that pervade her book and prevent its readers from ever fully appropriating it. *Testimonio*, as a call for solidarity and action, also shares something with advertising's use of a phrase such as 'the real thing' to sell Coca-Cola. Less cynically, these participants in the *testimonio* debate were also pointing both to language's opacity, and to what lies beyond language: 'the real thing' as in the French psychoanalyst Jacques Lacan's concept of the Real, the unrepresentable trauma (here perhaps the trauma of military rule and ethnic cleansing in Central America) that prompts, organises, yet also resists language. 'Subaltern Studies', then, consists in the careful reading of historical texts using the tools of literary analysis, in order to indicate the subaltern experience, affect, and agency that inevitably remain outside of those texts. Post-Hispanism will therefore pay *more* attention to the literary, with this recognition that literariness is not confined to literature. History (and historiography), too, may be a literary genre.

History

From language, through literature, we arrive at the third pillar of Hispanic Studies: history. We have already seen how interdisciplinary approaches to language and literature complicate the idea of history, by stressing the need to differentiate between history as what happens or is experienced and history as what is recorded or remembered. Because language is never fully transparent and experience never fully representable, there is an inevitable split between history as a form of writing or a production of memory on the one hand, and history as experience or affect on the other. Further, and despite the nationalist claim that history and aesthetics reinforce each other (that a national canon reflects a national history), we have seen an inverse relation between history and aesthetics: the more that literature is seen only in terms of aesthetic value, the more it becomes dehistoricised, regarded as the home of eternal and unchanging values; while the more that literature is viewed as the means by which social groups historically articulate their worldview, then the more its aesthetic value seems contingent and open to challenge.

This tension lies at the heart of disciplines such as Hispanic Studies, though it has been deferred by subspecialisation: in the distinction, for example, between the scholarly editing of texts (whose stress is historical) and their critical appreciation (for which history often falls by the wayside). Here Golden Age scholars and medievalists have often been in the vanguard of interdisciplinarity. Studying texts produced before literature emerged as a separate field necessarily entails following the connections between literature, history, and politics that have only recently become so evident again. It is no wonder that the critical approach known as 'new historicism', which consists in viewing all texts, literary or historical, as part of a network or continuum, emerged first in the study of the (English) sixteenth and seventeenth centuries. But as history is seen as a network, rather than a linear succession of events and achievements each of which builds upon the developments that preceded it, so the notion that it has any single unifying narrative line or plot slowly disintegrates. Again, this disintegration requires *more* attention to the historical, not less, now that earlier narratives no longer stand up to inspection.

In the end, and in place of pillars reaching to the sky, we could imagine Hispanic Studies as a ruined colonnade with masonry scattered over a wide area, occasional patterns emerging, but no guarantee that all the elements are present to rebuild the edifice(s) of which this masonry was once a part – indeed, no guarantee that the building was ever more than an unfinished folly in the first place. But rather than attempt this rebuilding, let us suspend our explorations, and consider new uses and activities for the space that has been set free. Let us examine some post-Hispanist alternatives to traditional Hispanic Studies.

BEYOND HISPANIC STUDIES

At stake in the debates and changes provoked by globalisation and the re-organisation of the disciplinary system is the extent to which new approaches can be productive, can produce new concepts within what emerges from Hispanism and Latin Americanism. As our brief reading of *Traffic* illustrated, the potential scope here is huge: as the US becomes demographically a Latin country, and as 'Latin spirit' (the food, drink, dance, music, and style associated with *latinidad*) infiltrates the UK and other corners of the globe, Hispanic Studies is likewise released from its disciplinary constraints. It is impossible to predict which ways post-Hispanists will turn, but here are some lines that they have been following recently.

Cultural studies

The premise of cultural studies is that 'culture is ordinary: that is the first fact' (Williams 1989: 4). What is meant by this is that the categorical distinction between culture as an autonomous, rarefied realm of (say) symphonies, literary masterpieces, and high art on the one hand, and the everyday activities of (for instance) shopping, eating, or socialising on the other hand, is a mistake. Watching television, or cooking, are also cultural activities, on a continuum with poetry readings, or ballet. All parts of this cultural continuum have to be analysed in terms of their political and historical function and context. For if culture is ordinary, it is also ubiquitous: most of what we do is invested in culture, and it is through culture that we negotiate the demands and desires of everyday life.

An example of this approach in Hispanic Studies is Jo Labanyi's examination of art as propaganda and propaganda as art in the posters and agit-prop theatre produced by the Republican side during the Spanish Civil War (Graham and Labanyi 1995: 161–6). Labanyi goes on to consider the political valence of such cultural artefacts: how much does a particular example of everyday culture arise from popular concerns, and how much is it an imposition on or distraction from those concerns? Cultural studies is divided between those who tend to stress the *accessibility* and so democratic possibilities of everyday culture, and those who tend to emphasise the imposition (by patriarchy, the state, or capital) of these forms upon people, and so the *alienation* that results. Do Venezuelan *telenovelas* (soap operas), for example, only reinforce and propagate gender stereotypes all the more effectively because of their popularity among women, or is their popularity a sign that women can find resources for resistance in their melodramatic plots? Is the Argentine passion for football an instance of ordinary people subordinating their individuality to the crowd in the name of distant, overpaid superstars, or does it bind working-class communities together to give them a sense of self-worth and identity?

Cultural studies shares much with sociology and anthropology: its conception of culture as a 'whole way of life' (Williams 1990: 325) is similar to anthropology's definition of culture, and, like sociology, it is interested particularly in the effects of modernisation. Yet cultural studies can be differentiated from 'straight' sociology or anthropology in that, first, it has less interest in political institutions or in studying societies as a whole, and secondly, its methodology is more likely to involve textual criticism or the study of signs (of whatever kind) than statistical analysis or fieldwork. But these are not hard or sharp distinctions: as we have seen, it is precisely the increasing fuzziness of disciplinary boundaries that enables interdisciplinary approaches such as cultural studies itself. Though it is true that there are places where cultural studies is gradually becoming institutionalised as a discipline in its own right, it is still on the whole a site where practitioners from disciplines as diverse as English, Languages, Film Studies, History, Communication Studies, and so on can meet and collaborate on projects that go beyond their particular specialisms

There are many who think that cultural studies has failed (so far) to deliver on its promise. This demonstrates the difficulties of interdisciplinarity even as it shows the need to move beyond old disciplinary boundaries. These boundaries are still well policed. In part, this is because of economic pressures: the same forces that encourage language-teaching to be dispersed across the curriculum (to boost financial profits) paradoxically also accentuate disciplinarity (as well as discipline) in so far as they devolve financial responsibility to individual university schools and departments (to locate the source of losses). In the UK, this parcelisation of the university structure into discrete budgetary units is encouraged by the governmental Research

Assessment Exercise, which assesses research output and allocates resources on the basis of disciplinary groupings. But in part it is also because the apparatus of intellectual life remains generally intact and strongly disciplinary: a discipline is as much a social as it is an intellectual formation, and consists also of a set of individuals who have had the same research supervisors, attend the same conferences, read the same journals and books, and are endlessly meeting each other (in person or in print), so re-affirming a corporate sensibility. This is true even when they argue, disagree, or cannot stand the sight of each other: such arguments and enmities (as well as consensus and friendship) structure a discipline such as Hispanic Studies.

Then there is the fact that truly interdisciplinary work of the type to which cultural studies aspires is *difficult*. Interdisciplinarity implies a serious attempt to understand (at least) two disciplines at the same time. If, for instance, a literary Hispanist reads a film such as Pedro Almodóvar's *Matador* as though it were a novel or play (by focusing on issues of character and plot that might seem to be transferable from other genres), this merely expands the borders of one discipline, assimilating film into Hispanic Studies. A properly interdisciplinary approach would, by contrast, require a grounding in the traditions of film theory and film history, to analyse the film at the interface of Hispanic Studies and Film Studies. All too often, however, cultural studies' interdisciplinary desire manifests itself as the wishful thinking of academics in (usually) traditional literary disciplines, trying to spice up their intellectual offerings by gesturing beyond their own disciplinary confines. This is the superficial and trendy side of cultural studies, which rightly draws derision in some quarters.

Yet the problem of applying approaches taken from one discipline to subject matters that have traditionally been the province of another may lead us to question the very rationale for 'Spanish' and 'Latin American' cultural studies. After all, the label 'cultural studies' itself derives from a tradition that originated in Britain (with figures such as Raymond Williams, Richard Hoggart, and E. P. Thompson), was consolidated with Stuart Hall's directorship of the Birmingham Centre for Contemporary Cultural Studies in the 1970s, and gained popularity in the United States in the 1980s and 1990s. What then is Spanish about Spanish cultural studies, or Latin American about Latin American cultural studies? Are 'Spanish' or 'Latin American' cultural studies simply the application of a British or US tradition to Spanish and Latin American texts? Alternatively, do they consist in the appropriation of disparate critical approaches from Spain and Latin America, which are then rebranded as 'cultural studies'?

But why in any case should there be a 'Spanish cultural studies'? This label links even this interdisciplinary movement once again to the nation state. The most obvious answer to this question of cultural studies' nationalisation lies with the publishing industry, which regards cultural studies as sellable. Another possibility might be that the difference between Spanish or Latin

American cultural studies and cultural studies *per se* is that the former are drawn to an engagement with the state form that often drops out of the latter's analyses. But perhaps a more consistent and interesting strategy would be to refuse the division of cultural studies into national (or area-based) specialisms, and to promote the hispanisation of 'mainstream' cultural studies, just as *Traffic* uncovers the hispanisation of 'mainstream' US culture. One effect of that hispanisation might be to reposition the state as a central problem for *all* cultural studies (see Beasley-Murray 1998).

Postcolonial studies

The problems facing Spanish and Latin American cultural studies demonstrate the importance of recognising the politics inherent in the relation between the person (or institution) studying a culture and the culture being studied. One of the contributions of what has become known as postcolonial studies has been to emphasise the intimate connection between a regime of knowledge and a regime of political dominance: colonialism always combined political control with the production of disciplines designed to understand the objects of that control.

Edward Said, for instance, shows how the disciplines constituting Orientalism (the study of the 'Orient') incarnate 'a Western style for dominating, restructuring, and having authority over the Orient' (Said 1979: 3). It is no great coincidence that the university's 'modern' languages are the languages of European colonialism (and so contrasted less with the 'ancient' Classical languages, than with the supposedly 'primitive' languages spoken by the colonised). English, German, French, Spanish, and Italian have been the languages in which, as far as the West is concerned, knowledge has been produced; Arabic, Breton, Nahuatl, Papamiento, and so on have mostly been the object of colonial curiosity at best and colonial suppression at worst. And colonial curiosity is spurred by the knowledge that what is under investigation is doomed by the political framework that makes that investigation possible: imperialism brings contact between cultures, and so the possibility of one culture knowing the other; but this contact also sounds the deathknell for most of those social organisations that have harboured and developed this diversity of culture. Certainly, imperial contact means the death of the 'authentic' and 'pristine' cultures of which European science and literature soon became enamoured; colonisers created many 'last Mohicans', and alternately derided and mourned these 'noble savages' living in the shadow of imminent extinction.

Beyond the study of language and culture, pioneering scientific expeditions (such as Alexander Von Humboldt's 1799–1804 voyage to Latin America, or the *Beagle* expedition that took Charles Darwin to the Galápagos islands) were also framed by colonialism or its legacy. Even economics found its ideal home in a Latin American setting, as some identified the very essence of *Homo oeconomicus* (economic man) in Daniel Defoe's fictionalised version of

Alexander Selkirk's stay on what (in homage to Defoe's fictionalisation) is now called Isla Robinson Crusoe. Colonialism has been the setting for European self-reflection from Shakespeare's allegory of encounter, *The Tempest* (1610–1611), to Sir Arthur Conan Doyle's drama of science pitted against primitive nature, *The Lost World* (1912) – or their Hollywood equivalents *Dr No* (1962) and *Jurassic Park* (1993). Postcolonial studies excavates this ground upon which the edifices of Western knowledge have been built.

As with cultural studies, postcolonial studies has tended to be an offshoot of (as well as a challenge to) English Studies. But the Americas were of course the first world region to achieve independence from Europe, and most of Latin America has been 'post'colonial since around 1825. And if the other side of postcolonial studies is to question how independent (or how 'post') postcolonial society can ever be, we could consider the entire tradition of reflection on Latin American identity (from Simón Bolívar to Eduardo Galeano and beyond) to be a contribution to this postcolonial debate. Some have argued that political independence from Spain merely ushered in an 'internal colonialism' whereby the creole and mestizo elite, descendants of the Spanish colonisers, continued to lord it over the native, Amerindian population. In some cases, as in Argentina, internal colonialism meant the more or less systematic extermination of indigenous populations; in other cases, such as Peru or Guatemala, rural indigenous cultures were simply marginalised or ignored by those living in the hispanised cities; while elsewhere, as in Mexico, some accommodation was reached between the twin heritages of Hispanic and indigenous culture. In every case, however, some ambivalence remained, even if the symptom of that ambivalence was repression or denial, and this marked the independent states' sense that they have, always, yet to achieve a coherent national culture.

If postcolonial studies often revolves around 'the failure of the nation to come into its own' (Guha 1988: 43), some of its insights are also applicable to the European nation states that likewise are somewhat frayed around their margins. Thus, within peninsular studies, there have been moves to consider Spain's relation to its autonomous regions in colonial and postcolonial terms. Moreover, the Iberian Peninsula as a whole is marked by a double postcoloniality: on the one hand, there are the legacies of the Arab occupation of much of southern Spain during the Middle Ages, echoed now by the impact of twentieth- and twenty-first-century North African immigration; on the other hand, there is the complex relationship between Spain and Portugal and their colonies between 1492 and 1898, whose oddest (if most symptomatic) moment came when the seat of Portuguese imperial government shifted to the colony itself, as the royal court was transferred to Rio de Janeiro (from 1807 to 1821), leaving the metropolitan centre, symbolised by the Palácio da Ajuda at Belém, an empty, unfinished shell. Hispanic Studies will be further transnationalised by analysis of both Spain and Latin America in the context of what we might call historical globalisation – the flows that traversed the

Mediterranean and the Atlantic both before and after Columbus's voyage of 1492 (see Gaylord 1999 and Dunkerley 2000). Post-Hispanism can produce a more nuanced position on the contemporary globalisation that provokes post-Hispanism in the first place.

Indeed, perhaps the most valuable contribution of postcolonial studies is the way in which it re-organises our conceptions of the global system. Postcolonial subjects are not alone in being split by their colonial heritage. Colonialism itself always induced ambivalence among the colonisers about their own status and the status of their 'civilisation', and postcolonial theory exploits this ambivalence. On the one hand, the aggression, determination, and technology that enabled Columbus, Cortés, and Pizarro (and later, Clive, Rhodes, or Reagan) to subdue native resistance cemented the notion of European (and US) superiority and historic, colonial destiny. Europe (and the First World) was to be the agent of history, and colonial (and neo-colonial) successes only confirmed the argument that any progress by 'the people without history' (Wolf 1982) would have to involve their copying European nation states. On the other hand (and even beyond the discovery of complex civilisations such as the Aztec and the Inca), this developmentalist ideology could give the colonisers pause for thought. Theorists from Frantz Fanon to Homi Bhabha have shown how the idea that the South should copy the North invokes a kind of panic: as apparently 'primitive' societies increasingly mimic and parody our own, the border between civilisation and barbarism becomes more uncertain, and so has constantly to be reinforced and patrolled.

The New Latin Americanism

If the edifice of traditional Hispanism has collapsed, this does not imply that what has been achieved within Hispanic Studies should now be abandoned. On the contrary: the point is that the study of Spain and Latin America can no longer be confined by disciplinarity. Post-Hispanism is a continuation of Hispanism, premised upon the argument that Hispanism has now to be an integral part of many areas of thought and research, rather than an optional extra. Take the relation between Hispanic Studies and Economics. Rather than accepting that Spanish is a linguistic option to be added to an otherwise self-contained discipline (as in the 'and Spanish' model: 'Business Studies and Spanish'; 'Marketing and Spanish' ...), post-Hispanism would indicate the ways in which current economic orthodoxies were first introduced, tested, popularised (and then found wanting), in Hispanic contexts. Indeed, this particular relation has been a focus of what I will call 'the new Latin Americanism', which arises from the responses of Latin American intellectuals to the challenge of thinking about culture in the shadow of capital's latest manifestations.

The roots of the new Latin Americanism are to be found in the so-called 'lost decade' of the mid-1970s to mid-1980s, when much of Latin America was ruled by military regimes. The brutality of the regimes in the Southern Cone (Argentina, Chile, Uruguay) seemed particularly shocking, because of these countries' traditions of respect for democratic processes. Even in Argentina, where there had been a history of military interventions into politics, little had prepared the populace for the 'dirty war' of 1976 to 1983, in which up to 30,000 so-called 'subversives' were murdered or forcibly 'disappeared' on the orders of the military junta. Meanwhile in Chile, from 1973 to 1989, under Augusto Pinochet around 3,000 citizens were likewise eliminated by the state, and many more tortured or forced into exile. In exile, whether in Europe, North America, or other Latin American countries, intellectuals gathered to compare and try to make sense of their experiences. New networks were formed within such communities and with solidarity organisations. Some of the critics and theorists who underwent this process of rethinking in exile include Néstor García Canclini, Ariel Dorfman, and Noé Jitrik. Within Brazil, Argentina, Chile, and elsewhere, intellectuals and writers such as Roberto Schwarz, Beatriz Sarlo, Ricardo Piglia, and Diamela Eltit also had to reconsider old certainties and reconceptualise the links between culture, criticism, and politics, often under conditions of clandestinity. In both cases, the experience of defeat prompted original and often adventurous strategies for understanding these Latin American developments and their relation to earlier models and expectations.

The 'lost decade' was no reversion to some former 'barbarism' buried in the Latin American psyche. Domingo Sarmiento's dichotomy between civilisation and barbarism (see Chapter 8) no longer held, if indeed it ever did, as military regimes brought together technological sophistication, terror, and economic innovation to produce new forms of civilised barbarism. 'Disappearances', for instance, whereby people were abducted from their homes or off the street, often led, we now know, to the victim being drugged, helicoptered out over the ocean, and then thrown overboard. This was technological overkill from regimes that did not have to go to such lengths to conceal their activities; in fact, concealment was not at issue here, rather the attempt to construct a new regime of (in)visibility. Whereas earlier regimes used technology to construct a *visible* state that would produce awe in the *public* sphere (as with the use of spectacle by Juan and Evita Perón (see Kraniauskas 1996)), since the 1970s technology has been used to construct *invisible* states that breach the boundaries between public and *private* spheres. And while the private was made public through technological implantation, the public was privatised as countries such as Chile became the testbeds for an economic revolution whereby public assets (from the social security apparatus to the national airline) were sold off, and the state allowed the logic of the market to prevail. These were the economic policies of what became known as 'neoliberalism', enthusiastically adopted by Reagan in the US and Margaret Thatcher in Britain.

The new Latin Americanists observed these phenomena, and while novelists such as Eltit, whose *Lumpérica* portrays an urban scene in which the public and private have been collapsed into each other and Piglia, whose *Respiración artificial* (Artificial respiration) centres around the difficulties of representing disappearance, tested the limits of what could be said and how it could be said, critics such as Nelly Richard and Beatriz Sarlo (and others published in their influential journals, the *Revista de crítica cultural* and *Punto de vista* (Point of view)) attempted a critique of these forms of power that did not make themselves visible for critique. Richard, for instance, analyses the iceberg that formed the centrepiece of the Chilean pavilion in Expo 1992, in Seville, to argue that its smooth, unmarked surface and semi-transparent, semi-opaque bulk symbolised perfectly the neoliberal attempt to present history and culture as somehow irrelevant (Richard 1998: 163–77). For the new Latin Americanism, getting a purchase on its object is like trying to climb the slippery sides of an iceberg, the new form of monument to a state that is mostly submerged, mostly hidden from view. And while Sarlo (1994) is torn between the desire to reconstitute a public sphere in which intellectuals might once more take up the privileged social roles they had at the beginning of the twentieth century, and the recognition that intellectuals now have to inhabit and write about shopping malls and video-game arcades, García Canclini (1995) examines the possibilities opened up by the fact that we are now citizens only by virtue of being consumers.

If Hispanic Studies has traditionally tied culture to the nation state (and built its edifice accordingly), the new Latin Americanism points to the changing relations between culture and the *market*. But post-Hispanism will also learn from the new Latin Americanism's observations that the state's collapse into the market, far from implying the absolute freedom of choice that neoliberalism associates with unregulated markets, can also coincide with the state's power becoming more absolute (albeit more invisible). At the same time, the transnational networks forged by those who have pioneered these analyses (from Santiago de Chile to Mexico City, Pittsburgh, PA to Manchester, England) offer examples of new ways of connecting and interacting, forming perhaps something like a globalisation from below. This is the globalisation evidenced also by perhaps the most interesting cultural and political movement of recent times, which stretches from Subcomandante Marcos's poetical/political reflections deep in the predominantly indigenous Mexican state of Chiapas, to the protestors of Seattle and Genoa (see Hardt and Negri 2000).

THE FUTURE OF HISPANIC STUDIES

Hispanic Studies is at a crucial, transitional moment, part of a wider transitional phase in the world as a whole. Hispanic Studies is changing, often in ways that I have suggested mean that it is more relevant than ever before, an indispensable aid to negotiate the traffic of contemporary globalisation. This is an exciting time. But it is hard to predict exactly what will happen next. What, then, is the future of Hispanic Studies? You are that future. It is up to you, as students of Hispanic Studies, to provide the future for which this book is only an introduction.

FURTHER READING

Beasley-Murray, J. 1998. Peronism and the secret history of cultural studies: populism and the substitution of culture for state. *Cultural Critique* 39, pp. 189–217.

Beverley, J. 1993. *Against literature*. Minneapolis: University of Minnesota Press.

Dunkerley, J. 2000. *Americana: the Americas and the world, around 1850*. London: Verso.

García Canclini, N. 1995. *Consumidores y ciudadanos: conflictos multiculturales de la globalización*. México: Grijalbo.

Gaylord, M. 1999: The true history of early modern writing in Spanish: some American reflections. In Sommer, D. (ed.) *The places of history: regionalism revisited in Latin America*. Durham, NC: Duke University Press, pp. 81–93.

Graham, H. and Labanyi, J. (eds) 1995. *Spanish cultural studies: an introduction. The struggle for modernity*. Oxford: Oxford University Press.

Greenblatt, S. 1980. *Renaissance self-fashioning: from More to Shakespeare*. Chicago: University of Chicago Press.

Gugelberger, G. (ed.) 1996. *The real thing: testimonial discourse and Latin America*. Durham, NC: Duke University Press.

Guha, R. 1988. On some aspects of the historiography of colonial India. In Guha, R. and Chakravorty Spivak, G. (eds) *Selected subaltern studies*. New York: Oxford University Press, pp. 37–44.

Hardt, M. and Negri, A. 2000. *Empire*. Cambridge, MA: Harvard University Press.

Kraniauskas, J. 1996. Political Puig: Eva Perón and the populist negotiation of modernity. *New Formations* 28, pp. 121–31.

Larsen, N. 1995: *Reading North by South: on Latin American literature, culture, and politics*. Minneapolis: University of Minnesota Press.

Nuffield Languages Inquiry 2000. *Languages: the next generation*. London: The Nuffield Foundation.

Pratt, M. L. 1992. *Imperial eyes: travel writing and transculturation*. London: Routledge.

Readings, B. 1996. *The university in ruins*. Cambridge, MA: Harvard University Press.

Richard, N. 1998. *Residuos y metáforas: ensayos de crítica cultural sobre el Chile de la transición*. Santiago de Chile: Cuarto Propio.

Said, E. 1979. *Orientalism*. New York: Vintage.

Sarlo, B. 1994. *Escenas de la vida posmoderna: intelectuales, arte y videocultura en la Argentina.* Buenos Aires: Ariel.

Sieburth, S. 1994. *Inventing high and low: literature, mass culture, and uneven modernity in Spain.* Durham, NC: Duke University Press.

Williams, R. 1989 [1958]. Culture is ordinary. In Gable, R. (ed.) *Resources of hope: culture democracy, socialism.* London: Verso, pp. 3–18.

Williams, R. 1990 [1958]. *Culture and society: Coleridge to Orwell.* London: Hogarth.

Wolf, E. 1982. *Europe and the people without history.* Berkeley: University of California Press.

Student comments

1   Eoin Barrett, BA Hons Hispanic Studies, MA in Hispanic Studies (Latin American Literature), University College Cork, Ireland, 1995–2001

I particularly enjoyed studying Latin American writers, such as Borges, as well as the poetry of St John of the Cross. These courses have introduced me to a world of knowledge across a range of disciplines and cultures. Hispanic Studies courses have provided me with the opportunity for employment, travel and adventure, and the benefits are becoming more apparent with the passing of time.

2   Michelle Bennett, BA Joint Hons French and Spanish, University of Wales, Swansea, 1992–1996

I began my degree at Swansea in September 1992 and chose to read Spanish (major) with French, and was offered a variety of courses. In my first year my timetable for the Hispanic side comprised language and translation classes, Modern literature and Hispanic history and culture, which provided a firm linguistic, literary and cultural foundation for the next three years of study. In the second year I was offered the opportunity to learn Catalan, which I accepted with excitement. Later in the year I was able to attain both a foundation and an advanced certificate in the new language. The classes were taught by a native Catalan teacher who was full of energy and enthusiasm. We were able to use a variety of resources including language laboratories, television and the International Thomson Corporation. We also studied a novel by the Catalan writer Mercè Rodoreda.

In my third year I attended the University of Murcia, together with three other Swansea students. We supported each other in finding accommodation and meeting new friends. During that year I studied twentieth-century literature, including poetry, and French drama. The university also provided a language class twice a week for all foreign students of a variety of nationalities. I made many friends and met many young people, arranging language exchange meetings in local cafés. In my final year I opted to study modern literature, Catalan, twentieth-century verse and translation. I thoroughly enjoyed my degree course at Swansea and not only learnt a lot about the history, culture and literature of Spain and Latin America, but also many invaluable skills, including essay writing, research and communication. It also helped increase my self-confidence beyond belief. I graduated in 1996 and did a PGCE course in Spanish/French later in the same year. I am currently Head of Spanish and Assistant Area-Coordinator at a school in Cornwall and I still derive a lot of pleasure from reading Spanish poetry and literature. I still visit friends I met in Spain during my year abroad in 1994–1995 and am now preparing A-Level students for their exams so that they may benefit from the same experiences that I had.

3   Joanne Bradbury, Joint Hons Spanish and French, University of Leeds, 1993–1997

I spent three months of the second year in St Etienne, France and my third year at the University of Salamanca, Spain. I selected to study the history of Spain 1492 to present day and the consolidation and democratisation of Spain. These were both excellent courses which covered in detail almost the entire history of Spain and were very insightful with respect to the behaviour, attitude and culture of Spaniards today. I found these options more objective than anything I felt I could learn from literature. In my final year I opted for Spanish in a business and economic context – by far the most valuable in terms of preparing for the job market. It provided an (optional) additional qualification from the Spanish Chamber of Commerce, which, due to the standard of the tutoring, we all did very well. Business language is the most useful to learn because it gave me the confidence to believe I could use my language skills in a corporate environment – a confidence I do not think I would have had without this opportunity. I felt I developed three very important abilities which I could take with me anywhere in the workplace:

1   Confidence – gained from speaking in front of my peers and in expressing my opinions.
2   Rational argument – I learnt to be able to prove a point rationally, backing up opinions with evidence.
3   Analytical skills – every aspect of life tends to deserve a certain amount of analysis.

I felt that studying languages enabled me to develop crucial transferable ability to analyse in a coherent, intelligent fashion.

I essentially just fell in love with Spanish culture and love knowing that I can just get on a plane and lose myself in a different culture without having a language barrier which can sometimes limit the experiences you can have. Although I do not use Spanish in my career as a web developer, I made lots of friends when on my year abroad in Spain whom I keep in contact with regularly and who have provided me with a wider range of experiences and viewpoints than I would have had if I did a straight degree without a period abroad. I will feel eternally grateful and privileged for that opportunity.

4 Eric Calderwood, third-year major in Hispanic Studies, Brown University, Providence, RI 1998–2002

I studied 'El neoclasicismo y la Ilustración', 'La estética y el compromiso en la poesía modernista'; 'Góngora, poetry and poetics'. I have learnt that the eighteenth century, far from being a period devoid of literary interest, is of essential concern to the student of Hispanic Studies. The eighteenth century, and in particular Kant's reflections on the meaning of the word 'Enlightenment', make what Foucault calls the 'ethos of modernity'. This century inaugurates the spirit of introspection, the tendency of the subject to reflect back on itself, that has persevered and continued to drive literary production to the present day. For the English speaker, Hispanic Studies opens the doors to an unexplored world of literary and cultural production. As a high school student, brought up in a tradition of literature in English, it is difficult to conceive how limited your scope of study is. Hispanic Studies illuminates the possibilities of names that previously languished in the darkness of the unknown: Góngora, Cervantes, Unamuno, Machado, Neruda, Cortázar. The Spanish language is the key that unlocks the mystery of these names and with them the dreams and landscapes of Spain and Latin America.

5 Adam Horgan, BA Joint Hons Latin and Spanish, University of Manchester, 1997–2001

I took courses on Chicano-Latino culture, and violence and representation in the context of the writing and films that came from periods of dictatorships in Chile and Argentina in the 1970s and 1980s, and the Maoist group Sendero Luminoso in Peru. In studying the culture and politics of Latin America, it is impossible to ignore the influence of the USA in the affairs of its southerly neighbours as well as the way in which Hispanic culture now pervades many of the states north of the Rio Grande. Some North–South American cultural hybrids are now commonplace: Ricky Martin on the radio, tortilla wraps at the supermarket, Buena Vista Social Club at the cinema or on CD. Hispanic Studies serves to further our understanding and appreciation of such phenomena and the cultures from which they originate. I am now studying for an MA in Latin American Cultural Studies at the University of Manchester.

6   Alistair Kanaan, MA Hispanic Studies, University of Aberdeen, 1995–2000

I started Spanish at university and from the third year on I studied Single Honours Hispanic Studies, which included Spanish language, Film in Spain, civilisation and barbarism, interpretation, translation, literature of the Civil War, Boom and Post-boom literature from Latin America, Basque studies. I really liked the film in Spain course as I have always been interested in the cinema, especially world and independent cinema. The course gave me an insight into how films can be used not only for entertainment (although this is always a key factor), but also as a form of social commentary and artistic expression. I liked the Latin American novel courses which included Borges, García Márquez and *La casa de los espíritus*. It was a great selection of quality literature. I enjoyed the lectures on the subject, but, moreover, enjoyed the texts themselves. Having studied and lived in Colombia for a year in the same region García Márquez lived in, I can appreciate much more the folklore and background he writes about. My favourite course was the literary translation course as I am interested in translating and the uses of language in varying contexts. The course was graded via an individual project which allowed for a greater focus on individual effort, which is much more satisfying as you are working on a text of your choice and translating into your own style. The work is 100 per cent your own and very rewarding. Knowledge of a language is an excellent thing to have. I love to travel and I am fascinated by Latin America, and speaking the language enables me to mix with the locals and fully appreciate the culture of the people. Spanish is also a very important language in today's modern business world. The literary courses open your mind to a whole range of texts that you would possibly not have read in this country and enable you to learn about other countries through their writers. I am interested in furthering my translation skills, so the translation course was very appealing and useful.

7   Kathryn Loosemore, BA Joint Hons French and Spanish, University of Wales, Swansea, 1995–1999

Arriving at university I had studied French to A-level standard but was keen to add another language to my repertoire. I decided to study beginners' Spanish. The first year was an intensive one in terms of language learning and I spent most of my time absorbed in the theory and construction of Spanish. Away from the language learning itself, my main interest in both French and Spanish was firmly rooted in literature. Although various literature modules I took covered a wide range of authors and periods, I soon found the twentieth century appealed to me most. In my final year I soon became absorbed in a module on modern Spanish feminist literature, which I found both satisfying and rewarding. As the only student taking up the module I had a great deal of freedom in terms of research and study. At the end of my first year I headed off to Salamanca for a month's intensive language coaching at a Summer school. This provided the oral and aural practice that I needed and also the confidence I required to take me to the second year. My third year was spent as a *lectora* in the official language school in León, Spain, where I taught English conversation and grammar to students, most of whom were studying English at university. I had taken a TEFL module in my second year in Swansea which prepared me well, giving me a wealth of ideas for classes.

Throughout my studies, literature remained my firm favourite in terms of area of study. The course that I found most rewarding was the module I completed on modern feminist literature. I was also able to explore literary theory and the interrelationship between psychology and writing. The general language classes were also rewarding in that they allowed me to develop my communication skills while tackling contemporary issues. After completing my degree in 1999 I began working for Reuters where I am currently employed as a market analyst in charge of the database for all financial instruments trading in Spain, Portugal and Latin America. Although I have now moved away from academia, the courses I studied have taught me many things that I have taken away with me. The overview I gained of Hispanic culture and history has served as a backdrop to my travels throughout Spain. On a more practical note, I now mostly work in the medium of Spanish. I am also studying Portuguese as part of my job. I am sure the confidence I gained through my studies at Swansea has allowed me to succeed in the career that I have chosen. My language skills play a vital role in my job. I have also gained a wider view of the world and a desire to explore and appreciate different ways of life.

8 Nikki Mackenzie, MA French and Hispanic Studies, University of Aberdeen, 1996–2001

I found that the Hispanic department offered a wide range of options in both Spanish and Latin American literature that really interested me. However, I chose most of the options in Latin American literature. These courses gave me profound knowledge not only of Latin American literature, but also of the culture and politics of Latin American countries. The courses traced the development of Latin American literature from the Regionalist novel to the novels of the Post-boom. Prior to studying the literature of Latin America, I had a very naïve, narrow view of the continent and its people. In fact, looking back, I was extremely ignorant. By studying Latin America literature, I am now also a lot more knowledgeable about the continent, its politics and culture. Studying Hispanic Studies has enabled me to travel, meet lots of different people and learn more about other cultures. It has also given me a greater appreciation of the literature and culture within the Hispanic-speaking world.

I am currently learning Portuguese at the University of Coimbra, Portugal, which will hopefully enable me to read Brazilian literature, in addition to the literature pertaining to the rest of the Latin American continent. This autumn I will begin an MA in European Languages and Literatures (Spanish and Portuguese) at the University of Manchester.

9 Carolyn McCafferty, BA Hons Spanish and Media, Trinity and All Saints College, Leeds, 1998–

I took film related modules in both my first and second years, which focused on cinema and society in Spain, Europe and Latin America over the last 50 years. I particularly enjoyed learning about the relationship between the cinema and Spanish society through themes such as the role of women, modernisation, and post-dictatorship Spain. Taking this course has contributed to my understanding of foreign films in their social, cultural and political contexts, and given me the perfect opportunity to indulge in my interest in cinema. As part of my intercalated year abroad in Las Palmas, Gran Canaria, I chose to dedicate my dissertation to a special study of Las Palmas International Film Festival. I was able to attend and participate in round table discussions, press conferences, meetings and so on. I was also given the chance to view many enlightening films which I would not have been able to see if they had not been included in the film festival. I managed to interview the director of the festival, Claudio Utrera, and gain useful information. I am fortunate to be taking a course that I am enjoying and which provides me with the opportunities to develop my skills and knowledge in both Spanish and the media.

10 Patrick Murphy, BA Hons Hispanic Studies, University College Cork, Ireland, 1997–2001

I enjoyed most of the courses that I took during my time in college with a slight preference for the more modern material. I studied seven stories from Latin America, history of the Spanish language, modern Spanish prose, pronunciation and phonetics, Cervantes's *Novelas ejemplares*, and language and form in the modern Spanish novel. The course on *Novelas ejemplares* was outstanding for its clarity and attention to detail. These studies have given me a different perspective on literature. Before coming to university I was limited to literature written in English. Studying Spanish has opened up a whole new world for me in literary terms. The study of any foreign language gives one insights into a different mindset, a different way of viewing the world. Studying Spanish has given me enormous satisfaction, going from the first faltering steps to a reasonable command of the language has been difficult but an ultimately rewarding experience.

11 Anna Sánchez, BA Hons French and Spanish, King's College London, 1991–1995

One of the courses I liked best was about the Spanish 'conquista' of America, which involved learning about the native peoples' accounts. I remember in particular their impressions of the conquistadors. They initially thought they were gods (the sight of the large ships floating on water was one deciding factor), but they began to doubt their belief when they witnessed the conquistadors' unrefined and ungodly behaviour. Another favourite was a course on drama and censorship and how the different layers of meaning inherent in drama (or literature in general) can overcome censorship. Because of its nature drama can remain a means of expression in a restricted society.

The language courses were for me a much needed opportunity to build a structure of grammar and rules about the Spanish that I already knew. Although Spanish was my first language (I left Spain for England when I was six years old) I could no longer spend enough time in Spain to rely on assimilation alone to retain the level of language. Studying the structure and grammar of Spanish has allowed me to remain fluent without spending long periods of time in the country. Studying these courses taught me that no opinion is 'right' or 'wrong' but each is valid provided it is backed up with argument and reason. Also, that literature is important as a tool of historical and social reference. On a practical level, Hispanic Studies has given me the skills and qualifications to do my ideal job – working in a foreign editions department of a commercial publisher where I take a printed English book and produce a Spanish edition of the same title.

Time chart

SPAIN

1469	Marriage of Ferdinand and Isabella.
1474	Isabella becomes queen of Castile.
1479	Ferdinand becomes king of Aragon. Dynastic union of Aragon and Castile.
1492	January: conquest of Moorish kingdom of Granada. March: expulsion of Jews who refuse baptism. October: Columbus reaches the New World.
1494	Treaty of Tordesillas divides the New World between Portugal and Spain.
1502	Expulsion of Moors who refuse baptism.
1512	Annexation of Navarre.
1516	Charles of Ghent, grandson of Ferdinand and Isabella, becomes king of Castile and Aragon.
1519	Charles is elected emperor of the Holy Roman Empire as Charles V.
1521	Hernán Cortés captures the city of Tenochtitlan, overthrowing the Aztec Empire.
1532	The Inca Empire falls to Francisco Pizarro.
1554	Philip, son of Charles V, marries Mary Tudor, becoming titular king of England until her death in 1558.
1555	Charles V abdicates, and his son, Philip II, succeeds as ruler of Castile and the Crown of Aragon, Franche-Comté and the Netherlands.
1563	Work begins on El Escorial, Philip's monastery palace outside Madrid. Beginning of the Dutch Revolt.
1571	Battle of Lepanto: a Christian fleet under a Spanish commander, Don Juan de Austria, defeats the main Turkish fleet in the eastern Mediterranean.
1580	Philip II becomes king of Portugal.
1588	The Spanish Armada sails for England and meets with disaster.
1598	Philip II dies and is succeeded by his son, Philip III.

1608	The expulsion of the *moriscos* begins.
1621	Philip III dies and is succeeded by his son, Philip IV.
1640	Independence of Portugal.
1648	Independence of the Dutch Republic.
1665	Philip IV dies and is succeeded by his sickly son, Charles II.
1700	Death of Charles II and end of Habsburg dynasty in Spain. Disputed succession of French claimant Philip V.
1702–1714	War of Spanish Succession.
1713	Peace of Utrecht ends international involvement in the war.
1714	Fall of Barcelona. Decree of Nueva Planta abolishes autonomous rights of the Kingdom of Aragon.
1714–1752	Foundation of Academies: Language (1714), History (1738), Buenas Letras (Barcelona, 1729, 1751) San Fernando (Art, 1752).
1746–1759	Development of the Enlightenment under Ferdinand VI.
1759–1788	Enlightened reign of Charles III.
1767	Expulsion of the Jesuits.
*c.*1768–1775	Establishment of settlements in the Sierra Morena.
1789	French Revolution quenches reformist zeal.
1792	Rise of Manuel Godoy.
1805	Battle of Trafalgar.
1808	French invasion causes the Peninsular War (1808–1814). Forced abdication of Charles IV at Aranjuez; Ferdinand VII proclaimed king, but confined at Valençay, France.
1812	Cortes of Cadiz promulgates liberal constitution.
1814	Return of Ferdinand VII to absolute power, except for a short period (1820–1823) of constitutional rule.
1833	Death of Ferdinand VII. Succession of infant daughter Isabella disputed by her uncle Carlos, causing the outbreak of the First Carlist War (1834–1839).
1843–1868	Reign of Isabella II characterised by political instability and government by mainly right-wing generals.
1868	Expulsion of Isabella II in the 'Glorious' Revolution.
1871–1873	Reign of constitutional monarch Amadeo of Savoy.
1872–1873	First Republic.
1873–1876	Second Carlist War.
1874	Restoration of Alfonso XII by Cánovas brings stability and spurious constitutionality.
1898	War with USA: 'El Desastre'. End of overseas empire.
1912	Assassination of liberal Prime Minister José Canalejas by an anarchist.
1931	Declaration of the Second Spanish Republic.
1936–1939	Spanish Civil War.
1930–75	Franco regime.

1975–	Death of Franco; accession of Juan Carlos I.
1978	Spanish constitution (the first democratic constitution since 1931).
1982	PSOE wins the elections and Felipe González becomes Prime Minister.
1996	José María Aznar wins the elections for the centre-right, Partido Popular.

SPANISH AMERICA

1765	Freeing of American trade to Spanish ports other than Cadiz.
1780–1810	Increasing pressure for freedom exercised by Francisco de Miranda ('el precursor') and Simón Bolívar ('el libertador').
1808	Power vacuum with imprisonment of Ferdinand VII stimulates urge towards independence.
1810	Effective independence of Argentina, confirmed in 1816.
1810–1822	Struggles for Mexican independence: Hidalgo, 1810; Morelos, 1820; Iturbide, 1820–1822. Independence secured, 1822.
1820	Bolívar finally liberates Greater Colombia (Venezuela, Colombia, Bolivia), and he and San Martín converge on Peru.
1822	Withdrawal of San Martín, leaving Bolívar in charge.
1823	Munroe doctrine of non-interference in America.
1824	Independence of continental Spanish America completed at battle of Ayacucho (Peru).
1827–1852	(Argentina) Dictatorship of Rosas.
1844–1848	(Mexico) War with USA ended with the loss of half the country's territory.
1861–1867	Intervention of France, Great Britain and Spain; imposition of Maximilian of Austria as Emperor by French. Successful resistence by Juárez brings execution of Maximilian (1867).
1876–1910	Dictatorship of Porfirio Díaz.
1895–1898	Struggle for independence in Cuba, culminating in Spanish-American War (1898). Loss of last Spanish possessions (Cuba, Puerto Rico, Philippine Islands).
1910	Outbreak of the Mexican Revolution.
1932–1935	Chaco War between Bolivia and Paraguay; Bolivia loses 100,000 men.
1954	Military coup of Alfredo Stroessner in Paraguay; he remains dictator until 1989.
1951–1955	Peronism in Argentina.
1959	Cuban Revolution.
1962	Cuban Missile Crisis.

1973	Pinochet coup against Allende's democratically elected government in Chile; start of Pinochet regime.
1976–1983	Military junta regime in Argentina.
1989	First democratic elections in Chile since 1970.
1994	Zapatista rebellion in Chiapas, Mexico.
1998	Pinochet arrested in London charged with human rights crimes by Spain.
2000	Pinochet set free and returns to Chile.

Index